JEWS

Also by Arthur Hertzberg

The Jews in America

Judaism

The Zionist Idea

The French Enlightenment and the Jews

Being Jewish in America

Jewish Polemics

The Outbursts That Await Us

Also by Aron Hirt-Manheimer

Jagendorf's Foundry

The Jewish Condition

JEWS

THE
ESSENCE
AND
CHARACTER
OF A
PEOPLE

ARTHUR HERTZBERG
ARON HIRT-MANHEIMER

HarperSanFrancisco
A Division of HarperCollins Publishers

The authors wish to thank Columbia University Press and
the Jewish Publication Society of America for the permission to quote
published material for which they hold the copyright.

HarperCollins books may be purchased for educational, business, or
sales promotional use. For information please write: Special Markets
Department, HarperCollins Publishers, Inc., 10 East 53rd Street,
New York, NY 10022.

HarperCollins Web Site: http://www.harpercollins.com

HarperCollins®, 📖 ®, and HarperSanFrancisco™ are trademarks of
HarperCollins Publishers Inc.

FIRST HARPERCOLLINS PAPERBACK EDITION PUBLISHED IN 1999

Designed by Joseph Rutt

Library of Congress Cataloging-in-Publication Data

Hertzberg, Arthur.
    Jews : the essence and character of a people / Arthur Hertzberg
and Aron Hirt-Manheimer. —1st ed.
        p.   cm.
    Includes index.
    ISBN 0-06-063834-6 (cloth). — ISBN 0-06-063835-4 (paper)
        1. Jews—Politics and government.   2. Anti-Semitism—History.
3. Christianity and anti-Semitism.   4. Judaism—Apologetic works.
5. Jews—Intellectual life.   I. Hirt-Manheimer, Aron, 1948–   II. Title
DS140.H47   1998
305.892'4—dc21   98-14250

99 00 01 02 03 ❖/RRD(H) 10 9 8 7 6 5 4 3 2 1

FOR OUR ANCESTORS

"The acts of ancestors point the way for their descendants."

מעשה אבות סימן לבנים

CONTENTS

Acknowledgments

The most pleasant of all tasks in the writing of a book is the one represented in these lines. When it is time for "acknowledgments" the book is done, the authors are feeling something between exhaustion and relief (and, of course, gratitude to God that they had managed to stagger across the finish line). Now that the manuscript is complete, we can add together the debts that we have incurred along the way.

This book exists because Aron Hirt-Manheimer came to Arthur Hertzberg with an idea that very quickly became a short précis of what this book might contain. Without a moment's hesitation one of the busiest literary agents in America, Patti Breitman, agreed to represent the book because, as she very frankly said to us, it is one that she wants to read. Patti not only sold the book, she read the manuscript, draft by draft, and she has made wise suggestions. We are absolutely persuaded that if she ever wants another career, she would make a great editor.

We have been equally fortunate in our editor, Mark Chimsky. Like all good editors, he has cajoled and occasionally even flattered the authors but, much more important, he saw very clearly that this book had to be written as a very direct and personal act of communication with the reader—and Mark had the courage to hold out for this view even as the last deadline extension was running out. We are also grateful to Mark's editorial assistants David Hennessy and Eric Hunt for their enthusiasm and efforts to bring this work to fruition. The publisher of HarperSanFrancisco, Diane Gedymin, and all her staff have been very supportive of this project at every stage.

The Talmud taught a long time ago that the works of man are prone to error. The accuracy of this manuscript depends on the help of friends, but we, of course, are responsible for the errors that remain. The entire manuscript was read by Chimen Abramsky, the Goldsmid Professor of Hebrew and Jewish Studies (Emeritus), at London University. He corrected some mistakes and made useful and important editorial suggestions. At several points along the way, we were helped by Dr. Gladys Rosen, formerly of the American Jewish Committee, Mark Friedman, formerly of Columbia University, and Azriel Rosenfeld, Professor of Computer Science at the University of Maryland and a scholar of the Talmud. Our special thanks for the many kindnesses of William Friedman, a friend and colleague of many years; to Linda Michaels, our gifted and devoted agent for foreign rights, to Hawa Ghaus, graduate assistant at New York University; and to Andrew Apostolou, who was especially helpful in the last stages of our work.

The only person who worked harder on this manuscript than its two authors is Carol Ivanovski, who kept typing and retyping at all hours of the day and night until she was satisfied that we got it right. More important she managed the authors, and put up with them, with extraordinary calm and forgiveness.

Each of the collaborators owes some words of personal thanks to those who were particularly helpful to him. Aron Hirt-Manheimer works every day in close association with his colleagues at the Union of American Hebrew Congregations, where he is the editor of its quarterly, *Reform Judaism*. He is very grateful for the friendship and encouragement of Rabbi Eric Yoffie, president of the UAHC; Rabbi Lennard Thal, vice-president and executive editor of the magazine; Joy Weinberg, managing editor; Hilary Ziff, assistant; and Rose Eichenbaum, photographer.

Arthur Hertzberg is especially indebted to Naomi Levine, senior vice-president at New York University, and Philip Furmanski, the dean of the Faculty of Arts and Sciences, for their encouragement and wise counsel. They and their associates at New York University have helped make it a warm and inspiring place in which to work. Arthur Hertzberg first started to think of writing a book about his own beliefs some years ago when he met and became friendly with Carl and Renée Landegger. The recurrent conversations with them have been illuminating and their help has made a substantial difference. Some of this book was drafted in Fribourg, Switzerland, in the home of Bluette Nordmann, whose friendship continues to sustain the Hertzbergs.

Edgar Bronfman and Arthur Hertzberg have a "special relationship." They have worked together for nearly thirty years on many public concerns and they are bound by deep personal friendship. Since 1991 Arthur Hertzberg has held the appointment as Bronfman Visiting Professor of the Humanities at New York University, with the support of the Samuel Bronfman Foundation and the very deep involvement of Edgar Bronfman. This book owes more than could easily be acknowledged to him, and to his wife, Jan Aronson.

Both the authors want to express their love and gratitude to their wives and families for their understanding and generosity of spirit. This book is for them.

Arthur Hertzberg
Aron Hirt-Manheimer

PREFACE

In the fall of 1940 I began my studies at the Jewish Theological Seminary in New York. Tuition was free because I had been awarded a scholarship, but I paid for my room and board by working nights as the desk clerk in the library. Those nights were exhilarating and full of surprises. I remember a Hasidic scholar in a black caftan and velvet skullcap standing before my desk beside someone who was writing a history of the Yiddish language. Nearby a Hebrew writer was waiting his turn to ask for a rare book of medieval poetry. In a few minutes the cast would change. The readers now included a scholar who wanted to see some fragments from the treasure trove of manuscripts that Solomon Schechter brought from Cairo a half century earlier, a refugee rabbi from Warsaw who was compiling an immense anthology of rabbinic commentaries on the Bible, and a young woman who was searching for material on female talmudic scholars in the Middle Ages. Most of the time I did not know the religious or ideological convictions of these readers. The library was open to anyone who cared to belong to the community of Jewish learning. This was not limited to Jews. Indeed, early one evening Louis Ginzberg, the talmudist who was the seminary's leading light, came in accompanied by his friend George Foot Moore, a renowned Christian scholar of religion at Harvard. They had come to look at a rare text. But most of the readers who came night after night were Jews of varying beliefs and ideologies. They exchanged ideas and often helped one another with a reference. They were all rooted in Jewish memory and Jewish learning.

My nights as clerk at the library reinforced what I had already learned in the home of my parents. My father and mother were the rav and rebbetzen of the Hasidic community in Baltimore. And yet "everybody" came to our home. At the table I met Hasidic rebbes who stayed with us when they came to visit their adherents and Reform rabbis who came to discuss the writings of Martin Buber with my father and young people establishing a new Conservative synagogue who needed a Torah scroll but could not afford to buy one. Without hesitation, my father loaned them one of the Torah scrolls from his synagogue. Some days later, a couple of his congregants asked him why he had helped these "heretics." My father answered them very directly: "If thirty Jews do not hear the Torah read on Sabbath morning, will that make you feel better?" This spring, fifty years later, I will be scholar-in-residence at their synagogue, to which many hundreds now belong. We shall be remembering its beginnings and my father's help when they were few and in need.

With Aron's help and partnership, I have written this book to express what I learned in my father and mother's house and during those nights when I sat at a desk in the JTS Library surrounded by all kinds of Jews. My parents taught me to embrace them all and never to imagine that the Jews would be better off, and that decency would be strengthened in the world, by casting out anyone with whom I did not agree.

I have written a number of books and innumerable essays in the course of a career of more than a half century. They have been monographs in history and religion, think pieces and polemic essays, but finally I am compelled to speak directly for myself as a Jew. I am profoundly and passionately persuaded that I was raised in the true mainstream, in the home of parents who loved and valued all kinds of Jews, and who learned from their Jewishness that all people are God's children. This mainstream tradition has been distorted in recent years by raucous voices on the religious right, who insist that only those who belong to their brand of religion are the true Jews, and by those on the left, who assert that being Jewish requires no learning and no obligations because the past is irrelevant to the new age. I hear almost every day from people who tell me that being a Jew does not matter to them or, at best, that it is enough that they feel Jewish without knowing much about what it means. I cannot be silent when the self-righteous or the ignorant keep asserting that they speak for Judaism.

This book, which is so different from all the others I have written, is the debt that I owe to my parents and to my teachers. They have taught me to understand the authentic mainstream of Jewish experience. It is an ancient river, and its strong current will continue to sustain the Jews.

Arthur Hertzberg
January 1998

There is an old saying: "Two Jews, three opinions." So how is it possible for two Jews to write a book on the essence of the Jewish character in one voice—and remain friends?

The simple answer is division of labor. When we teamed up to write *Jews,* Arthur Hertzberg and I agreed that his viewpoint and scholarship would drive the arguments put forth in this book. In fact, he dictated almost the entire first draft! I then rendered the transcript into a workable text, which we revised and edited together to our mutual satisfaction.

But the success of our collaboration goes much deeper than the practical question of who did what. If we had not shared the same language of the heart, this work never would have come to completion. Though we are a generation apart in age, Arthur Hertzberg and I are kindred spirits. We march to the same drummer. Once, when Arthur tapped a certain rhythm on the table, I recognized it immediately as the tune my father had tapped as I was growing up. I know now that it belongs to a Hasidic *niggun* (melody). Our immediate ancestors were, in fact, Hasidic Jews from Poland. We both lost grandparents in the Holocaust, and we both immigrated to America as children who spoke only Yiddish. He arrived in 1926 from Poland, I in 1951, when my survivor parents were finally released from a displaced persons' camp, my birthplace, in occupied Germany.

This book has both our names on the cover because, in the writing, it is a true collaboration. Nonetheless, as you will observe, we have used the first person singular in order to replicate my experience of "hearing" Rabbi Hertzberg's voice, especially when he recalls encounters with some of the greatest Jewish thinkers of the twentieth century. This approach also follows the ancient Jewish tradition of oral transmission from rabbi to disciple.

Arthur Hertzberg brings to this book more than a vast academic knowledge of Jewish religion and history. The pages that follow reflect the major influences in his life: his identification with the Hasidic world of his youth; his years as a pulpit rabbi in the Conservative movement; his career as a professor at Columbia, Dartmouth, and New York University; his literary expertise as author of eight previous books, as an editor of the *Encyclopedia Judaica*, and as a frequent contributor to *The New York Times Book Review*, *The New York Review of Books*, and many other periodicals worldwide; and his public life as a former president of the American Jewish Congress and vice president of the World Jewish Congress.

Even as Arthur has come to be regarded by many as an elder Jewish statesman, he remains in his own eyes "a Hasid in modern dress." His father, Zvi Elimelech Herzberg, was the rabbi of the Hasidic community of Baltimore, Maryland, from the 1930s to 1971. Every morning before going off to public school and then to college, Arthur studied Talmud with his father. The boy was also encouraged by his father to read Yiddish and Hebrew periodicals so that he would be aware of the issues facing the entire Jewish community. Arthur would continue this two-track education. He received his first rabbinic ordination (Orthodox) at age eighteen and his B.A. from Johns Hopkins University a year later. He went on to receive a second ordination from the Jewish Theological Seminary (Conservative) and his Ph.D. in history from Columbia University. Arthur became a close disciple of Professor Louis Ginzberg at JTS and Professor Salo Baron, the eminent historian, at Columbia. Arthur's first book, *The Zionist Idea*, became a classic; it is still in print after forty years. Its introductory essay is widely regarded as a masterpiece of critical analysis of modern Jewish history.

Only by working so closely with Arthur on this book did I come to understand the core of his emotions. All his life he has mourned the loss of the Jewish world of his ancestors in eastern Europe. Every morning he wraps himself in a large, old-world tallis (prayer shawl) and attaches tefillin (phylacteries, little black boxes containing passages from the Hebrew Bible) to his left arm and forehead. His most prized possession is the set of tefillin that he received as a bar mitzvah gift from his grandfather, who was murdered by the Nazis in Lvov in 1943, together with the rest of his family. Every year on the eve of Yom Kippur, Rabbi Hertzberg lights thirty-seven candles in their memory. He never prays alone; they and all their ancestors are his minyan.

The loss of almost all my relatives and the suffering of my father and mother in Nazi concentration camps are the formative events of my life. But what am I to make of this dark legacy? Should I be angry with God, as my father was for the rest of his life? Should I be thankful to God, as my mother is, for having saved her from almost certain death? Or, perhaps, is it best for me to go on being a committed Jew without giving God much thought at all? In working with Arthur Hertzberg on this book, I now can understand that theological formulations are much less important than finding the courage to begin over again as a Jew. This act of will is today, as always, the essence of Jewish faith.

After every great catastrophe, the direct descendants of the survivors—those who chose to remain Jews—broke new ground and rebuilt Jewish life. The generations that followed the destruction of the Second Temple created the Talmud, the greatest body of Jewish literature since the Hebrew Bible. The children and grandchildren of the Jews who were expelled from Spain in 1492 radically altered the course of Jewish history. And now again, one generation after the Holocaust, we are at the beginning of such a cycle.

Arthur Hertzberg and I have written this book because we are commanded by Jewish tradition to be among the builders. We hope that in the century to come Jews will learn to live in peace with one another and with the world.

Aron Hirt-Manheimer
January 1998

INTRODUCTION

The Jews are a peculiar people. In age after age they have been expected to disappear, and yet they persist. In age after age they have been few in number, and yet they have seemed large to themselves—and to their enemies. In age after age the beliefs and values of the Jews have challenged, and often irritated, the majority society. In age after age large numbers of Jews have been murdered or have been forcibly converted or have deserted their faith by choice, but enough have elected to carry on their Jewish otherness to continue the journey.

No one doubts—not even their enemies—that the Jews have been the most creative of all the small peoples in human history. From the prophets of the Bible to the rabbis of the Talmud to the poets and philosophers of the Middle Ages to the writers, musicians, and scholars of modern times, the Jews have always been startlingly important in the spiritual history of humankind. Why this is so remains a mystery. Some have found the answer in the destiny that God ordained for the Jews. Others have found it in the persistent pressure to which Jews have been subjected, almost always, by anti-Semites. We find it in the continuity of the character of the Jews.

To be sure, many centuries of faith in their chosenness and many centuries of resisting their enemies have been the major forces in fashioning this character, but the Jewish nature now has a momentum of its own. What we are describing in this book is how that character was fashioned and how it changed, even as it has remained essentially the same since the time, some four thousand years ago, of the founding patriarch, Abraham. In age after age Jews have followed after Abraham—by being different, by insisting on their otherness.

This book runs counter to polite and politically correct portraits of the Jews. It dares to define the lasting Jewish character. Such heresy is sure to evoke worried reactions from some Jews, and non-Jews, who will accuse us of producing a reactionary and damaging work. Indeed, a number of publishers in the United States and in Europe turned this book down, fearing that it would bring the wrath of the Jewish establishment upon them. Obviously, defining the Jewish character is cause for trepidation: it is the breaking of a post-Holocaust taboo.

This fear of stereotyping is curiously absent when applied to other national cultures. Alexis de Tocqueville's observation in the 1830s that Americans are essentially a pragmatic and problem-solving people is quoted regularly, more than a hundred and sixty years later, in profiles of the American character. It is just as common to speak without hesitation about the French, German, or Italian character. In fact, twenty-five years ago Luigi Barzini's book, *The Italians*, in which he described the "great motifs" and "constant characteristics" of the Italian people since time immemorial, became an international best-seller. No one took exception to his observation that Italians have an irresistible propensity to fall under the spell of dictators, from Julius Caesar to Benito Mussolini. Yet to speak about the continuing Jewish character causes instant discomfort to many Jews.

One might say that the problem lies in the complexities of defining Jewishness. At various time Jews have been classified as a religion, a culture, a nationality, a class, a race, or a combination of the above. In fact, the anxieties that this book provokes have nothing to do with the endless debates about what or who is a Jew. It goes deeper. Our insistence on saying, publicly and in many languages, that there is a definable Jewish character contradicts the counter message that Jews, in various degrees of assimilation, have been sending for some two hundred years, since the beginning of their emancipation in Europe: that they are good French people, good Germans, or good Americans who are essentially just like everybody else.

There is another, darker, reason for this visceral rejection of defining Jewish group characteristics. It derives from the legacy of Jew-hatred that in our own time reached such ferocity it nearly destroyed European Jewry. We understand, therefore, why many Jews deny the existence of common Jewish traits. Anyone who makes such a claim, they say, is either an anti-Semite who defines us by exclusion or a misguided or self-hating Jew who is strengthening the hand of the enemy. Only those who bear us malice would want to define us as different— as other. This cautious and defensive posture is understandable, but it does not refute our thesis that there is a definable Jewish character, which began with the first Jew, Abraham, and continues to this day. It is our goal to describe Jews as they really are, and not as Jewish defense agency publicists might want our people to be portrayed.

Make no mistake, ours is no facile portrait that reduces Jewish identity to its lowest common denominator or to a handful of clichés. Our aim is to clarify, not to simplify. To paint our portrait of the Jews, we have created a conceptual framework in which the Jewish character is depicted by three prime concepts: the Jew as the chosen, the factious, and the outsider. Some Jewish readers will not recognize themselves in the portrait that emerges from the interplay of these elements. It is not the image they want the world to see. It is "too Jewish." Throughout their history, the Jews have divided into two camps: those for whom the survival of their Jewishness is central to their lives, and those for whom the ideal is fitting into the majority culture. Readers who fall into the second category will likely feel estranged from our depiction of the essential Jew. They may, however, recognize a parent or grandparent—or a child of theirs who is now on a journey to find his or her Jewish self.

The critical difference between this book and other contemporary works on the subject is that most authors typically have written about Jews from a modern perspective looking backward. We have taken the opposite approach, beginning at the very source of Jewish identity. The essential Jewish character, we believe, was already present and formed in the person of Abraham. It was reinforced for many centuries by Jews who were willing to bear the indignities of exile or even accept martyrdom rather than give up their faith in the one God. We view the Jewish character as an ancient river surging down into a delta—the delta being the modern age—where it diverges into numerous streams. But the impulse flows from the river. It is not the delta that makes the river; it is the river that makes the delta, and its momentum has sustained the Jewish people to this day. Therefore, we insist that the most fruitful approach to understanding Jewish identity is to begin with the basic sources, the Hebrew Bible and the Talmud, the record of eight centuries of commentary and redefinition of the meaning of the Scriptures. In this book we describe the essential and enduring characteristics of the Jews through portraits of pivotal individuals, past and present, who embody the struggles, the ambivalences, and the longings of the Jewish people at critical moments of their history. These striking personalities have made a difference because each represents a lasting element of the Jewish character. It must be remembered, however, that the Jewish people exists today because of the tenacity and courage of the Jewish masses who have chosen to continue the journey no matter how treacherous the terrain.

In this book we dare to say that Jew-hatred is not some irrational prejudice that affects the non-Jewish world. It has a cause. At its root, anti-Semitism is an angry reaction to the Jews, who have been among the most persistent dissenters in every society in which they have lived. We reject the assertion of Jean-Paul Sartre in his post-Holocaust book, *Anti-Semite and Jew,* that the Jews would have assimilated long ago into surrounding cultures were it not for anti-Semitism. Sartre insisted that the Jews do not have an independent existence; they are an invention of their enemies. Not so. It is a serious mistake to dismiss Jewish religion, culture, and history as irrelevant. Jews have deep within them the determination to remain other and to live, often precariously, as a minority, on the margins of alien cultures. The Jews are self-created and continue to exist by choice.

We reject the conventional modern argument that those who hate Jews are satisfying their own need for a scapegoat upon which to heap their anger. Why do they target the Jews? The answer given a century ago by the founders of modern Zionism, Leon Pinsker and Theodor Herzl, is that anti-Semitism is the most pervasive expression of xenophobia—hatred of the stranger. But Jews are no ordinary strangers. The tensions that affect the Chinese Diaspora scattered among the nations of Asia is not comparable to the Jewish experience in exile. Group conflict does not account for the demonization and dehumanization of the Jew. It cannot explain the Holocaust, which had deep cultural, theological, and racial roots.

In the immediate aftermath of the Holocaust, social scientists explored the minds of anti-Semitic mass murderers for signs of personality disorders. In a study sponsored by the American Jewish Committee in 1950, Theodor Adorno and Nevitt Sanford defined "the authoritarian personality" and linked it to the Nazis. This, too, is a flawed argument. The Nazi machine was not powered by people with personality disorders; the bulk of the Germans and other Europeans who collaborated in the slaughter were otherwise ordinary people. Something else was happening. That "something" has not been grasped by most modern interpreters of anti-Semitism because their theories are derived mainly from secular assumptions. To blame anti-Semitism on the need for scapegoats or on authoritarian personalities is to project latter-day interpretations upon the past.

All these explanations avoid the critical question: Do the Jews make any contribution to anti-Semitism? The answer is, fundamentally and unavoidably, yes. Their contribution to Jew-hatred is that they insist on being Jews; by definition they challenge the dominant dogmas. According to rabbinic legend, Abraham began his rebellion by breaking the idols of his father. He insisted that the One God is true and paganism is false. He challenged the culture around him. When the Jews encountered Hellenistic culture after Alexander the Great conquered the Near East, Jews were the lone dissenters. When Christianity became the state religion of the Roman Empire, the Jews refused to accept the new dispensation. In medieval Europe, nobody would have doubted even for a moment the divinity of Christ, until a Jew showed up. So long as Jews cling to their own faith and their own values, they call into question the majority faith and culture. Even Jewish unbelievers, such as Franz Kafka in Prague or Sigmund Freud in Vienna, challenged the seemingly self-evident beliefs and values of conventional society. So, what is anti-Semitism about? It is the fierce and often murderous anger of majorities against a people whose very existence keeps calling their verities into question.

We understand why Jews have preferred explanations of anti-Semitism that focus on the moral imperfections of non-Jewish majorities. It is more comforting to believe that the Jew-haters, in all their wickedness, have no shred of a reason—even a bad one—for their angers. It is far more difficult for Jews to accept the idea that anti-Semitism may be, fundamentally, the heat of a cultural clash.

What we are saying should not be taken as a justification for anti-Semitism. Far from it. Jews have the right to be different and to dissent from the majority culture. They have the right to demand that the majority culture accept them, and other people in the minority, for who they are. The test of a democratic society is its capacity to deal justly with people who are different, and especially those who question the majority's most deeply held assumptions. Any society that cannot deal with the dissenting other can quickly become a killing ground. Anti-Semitism and all other group hatreds will disappear only when people are willing to accept men and women from different cultures as their equals. The solution to anti-Semitism requires that Jews come to the table and say to their persecutors: Yes, we are different. When anti-Semites hear Jews and their friends saying that the Jews are really "just like us," they know this to be false, and therefore they are unmoved by appeals for tolerance. Albert Einstein made this point very plainly when he wrote in 1921, "It suffices that we [Jews] form a social body of people which stands out more or less distinctly from the rest of humanity, and the reality of which is not doubted by anyone."[1] Jews can defend themselves in this long and deadly debate only by insisting on their right—and the right of other minorities—to be different.

Jews, of course, have no monopoly on being persecuted. But they have existed under attack in more places and over more centuries than any other people. Very early in their history Jews began to invent ways of surviving in hostile societies. The first Jew, Abraham, tried to protect himself in the court of Abimelech, the king of the Philistines, by pretending that his beautiful wife Sarah was really his sister. Abimelech was clearly interested in acquiring Sarah for his harem, and Abraham's deception saved Abraham from immediate violence and bought time for God to intervene and save them both. The newborn Moses survived Pharaoh's decree that all the Jewish male children should be killed because his mother and sister put the infant in a box in the river where Pharaoh's merciful daughter was sure to find him. So it has gone, age after age. Jews have been forced to be clever and to employ schemes that the weak must devise to outsmart the strong, even as they have placed their hope and trust in God to rescue them from peril.

In the modern era the great passion of Jews for equality owes much to the pent-up desire to be able to throw off all the habits that had helped them survive when they were unequal and unprotected. Jews rejoice in societies where there is equal protection under law for all because so much of their experience has been distorted by persecution and powerlessness. Jews fought to leave the shtetl—that warm, inner home where they lived an intense life of their own—because it was a place of weakness and deprivation, a place where so many had to live as *Luftmenschen*, as people of no settled occupation who survive, usually unsuccessfully, on nothing more substantial than air. The "new Jew," whom the Zionists imagined, was constructed as unbowed, strong, and straightforward to a fault. Jews have long been tired of being the clever *Luftmenschen*.

The life of weakness and suffering bred into the Jewish soul a pervasive sadness. Jewish religious law rules that no joy is ever complete because one is commanded to remember, even at the happiest occasions, the destruction of the Holy Temple and the exile from the Holy Land. The music of the traditional liturgy is in the minor, mournful key. In eastern Europe until a few generations ago, at every wedding there was a *badchen*, a man who improvised songs in honor of the bride and groom. These were no joyous tunes, and the words were not celebrations. The *badchen* told the new couple that life was full of sorrow and that if they were to find happiness, it would represent a wondrous exception. But there was always hope. The Messiah kept tarrying, but he would come and bring the "end of days," when all the world's ills would end and all humanity would live always in peace. That hope has been the saving grace.

Even in the worst of times, there has been hope. In Theresienstadt, a Nazi concentration camp near Prague, a group of starving Jewish women recorded their most beloved food recipes into a copybook. They argued about the proper way to prepare noodle pudding or plum strudel or caramel bonbons. The making of a cookbook was an act of defiance and a protest against despair. Someday the Nazis would be defeated. The hidden recipes would be recovered. We are reminded of a Jewish folksong that describes the menu that God will serve at the feast celebrating the coming of the Messiah. These women in Theresienstadt had their own menu for the day of redemption: at home again, feeding their husbands and children in their own kitchens.

In Auschwitz a Jewish inmate stepped into line for roll call wearing his prayer phylacteries, the small black boxes containing biblical verses, tied to his left arm and to his forehead. He had not prayed earlier because *Shachrit,* the morning service, does not begin until daybreak, but the work details had to line up at five, before dawn. The kapos, Jews who had been selected by the Nazis as enforcers, beat the man for daring to defy the rules of the death camp. Perhaps these kapos were beating him because they were ashamed that they had not found the courage to be like him. Or did they hope that they themselves might survive if they obeyed the Nazis? We cannot know. We do know that the inmate with the phylacteries refused to give in. The same scene was replayed the next morning. This man would not give

an inch to the enemy and accepted martyrdom. He would not surrender the hope that his values would live on.

Another story: Private Schultz (we do not know his first name)
was a German soldier assigned to a killing squad. He refused to fire on
civilians. What happened next is recorded on film. Schultz was
ordered to the other side and summarily executed along with the other
victims. Like the man who wore phylacteries, this German chose to be
himself: he could not kill innocent civilians. Across Europe some gentiles risked their lives to protect Jews, and some of them died in Nazi
death camps. These righteous gentiles were a source of hope, and they
are honored at the Holocaust memorial at Yad Vashem in Jerusalem.

Jews have been able to keep going because they have refused to
believe that their destiny is an endless repetition of defeats and disasters. Jewish history is not a repetitive Greek tragedy, a human tread-
mill from which one can never exit. Central to Jewish belief is the conviction that at the "end of days" Jews will be around to experience the
miracles and wonders of the coming of the Messiah. It is that hope of
redemption that gives Jews the courage to continue their journey.

Rabbinic imagery, even as it remembers the sorrows, does allow a
foretaste of the restored world. The table on which a family lives in
unity and in peace is an act of restoration; it is a piece of the altar in the
ancient Temple in Jerusalem. There is in the Talmud the wonderful
image that the synagogues and houses of study of the Diaspora, no
matter how poor or precarious, will be replanted, in messianic days, in
the land of Israel. The most memorable Yiddish song during the
Holocaust begins with the line *Zog nisht keinmal az du gehst dem letzten
veg*, "Never say that you are on your final journey." For the believing
Jew, there is always the promise of a brighter future. And for those
nonbelieving Jews who have been in the forefront of all the liberal ideologies and movements, the struggle to build a better society is an act
of hope.

And what of the Jewish future? How will it differ from the Jewish past? Deep problems threaten the future of the Jewish people. The rates of intermarriage and assimilation in the Diaspora are extremely high and rising almost everywhere. Worse still, the most vehement Orthodox factions are ever more at war with the religiously liberal elements of the Jewish people. This passion for rejectionism and separatism is fueled by the notion that we have entered the "time of the Messiah." All kinds of acts, no matter how irrational or reckless, are justified because the messianists must clear the path for this final event. Indeed, this messianic fervor among a small but vocal minority is approaching the intensity aroused in the seventeenth century by the followers of the false messiah Shabbetai Zvi. As we shall show, the new Shabbateans pose the most serious threat to the future of the Jewish people. But there is hope, and it is to be found by looking at the Jewish experience through the lens of the rabbinic authors of the Talmud. They were indifferent to chronology and regarded all of Jewish experience as contemporary; past and present are one, just as God is One. The sages Hillel and Rabbi Akiva are counterposed in the Talmud as debating a point of Jewish law, even though they lived generations apart. It is of little importance who preceded whom or who lived in what age. The righteous and the wicked reappear in every generation; right and wrong do not change, and the struggle between them continues to the end of days.

The present has meaning only to the degree that it echoes the resonances of all of the Jewish pasts. I remember that after 1945, my father would never speak of the world of eastern Europe in the past tense. He never said, *in Raishe hat men gezogt*—"they used to say in Raishe." To the end of his days, my father always said, *in Raishe zogt men*—"they say in Raishe"—in the present tense. By an act of will, he would keep that culture alive. What was the meaning of my father's charade? Of course, he knew that the Jews of Poland had been murdered, but he refused to think of them as victims who were dead and gone. Of course, he grieved over their deaths, but he remained united with the people who had been murdered. My father revered their lives as even more sacred than their martyred deaths. Every time he talked of them in the present tense, they lived through him.

The tragedies do recur. In the words of the liturgy, "we suffer for You every day," but there is light and hope. Jewish believers have an abiding faith in the coming of the Messiah. In secular terms this drama of an end of days—a time of universal peace—is the greatest creation of the Jewish spirit. But whether God centered or human centered, the messianic idea has been central to Jewish consciousness. At the end of days a brighter world will arise, and a future generation will experience that glorious time. As long as that hope lives on, so will the Jews.

CHAPTER 1
THE CHOSEN

Some years ago I was invited to the Vatican, to the office of an archbishop who sat two doors away from the private apartment of the
pope. The conversation went well—so well that the archbishop asked
me whether I would want to see the pope. He then added that I would
have something in common with His Holiness, because, like him, I
was born in Poland. The archbishop presumed that I would be able to
communicate with the pope in our native language. I replied that my
native language was Yiddish and that I remembered only the little
Polish that I had picked up on the street. The archbishop was curious.
He wanted to know what Polish I remembered, so I told him. The
words that still stuck in my mind, sixty years after I left Poland, were

those that were flung at me by the children who chased me down the street screaming *"parzhive zhid,"* "dirty Jew." Suddenly the atmosphere cooled. The archbishop seemed to fear that I might tell the pope the same story—he was right, I would have—so the meeting with the pope never took place.

I did not want to leave the archbishop with the impression that we could not be friends, so I told him another story. At the age of sixteen I was finishing high school in Baltimore and desperately needed a scholarship so that I could go on to college. It was 1937; the Great Depression had not yet lifted, and my parents had no money. It was also a time of the rising power of the Nazis in Germany and ever-increasing anti-Semitism in the United States. With some trepidation, I went to an interview that would decide my future. The interviewer was a professor from Johns Hopkins who had been born in Germany and was clearly very much a Christian. He treated me kindly and with a seemingly instinctive understanding of my nervousness. He knew, both from my resumé and because I made a point of telling him, that I was the son of the rabbi of the Hasidic community in Baltimore and that I was personally a religious Jew. At the end of the interview the professor told me that he had chosen me for the scholarship. A few days later I got the official notice, so I telephoned the professor's office and asked to see him.

At our second encounter I thanked him profusely and even found a way of saying how deeply moved I was that someone of his background had shown particular concern for a rabbi's son. He did not respond. As I was getting up to leave I assured the professor that I would always be grateful and asked him what I could do to express my gratitude. He answered very quietly and very solemnly, "Young man, one of these days you will be sitting at the other side of the table. When you become the one to make the decisions, remember to help the littlest and the least." At the age of five I had run from Christians, but eleven years later a Christian believer had helped me—because he was a Christian.

The archbishop was comfortable again, and our meeting continued. But I knew that I had upset him because I spoke with a frankness that is uncommon in such encounters. Jews are supposed to be "nice," and here I was telling him that I had escaped a mob of Polish kids who had been taught that I was personally guilty for the death of Christ.

I didn't tell the archbishop how my childhood story ended. I succeeded in outrunning my pursuers (for many centuries Jews have become adept at finding places to hide). When, breathless and trembling, I burst into our house, my mother calmed me down. She told me that it was wrong of these Polish children to want to hurt me because I was different. So I asked her: Why are we different? My mother did not hesitate for one second. We are different, she explained, because God wants us to be. He wants us to behave better than those who try to hurt us. You are different, she added, because your parents expect you to study these holy books—she was pointing to my father's library of sacred Hebrew texts—so that you might know what God expects of Jews and what we expect of ourselves. Still afraid, I headed back to *cheder,* the traditional Jewish school that had existed for hundreds of years in my native Lubaczow. But I was sure that learning Hebrew, God's own language, was worth running the gauntlet every day.

This personal drama in 1926 reenacted an age-old story. That day, at age five, I learned from my mother what Jews have always known. Their basic emotion is pride, not fear. Affirming Jews cleave to their Jewishness in the conviction that they are the chosen people. This may be a delusion, or at very least an exaggeration, but this is at the very core of their self-image. It has given us the courage, in age after age, to go on and to raise our children within our tradition and community.

What evidence do Jews have to support so outrageous a claim? The best "proof" is that even our enemies believe some version of this assertion. The apostle Paul accepted this truth when he said of the Jews, "God has not rejected the people which he acknowledges of old as his own" (Romans 11:2). Islam is likewise rooted in the belief that God's first revelation was given to the patriarch Abraham and that the ancient Hebrews were God's first messengers. And so most Christian and Muslim theologians would agree that God first addressed the world in the language of the Hebrews.

Even the tragic, and demonic, shadow of this accepted truth bears witness to the unique importance of the Jews, who have been cast as the special enemy of Christianity and, increasingly, of Islam. The Church Fathers, who fashioned Christian dogma in the second century, explained the failure of the Jews to accept Christianity by saying that the devil had taken control of the Jews and made of them the "synagogue of Satan." In the course of the centuries, the demonic image of the Jews kept appearing and reappearing in ever nastier permutations, but the basic accusation remained the same. The Jews supposedly possessed the unique capacity to subvert Christianity and, indeed, all of humanity. Even today in Japan, where there are almost no Jews or Christians, the anti-Semitic forgery *The Protocols of the Elders of Zion*, which accuses international Jewry of conspiracy to take control of the world, continues to be read. Clearly, in the midst of centuries of intense and ceaseless discussion of the Jews, it has not been difficult to conclude that humanity as a whole regards the Jews as a people unlike all other peoples.

But do Jews themselves really believe in the doctrine of chosenness? Religious believers, of course, have no problem in thinking of themselves as part of the chosen people; it is the central affirmation of the Jewish faith that God had singled out their ancestors and entered into an eternal covenant with them. The blessing Jews recite before reading the Torah includes the words: "Blessed are Thou O God who chose us from among all the nations." But it is not only Jewish believers who count themselves as chosen. I have heard Jewish agnostics, who do not believe that God ordained a special relationship with the Jews, insist that the Jews are the *self-chosen* bearers of a unique, incandescent message. Israel's first prime minister, David Ben-Gurion, said toward the end of his life,

> My concept of the messianic ideal and vision is not a metaphysical one but a socio-cultural-moral one.... I believe in our moral and intellectual superiority, in our capacity to serve as a model for the redemption of the human race. This belief of mine is based on my knowledge of the Jewish people, and not on some mystical faith; the glory of the Divine Presence is within us, in our hearts, and not outside us.[1]

As a Zionist, Ben-Gurion devoted his life to a great Jewish task—the creation of a modern Jewish society in a reconstituted Jewish state. Like most Zionists, he had to feel that he was not simply fighting a battle with Arabs over real estate. He was leading his people, through Zionism, to be a moral example for all of humanity. Is that not a modern version of Jewish chosenness? I once had the boldness to twit him by suggesting that his "theology" amounted to saying, "There is no personal God, but He chose the Jews and He promised them the Holy Land!" Ben-Gurion smiled as if I had found out his secret.

Even many Jews who have spent their lives outside the Jewish community have not shaken off this notion of being part of an elect people. It was bred into their bones by their ancestors, who were sustained in all their travails by the unshakable faith that God had chosen the Jews as a "kingdom of priests and a holy people." This biblical definition—that Jews have a special destiny—is at the very core of the self-image of Jews. It is why so many Jewish parents want their children to marry a Jew.

The Jews did not invent the concept of chosenness. The idea probably goes back to prehistoric cave dwellers at the dawn of religious consciousness. Those with a definable set of beliefs considered themselves the in-group. They were the true humanity; all others were lesser beings. They were the community of the elect, the elite; the others were primitive and inferior. The notion of chosenness, thus, has a long history—and one that has often been bloody. It has been used as justification for the assaults by the bearers of "truth" upon the supposedly benighted, nasty beings who do not belong to the enlightened.

Christians have attacked and executed heretics for traducing the true faith, and they have persecuted Jews for rejecting God's truth when it appeared among them in Jesus. The Nazis murdered six million Jews in order to cleanse the world of a supposedly inferior race. The Jews thus have been among the prime victims of the doctrines of religious and racial superiority. But let us not forget that in the conquest of the land of Canaan, Jews, too, gave themselves the right to annihilate another people. The commandment is repeated several times in the Bible that the idolatrous peoples who dwelt in that land must be destroyed so that no trace of their gods or of their immoral practices should remain. The conscience of the Jews was troubled by this history.

The Jewish ambivalence about the meaning of chosenness is already evident in Deuteronomy (7:7). God says, I chose you not because you are more numerous or powerful, and not because you are morally, spiritually, or intellectually superior. You are not. I chose you out of my unknowable will. The prophet Amos echoes this assessment in the name of God: Only you have I known from among the nations of the earth. But you are no better to me than the children of the Ethiopians (9:7), and the prophet Amos adds, God loves you no more than the Philistines (8:8). Imagine what a come-down to be told that God has equal love for your most bitter and powerful enemy! Amos defined chosenness not as merit but as responsibility, even as an affliction. God expects Jews to live intensely, creatively, decently, in the moral vanguard of humankind. Chosenness is the ever-present, and inescapable, discomfort caused by conscience.

To be sure, the older chauvinistic view never quite died out. A Jewish right-wing minority in Israel today thinks that power and conquest will solve the "Palestinian problem." The chosen people, so these ultranationalists insist, has to expel the Palestinians from the land that was owned by Jews in antiquity. No matter how long these "squatters" have dwelt in Palestine, they have no valid title to the land that God promised to the Jews. Right-wingers make this argument knowing full well the consensus in the Talmud: the pitiless conquest of the Promised Land happened long ago. This was a one-time event; it is forbidden ever to repeat such conduct. The rabbis of the Talmud arrived at this position by ruling that the original command applied only to "seven nations," the tribes the Israelites encountered when they invaded the land of Canaan, and these tribes are long gone. Maimonides made this position unmistakably clear in his Code of Jewish Law, in which he wrote that all the injunctions about "seven nations" are no longer operative because "their memory is now forgotten" (Yad Hachazakah, The Laws of Kings, 15:4).

This debate about the meaning of chosenness, of God's special covenant with the Jews, is no abstract issue. It is at the heart of the controversy that continues to surround the memory of Dr. Baruch Goldstein, the messianist who sprayed machine-gun fire at Muslims in prayer at the holy burial ground of the patriarchs and matriarchs in Hebron. In February 1994, Goldstein killed twenty-nine Muslims, and he himself was beaten to death by enraged survivors. The large majority of Jews both in Israel and abroad were horrified by Goldstein's assault on a congregation in prayer; for most Jews, this act was the antithesis of everything they had always believed about themselves— that Jews are lovers of peace with special reverence for people of faith. But Goldstein's grave has become a place of pilgrimage for some Jews who regard him as a martyr to an ancient cause: the clearing of the land of Israel from all intruders so that God's chosen people may have the dwelling place prescribed in the Bible. For most Jews, including myself, the memory of Baruch Goldstein evokes profound shame.

What benefit, then, have we Jews derived from being God's chosen people? Perhaps the biggest plus is that it has elevated us in our own minds. We are not merely another obscure little people in the global human family. Since Sinai, the Jews have viewed themselves as central players on the world stage. Even when forced to live in squalid ghettos, Jews always remembered who they were and knew they had to be at their best. On the holy day of Sabbath even the poorest Jews imagined themselves as royalty. This sense of themselves as aristocrats of the spirit reflects a belief that what Jews do is of transcendent significance to the whole of the human enterprise. These assertions may rightly be viewed by others as signs of supreme arrogance. The enemies of the Jews say chosenness really means a Jewish quest for world domination; Jews say it is a mandate to struggle for universal justice and peace. I say it is both a sense of moral mission and a survival mechanism that brings us both comfort and tribulation.

The idea of the Jews as God's chosen people has invited mockery in every age. The Romans derided Jesus with a crown of thorns: If you are the "king of the Jews," leader of the chosen people, why are we about to crucify you? In the Middle Ages, Jews were forced to wear distinctive clothing so they could be recognized instantly—and treated with contempt. The Nazis mocked Jewish claims to chosenness by taking fiendish delight in proving they could treat Jews like vermin. Even as they walked their final steps toward the gas chamber, many Jews clung to their faith and defiantly recited "*Shema Yisrael*," "Hear O Israel . . . God is One." They would die as Jews. They would continue to believe that they and their people mattered, even when they were overwhelmed by defeat and God seemed far away.

Whatever the theories, even contortions, by which the Jewish doctrine of chosenness is justified, the question remains: Why would God want to bother at all with the world after its creation? The ancient rabbis settled this quandary to their own satisfaction. They suggested that when God created the world out of cosmic chaos, a piece of this creation was left unfinished. God wanted to give humans the grand and holy task of bringing some order to their world. At the very least, they would strive to control the chaos within their own souls. It was self-evident to the rabbis that God's prime partners in this cosmic endeavor were the chosen people. The Jewish believers, therefore, had no trouble at all with the question of why God bothers with humanity, and especially with the Jews. God created man and woman to be part of the divine enterprise—to tame the world—and Jews were to lead the way. Therefore, even those who had lost or abandoned the ancient faith still felt the momentum of the ancient rabbinic assertion that the central task of Jews, the very purpose of their lives, is to play a transcendent role in the perfection of the world.

Let us not imagine this Jewish idea to mean that the center of the religious enterprise is to satisfy a person's need for inner peace or, for that matter, spiritual fireworks. From its very beginning, Judaism has disdained emphasis on the self. Of course, the desire for self-fulfillment has always been deeply embedded in human nature. At the very dawn of religion, men and women appeased the gods by offering precious sacrifices so that the gods would favor them with fertility and happiness. But the biblical prophets kept insisting that such sacrifices are empty gestures because God is not in the business of granting humans peace of mind. The God of the Bible demands an absolute commitment to justice and compassion. That commitment is uncomfortable and burdensome. Those who live under this law must ask themselves constantly if they have done their moral duty to others. Here again, chosenness is a burden and a discomfort.

The closest that people can come to having peace of mind is in the somber dictum of Rabbi Israel Salanter, the nineteenth-century moralist: To save your own soul you must save somebody else's body. Israel Salanter understood basic Judaism better than the innumerable popularizers of our time. He remembered that on sending Abraham into the world, God said, "Go forth from your land and from your place of birth to the land which I will show thee . . . *and be a blessing"* (Genesis 12:1–2). God did not send Abraham to Shangri-la or to some protected retreat where he would be content and at rest. God was not offering Abraham inner peace through yoga exercises or kabbalistic meditations. Yes, Jews might meditate and reflect on their deeds; they might dance to express their joy in being alive or to celebrate the privilege of being God's partner, but none of this is the central content or meaning of Judaism. Such activities are decoration; they are not the essence of Judaism or of the Jewish character. On the contrary, Abraham was commanded to go out into the world to be a blessing to those around him and ultimately to all of humanity. Abraham and Sarah were sent on a journey so that they might help and protect the hungry, the weak, and the defenseless. Jews are forbidden to walk away from society, from the rest of the world, to busy themselves with self-perfection. From Abraham to Israel Salanter to this very day, those for whom the center of the religious enterprise is the "hungry i" are essentially sacrificing the authentic values of Judaism on the altar of their own desires.

In modern times the most pointed encounter with the idea of chosenness occurred not among the Jewish faithful, but among the Jewish nonbelievers. By the beginning of the nineteenth century, the central concern of European Jewry had moved from waiting to be redeemed from their exile by God to a vehement push to be admitted as equals into the larger society. It was no longer enough to keep hoping for the Messiah to appear and end their suffering. A growing number of Jews wanted to take control of their own destiny and possess a fair share in the world of the here and now.

The most intricate permutation of the Jewish chosenness doctrine was fashioned by nonbelieving Jewish intellectuals who joined the ranks of the great revolutionary movements of central and eastern Europe. These men and women demonstrated a special passion for remaking the world, and they were willing to accept martyrdom as the price of realizing the promise of a better life for all. Their ranks included Samuel Aaron Lieberman (1845–1880), an early Socialist and Hebrew writer who attributed his progressive ideology to ancient Jewish culture, particularly to the theme of messianic redemption. In his manifesto to the "wholesome and faithful Jews" (1876), he insisted that the true leaders in the movement toward a Socialist society of universal justice were not the Jews who wanted to assimilate out, but those "enlightened Jews," the Hebraists, who identified with and cared about the Jewish people. They had joined the vanguard of a new elite, "suffering servants" of the revolution, to perform the task that prophets and rabbis had set for humanity: to regulate the moral chaos of society by creating a just order.

One of the most striking examples of this new version of chosenness was in the way the Jewish Socialist Bund defined itself at its founding meeting in 1897. Organized in Vilna, the Bund quickly became the most powerful organization of Jewish workers in all of czarist Russia. At its inception, the Bundists declared themselves to be antireligious, antinationalist, and anti-Zionist. Their avowed purpose was to engage in the wider struggle of Russian workers to overthrow the oppressive ruling class. The banding together of Yiddish-speaking workers was solely a matter of convenience; it made communication among them easier. The Bund did not plan to foster Jewish unity or to cultivate the Yiddish language and culture. But within a few years the Bund split, as some of its leaders began to extol the virtues of Jewish folk ties and the importance of Yiddish popular culture. They asserted that Jews had a unique role to play in the revolution because, as a long-persecuted people, they brought a disproportionate amount of energy to the cause. These more Jewish stirrings ran counter to the overarching socialist ideal of creating a proletarian society in which all separate national identities would disappear. The Bolshevik leaders Vladimir Lenin and Josef Stalin called the Bundists "Jewish national deviationists." Georgi Plekhanov, "the father of Russian socialism," mocked these Jewish socialists as Zionists who did not get on boats in Odessa and sail to Palestine because "they were afraid of seasickness." The Bundists had abandoned the Jewish religion and all the holy books in Hebrew, but they clung to Yiddish as the national language of the Jews and they celebrated the Jewish proletarian as the vanguard of the revolution. All this reminded Plekhanov of some old ideas about the lasting distinctiveness of the Jews. Plekhanov was right.

The question of chosenness caused debate within Zionist circles as well. Theodor Herzl, the founder of the modern Zionist movement, did not much concern himself with this issue. His dream was to transform the Jews into a national entity with a state of its own and to make of them a "normal nation." But Herzl's most important ideological opponent within the Zionist camp, Asher Ginsberg, who wrote under the pen name Ahad Ha'am, was a convinced defender of the doctrine of chosenness, even though he defined his own connection to Jewishness in cultural rather than religious terms. Ahad Ha'am insisted that the central affirmation of Jewish self-consciousness was the doctrine of chosenness. Jews had fashioned their own, unique values, and only those who shared this ethos and this self-consciousness would ultimately remain Jewish.

Ahad Ha'am found particularly offensive the idea proposed in a 1909 book, *The Synoptic Gospels,* by the early Jewish reformer Claude Montefiore, that the ethical teachings of Judaism and Christianity were identical. In a critique of the book, he wrote,

> History has not yet satisfactorily explained how it came about that a tiny nation in a corner of Asia produced a unique religious and ethical outlook, which though it has had so profound an influence on the rest of the world, has yet remained so foreign. . . . But every true Jew, be he orthodox or liberal, feels in the depths of his being that there is something in the spirit of our people—though we do not know what it is— which has prevented us from following the rest of the world along the beaten path, has led to our producing this Judaism of ours, and has kept us and our Judaism "in a corner" to this day,

because we cannot abandon the distinctive outlook on which Judaism is based. Let those who still have this feeling remain in the fold: let those who have lost it go elsewhere. There is no room here for compromise.[2]

In other words, Jews who do not want to remain a distinct people with a distinct moral message to the world should remove themselves from the Jewish enterprise because they are deluding themselves about the meaning of being a Jew.

The Jewish belief in chosenness, even at its gentlest, has always suggested that Jews, at least ideally, live on a higher moral plane than their neighbors. Jewish intellectuals usually have insisted that this difference is not born of defiance. But historically the Jewish masses have made no such distinction. They have taken consolation in the belief that they were better than their enemies, as my mother taught me when I escaped from the rocks and sticks of my pursuers in Poland. Jews often have taken pride in their unique talents to outfox those who would try to harm them.

Yiddish literature and lore often contrast Jews and "goyim" to show that the chosen people, in all their sufferings, are nonetheless superior to the gentiles. The oft-used Yiddish expression *shicker vee a goy*, "drunk as a gentile," forms the basis of the following story: It is Rosh Hashanah, the Jewish New Year. Reb Levi Yitzhak of Berdichev senses that the trial of the Jews before the heavenly court is going badly, so he stops the service and orders the shammas, the sexton, to look under the benches of the synagogue. The shammas asks, "For what?" "To see how many drunkards you can find," answers the rebbe. The shammas pauses and asks, "On this holy day do you really expect to find drunk Jews beneath the pews?" But the rebbe insists, so the shammas complies and reports that not a single drunkard can be found. At that point, the rebbe turns his eyes heavenward and says,

"Dear God, we Jews may be a simple people, but look at the difference between our New Year and theirs. On their New Year, they are laid out drunk head to head, head to toe. On Rosh Hashanah no Jew would even dream of such a thing. Are we not a better people? Are we not the people closest to you? Do we not deserve a good year?" This plea is part chauvinism and part complaint, but mostly it is a bit of consolation—a bone to the underdog of society.

IF DOGS COULD TALK

Sigmund Freud observed that Jewish humor and folklore often express the need of the powerless to take revenge on their oppressors. The Jewish joke is a well honed means of diminishing those who have the power to beat you, expel you, or kill you. There is the joke, for instance, about the Poritz, the Polish count, who goes off to Paris to gamble. He comes back with a dog and says to his Moshke, his house Jew, "Teach my dog how to speak in one month or I'll have you hanged." The Jew runs home and tells his wife the terrible news. She says, "You have to go back and convince the count to drop this crazy demand." He talks to the Poritz and comes back beaming. "Nu," says his wife, "did he give up on the idea?" "No," says her husband, "but he extended the deadline for a whole year." "So in a year the dog will talk?" she scolds. "You don't understand," he says, "in a year maybe the Poritz will forget; maybe he'll die; or, who knows, maybe I'll teach the dog to talk."

The Jewish leader Nahum Goldmann created his own ending to this joke by imagining what might have happened at the end of the year. The Poritz summons the Moshke. "Is my dog talking yet?" he demands. "O great Poritz," says the Jew in a whisper, "I have a story to tell you. The dog did start talking last week, and this is what he said: 'The master received me as a gift from the madame of the most expensive brothel in Paris, where he gambled away his wife's jewelry, which he had taken to Paris to have repaired. Instead, he sold the gems and brought back fakes.' At that point, the Poritz says, "Oh my god, I can't afford to have this story told." And the Moshke says, "Not to worry, I did away with the dog."

For most of their history in the Diaspora, Jews had been powerless, but they came to believe that, even in the worst of times, everything would work out in the end. While they might lose some, the majority would survive by their wits and by the grace of God. Such hopefulness was rooted in the idea of chosenness, which assured the Jews that all is never lost, that God would intervene. In the past they had always managed to ride out the storm. In the face of Nazism, this confidence was a trap. Jews were dealing with an ideological war of a kind they had never known. The only possible defense was flight, but many Jews waited too long for the situation to improve and the trouble to pass. Others fled or tried to flee, but they could find no refuge. The nations of the world had shut them out. That is why, immediately after the Holocaust, winning a Jewish state—one place that would welcome all Jews at all times—became the driving force uniting the Jewish people.

In America the attachment of Jews to chosenness lacked the bitterness and resentment associated with the European Jewish experience. The deeply ingrained anti-Semitism of the old world never took root on this continent. Throughout Europe, Jews had been the subject of discrimination by law. State after state had expelled them (England in 1290, France in 1394, Spain in 1492 . . .). Jews did not always receive full equality in colonial America, but they were never excluded from the economy or even from politics. America was an expanding frontier and an immigrant society. It needed newcomers. An outsider eventually could find a place in this nation, which had drafted a constitution based on revolutionary principles, granting full equality to all its citizens. Consequently, from the very beginning, Jews were more respectful and obedient to civil authority in America, and there was very little of the us-them mentality so prevalent in Europe. Gentiles were not perceived as the enemy. Chosenness in America did not become a defiant reaction of a persecuted minority needing to cheer itself up by saying, under its breath, I am better than you are. Rather, it became a moral challenge: we are going to prove that we are worthy of complete acceptance by showing how righteous and wonderful we are. American Jews have expressed this stance most tangibly through their passion for charitable giving.

WRESTLING WITH GOD AFTER THE HOLOCAUST

More than any event since the destruction of the Second Temple in Jerusalem, the Holocaust put the notion of chosenness to the test. If the Jews are God's chosen people, why have they repeatedly been the target of the worst excesses of human depravity? When news of the *Shoah* (Hebrew term for the Holocaust, meaning "catastrophe") reached my father in Baltimore, he declared, "We should go back to Mount Sinai as a delegation and say, 'Dear God, we, your chosen people, have carried your Torah around for three thousand years. We have come now to give it back to you. We implore you, God, to choose somebody else. Let them carry the burden.'" Of course, he did not mean what he was saying, not literally. My father was standing in a long line of Jews, beginning with Abraham, who called God to account. He was crying out, Why have You allowed these horrors? Why have you done this to us? And my father knew that, unlike Job, he would hear no voice from a whirlwind responding to his outcry, but he had to speak. He had to wrestle with God.

Some Jews, both religious and secular, have tried to make the point that the continuing survival of the Jewish people, even after the

Holocaust, is proof of Jewish chosenness. For the Zionists, the miracle is the rebirth of the Jewish state after almost two thousand years of exile; for the ultra-Orthodox it is the recreation of the shtetl way of life in various places in the new world, and especially in enclaves in Israel, after its near destruction in eastern Europe; and for the semiassimilated, it is the continuing importance of the Jews in Western culture.

I dissent from all these "explanations." The chosenness of the Jews is a mystery. Only God knows the purpose of setting apart an obscure tribe to suffer and to achieve more than could be expected from so small a band on so stormy a journey. All that we Jews can know about ourselves is that after every tragedy we have always made new beginnings.

Jewish chosenness is not an enviable state. Sir Isaiah Berlin, who was perhaps the most brilliant British intellectual of this age, kept insisting that the Jews would be better off becoming a normal nation like the Albanians (his example) and not this unique people that spawned so much brilliance and creativity. Berlin added a striking metaphor to his argument. The healthy oyster, so he said, lives and dies in a state of normalcy and never produces a pearl. The pearl is a result of disease in the oyster. Berlin wondered if given the choice the oyster would prefer to suffer the disease in order to produce the pearl. So it is with the Jews: between persecution by their enemies and their own self-image as a chosen people, they have produced men and women of genius, but has it been worth the price? Berlin said that he would have preferred to be a normal Albanian than a creative Jew.

As one of his friends, I was not persuaded that Isaiah Berlin really wanted the Jews to transform themselves into imaginary Albanian peasants. Berlin knew, and took pride in, a vast number of Jewish men and women of talent and genius, from Chaim Weizmann to Albert Einstein. Did he really want them, and himself, to disappear? Did he really think that Jews would ever be content to live in the bliss of quiet and complacency? Yes, a vacation from the intensity of Jewish life might be nice, but not a permanent vacation.

There is no quiet life for Jews anywhere, at least not for long. The only question is whether one lives among the tempests with purpose and dignity. We Jews know why we suffer. Society resents anyone who challenges its fundamental beliefs, behavior, and prejudices. The ruling class does not like to be told that morality overrules power. The claim to chosenness guarantees that Jews will live unquiet lives. I say it is far better to be the chosen people, the goad and the irritant to much of humanity, than to live timidly and fearfully. Jews exist to be bold. They cannot hide from the task of making the world more just and decent. In a society without law, where brute power prevails, no one is safe, and most often the Jew is the least safe of all. The Jew, therefore, must stand up for a society that is bound by human morality and speak truth to power.

Modern Jews are offended and embarrassed at the suggestion that Jews are in any way special or unique. They want the gentile world to admire them for their talent and creativity, not because of some ancient calling. And yet, it cannot be denied that the very Jews who insist that they are "just like everybody else" want everyone to know that one in seven of the winners of Nobel Prizes are Jews, even though this small people is less than one-fifth of one percent of the world's population. Books about "the Jewish contribution to civilization" have been coming off the presses in large numbers for many decades, much to the delight of Jews who are repulsed by the very idea of a chosen people.

It has been necessary to tell the story of the role that chosenness has played in Jewish consciousness through the ages, even when prettified and sanitized for political correctness, so that we can continue a candid discussion of the essential character of the Jew. The doctrine of chosenness is so deeply embedded in the soul of Jews that it persists among those who no longer believe in the faith of their ancestors. Paradoxically, these men and women would deny that Jews are different from other Americans, but still they cannot bring themselves to abandon an idea that has defined Jewish existence since the Jews encountered God at the foot of Mount Sinai.

Jews continue to make themselves gloriously miserable by striving to be worthy of their chosenness.

CHAPTER 2

A HOUSE DIVIDED

In my student days at the Jewish Theological Seminary, Rabbi Mordecai Kaplan tolerated but did not like my dissents from his views. Even then I was arguing for chosenness as he was insisting this was an antidemocratic idea. One day he got back at me. I was to give a talk in class, so I tried to be very clever and self-protective by producing remarks that were a summary of what Kaplan himself had said on the subject four days earlier. As I delivered my presentation, Mordecai Kaplan sat impassively, and then he demolished everything I had said, point by point. Afterward, I said plaintively, "But, Dr. Kaplan, I don't believe this stuff either, but this is exactly what you said on the subject last Thursday." He looked me straight in the eye and said, "But, Arthur, I've grown since Thursday." The august Mordecai Kaplan was in disagreement with himself in order to prove me wrong.

Two decades later I was working closely with another legendary Jewish leader, Nahum Goldmann, who served for many years as president of the World Jewish Congress and of the World Zionist Organization. I admired his capacity for maintaining an amiable relationship with factional representatives who loathed one another. One day I was in the chair at a luncheon in his honor and introduced him as the only man I had ever met who could be at one and the same time the head of the establishment and the leader of the opposition.

We Jews make jokes about our divisions, but throughout our history they have been very serious and often very tragic.

The widespread notion of world Jewish unity is a myth that has long been exploited by anti-Semites. The classic example is *The Protocols of the Elders of Zion*, devised by agents of the Russian secret police in the last decade of the nineteenth century to prove the existence of a backroom, international Jewish conspiracy intent on world domination. Still in print in many languages, *The Protocols* remains a mainstay of anti-Semitism. In Arabic, it is widely read in the Middle East. In America the anti-Semitic Nation of Islam, led by Louis Farrakhan, distributes an edition to its members and to anyone else who will stop at one of its displays. In German and other European languages, *The Protocols* are the bible of the neo-Nazis. Those who take *The Protocols* as truth believe the charge that Jewish capitalists are planning to enslave the world. Yes, there is a cabal, but its members are not Jews; they are Holocaust deniers and other anti-Semites who run a worldwide industry of hate literature in print and on the Internet.

∞   ∞   ∞

At the beginning of the Nazi era, the story is told of the conversation between two German Jews as they are riding together on a bus. One notices that the other is reading the Nazi newspaper *Der Stürmer* and says, "Excuse me, but why are you reading that anti-Semitic rag?" The second Jew answers, "Because in the Jewish press I read about how Jews are at each other's throats and I get depressed. But when I read in *Der Stürmer* that Jews are rich and powerful, organized and unified, and control the world, I feel encouraged."

The Jewish people has been a divided house from the very beginning. The hallmark of Jewish history has been the tension between the quest for a unified people and terrible factionalism. The ancient biblical kingdom lasted as a united realm only through the reigns of David and Solomon, fewer than one hundred years. When Jews, on occasion, did have the semblance of a united structure, it was short-lived. In the Diaspora, where official Jewish leaders sometimes did exist, such as the exilarch in Babylon in the first to the twelfth centuries or the councils of the Lands in Poland and Lithuania in the seventeenth and eighteenth centuries, these authorities usually were appointed by the rulers to collect special, and very heavy, taxes from the Jews. A central authority without outside pressure rarely existed in Jewish history.

Jewish factions clashed over many issues. In biblical times, the primary battle raged between Jews who worshiped one God and the Jews who adopted the pagan idols prevalent in the land of Canaan. In Hellenistic times the fundamental break was between those who wanted to assimilate into the world culture of the Greeks and those who refused to abandon the faith and ways of their ancestors. In Roman times the dividing line was between those who were willing to make peace with the occupying power and those who demanded independence at any cost. On the surface, these quarrels appeared political and cultural, but they were rooted in battles of a religious nature. The fundamental issue, in many permutations, was always who is the true heir of biblical revelation? It was a struggle about legitimacy and the power that it conferred upon the winner.

As anyone familiar with the Bible knows, this conflict began in the household of Abraham and Sarah. Which of their sons, Ishmael or Isaac, had the rightful claim to the birthright—that is, to God's blessing? The Bible deemed Isaac the legitimate heir, even though he was the younger son. (The Koran restored the birthright to Ishmael, his older half-brother who was the son of the bondwoman Hagar.) In the next generation Jacob wangled away the birthright from his older brother Esau, thus reinforcing the pattern of younger sons laying claim to the mantle of leadership. Again in the following generation, two of Jacob's younger sons, Judah and Joseph, became the progenitors of the southern and northern kingdoms after the death of King Solomon. By what right did these younger sons appropriate their brothers' birthright, violating entrenched norms of inheritance? By what right did they claim to be the true heirs of the blessing that God bestowed upon Abraham? The answer lies in the character of these individuals, not their birth order.

In the Bible primogeniture was overruled when the younger son was found to be the *ish haruach,* the one upon whom God had conferred a special spirit. These younger sons shone by their divine election, their spiritual excellence. Sometimes all the children in the first family were bypassed, as when Moses handed the mantle of leadership to Joshua, who was from a different tribe. Why Joshua? Because, after Moses, God had chosen to speak to him. The descendants of Aaron became the *kohanim;* they inherited priestly status, but their leadership was challenged by the prophets, who spoke directly in the name of God, and later by the rabbis, who claimed to hold the key to the meaning of Scripture. The authority of the prophets or the rabbis was not inherited. They were the vessels through whom God chose to speak. The *ish haruach* model of succession set up a contest between competing powers who claimed to be the legitimate messenger of God's truth. Not surprisingly, the clash between these holy vessels led to fierce factionalism, and it has not subsided to this day.

Even in periods of relative calm, no single rabbinic authority was universally respected. In the second century of the common era, Rabbi Judah the Prince, the redactor of the Mishnah, the basic text of rabbinic laws, was undercut by his rabbinic detractors. In the thirteenth century, the disciples of Maimonides were excommunicated by a rival faction, which regarded their teacher's opinions as heretical.

In our own day, just as in antiquity, rabbinic authority gained legitimacy not by appointment but by individual merit. From the 1940s to the 1980s Rabbi Joseph Soleveichik, who never headed a yeshiva (school of talmudic studies), was widely accepted among the modern Orthodox Jews in America as the dominant religious legal authority. The more rigorously Orthodox addressed their questions to Rabbi Moshe Feinstein, the head of a minor yeshiva. In Israel, the leading talmudic figure was Rabbi Shlomo Zalman Auerbach, who served, until he died in 1995, as the head of a small yeshiva. The reputations of the official chief rabbis of the Holy Land have been mixed. The first to hold that office, Rabbi Abraham Isaac Kook, was widely revered as a holy man and a great scholar, but even he was not accorded total respect and obedience. Jews do not automatically revere high religious office. They keep disagreeing about who is learned enough or pious enough to be worthy of true respect. I would bet that if Ribbono shel Olam (God) came to town disguised as a rabbi, he would face opposition from the faction in the congregation that does not like the rabbi. Jews judge one another harshly, and sometimes not even God makes the grade.

An old rabbinic story makes this point strikingly. It is based on the myth that God created a primal ox and a huge fish, the Leviathan, so that they might be served at the end of days when the righteous will make a feast to celebrate the coming of the Messiah. So, some rabbis asked, why did the Lord have to provide both the ox and the fish? Is it not written that a true feast is held with meat as its main course? Another rabbi responded that the fish was necessary because at the end of days God will be the one who slaughters the ox, and there will be people at the party who will not trust the Lord to have prepared the meat according to all the stringencies of the Jewish dietary laws!

Jewish factionalism was usually at its sharpest when threats from the outside required just the opposite. Never, in any of the major crises in Jewish history, was there a unified response. In the second century B.C.E., Judea was ruled by the Syrian Greeks and an elite class of Jews—priests and other officials who had adopted Greek culture. The revolt of the Maccabees (their victory is commemorated in the holiday of Chanukah) was just as much a civil war as it was a struggle of the Jews against an outside oppressor. A family of priests from the countryside, the Maccabees, led the battle against sophisticated Jews in Jerusalem, who had adapted to Hellenistic ways. The Maccabees cleansed the Temple because Jews had introduced idols, the symbols of Greek culture, into the sanctuary. These Jewish "Hellenizers" were simply being proper citizens. In the normal practice of Greek culture the way to make peace with a foreign power was to exchange idols—they accepted your God into their pantheon and you adopted theirs. The Maccabees won the war, but within three generations of assuming power, their descendants would embrace Hellenistic culture. And so the struggle for Jewish legitimacy heated up again, as another faction rose to challenge the reigning power in Jerusalem.

Never was factionalism among the Jews more intense than during the great revolt against Rome, which began in 66 C.E. Before Jerusalem was destroyed four years later, in 70 C.E., the factions within the besieged city fought one another murderously, down to the dramatic moment when the Zealots, who led the revolt, burned the supplies of grain in the city. The Jewish inhabitants then had no choice but to fight desperately to break the siege. Such disasters have seldom moved the warring Jewish parties to seek compromise. Even today, in the modern State of Israel, these battles have continued.

Since Israel's famous victory in the Six-Day War of June 1967, a vociferous Jewish minority has adopted the view that the decisions of the state are not binding upon them; they answer only to the higher law of God, as they define it. The immediate and most contentious issue is the policy of the government toward reconciliation with the Palestinians. The return of any land on the West Bank is, in their view, forbidden because God commands that the Jews must possess all of the Holy Land. This is a question of transcendent importance because we are supposedly living in the days of the Messiah, and the political events of this moment are either hastening or delaying the glorious day when he will appear on earth. To the new zealots a government that makes any move toward compromise on these territories is transgressing a divine commandment, and any Jewish leader who signs an agreement to return part or all of the West Bank to the control of Palestinian Arabs is guilty of high treason. So, Yigal Amir justified killing Israeli Prime Minister Yitzhak Rabin in 1995.

Most Jewish messianists reject assassination as a tool to bring redemption, but a core group, an irreducible minimum, remains fervent and defiant. The Yigal Amirs of Israel will not hesitate to make war on their enemies. The Jews will have to live with the tension between the gentler messianism of those who advocate peaceful waiting and the aggressive messianism of those zealots who would kill to hasten the coming of the Messiah. Those who teach young Jews that killing is a religious act are as guilty as the assassins whom they are breeding. The very worst aspect of such violence is that it is done in good conscience by people who think that they are carrying out God's will when, in fact, they are committing *hillul Hashem*—a desecration of God's name. Sometimes, in my most discouraged days, I wonder if these angers will persist even in the days of the Messiah. I awake from such despair and say that it must end then, for what good is a Messiah who cannot make peace among the Jews?

Given their long history of internal strife, it may seem ironic that one of the fundamental tenets of Jewish life is the talmudic injunction "All Jews are responsible for one another." The truth is that the vast majority of affirming Jews feel a strong sense of belonging to one another. When observant Jews travel abroad, they tend to seek out other Jews, and they are often invited home for a Sabbath meal or to the synagogue for worship. When someone who is not born a Jew is being formally admitted to the faith, we do not say to that person, "You are now being added to the roster of the believers in Judaism," for that is self-evident. The rabbis pronounce at this solemn moment a very simple formula: to a man they say, "You are our brother," and to a woman they say, "You are our sister."

Throughout most of their history, Jews have lived as a minority, often under attack. To survive they have depended on one another;

hence Jews who fail one another commit an unforgivable sin. When two hundred and seventy-five thousand Jews left Spain in 1492, most Jewish communities received the refugees with kindness and support; other Jewish communities, afraid that these newcomers would be too visible and make trouble, turned them away. But the overwhelming Jewish experience through history has been that Jews have accepted responsibility for their people; this has been essential to Jewish survival. And so, in the mass migration from Europe to the United States between 1882 and 1914, the Jews coming to America presumed that those who were already here, both their relatives and the long-established community, would help them. Some failed the newcomers, but most did not. Whatever else Jews may be, at their very core they are, and remain, an extended family.

One of the most painful discussions within the Jewish community is the question of the behavior of Jews in the free countries during the Holocaust: Did the Jews who were not immediately affected by the Holocaust—particularly those in North America and in Palestine—do enough to save the Jews of Europe? The critics admit that the American Jews were stifled by anti-Semitism and that the Jews of Palestine were under the control of the British, who severely restricted Jewish immigration in 1939. Nevertheless, the charge that these communities did not do enough has enormous power and resonance.

The anger is even greater at the non-Jewish majorities in the various occupied countries that stood by or even collaborated. Those who helped Jews survive are remembered with gratitude. Jews have persevered because they often have found some help outside the Jewish community; the occasional bishop or duke who defended or sheltered them is accorded a special place of honor in Jewish history.

But the basic Jewish feeling is that, in the last analysis, Jews depend on one another. In 1945, at the end of World War II, the world Jewish community mobilized its resources and rose up, united, to help create the State of Israel. In 1948 the first act of the newly established Jewish state was to adopt the Law of Return, guaranteeing that any Jew who comes to Israel will receive citizenship upon demand. This law is an affirmation of the talmudic principle of Jewish communal responsibility. Throughout the ages, the commandment to "redeem captives," that is, to save Jews from imminent danger, has been so central that even synagogues and scrolls of the Torah could be sold to raise the money with which to pay ransom and save lives. Israel remains a place of refuge for any Jew in need. The port of Haifa and Ben-Gurion Airport near Tel Aviv are the holiest Jewish sites in the world. Here the young women or men in uniform who are inspecting passports will never say that Israel already has too many Jews.

Even as Jewish visitors walk past the passport desk at Ben-Gurion Airport, proud to be stepping onto the soil of the Jewish state, they are not—almost no Jew is—uncritical admirers of everything that Israel is doing. Jews could not be otherwise, for they are by their very nature a people of critics. Chaim Weizmann, the first president of Israel, once said that the difficulty of his job is not that he is the president of several million citizens; he is the president of several million presidents! But no Jew can walk out of the customs shed into the bustle of the street without the feeling of having come home. This does not mean that the visitors from the Diaspora are not deeply American or Dutch or Italian and that they are not patriots of the countries from which they came, but entering the land of Israel evokes one of the deepest Jewish emotions. This is the home in which the extended family had its beginnings. Never mind the more recent memories of the shtetls in Poland or the mellahs in Morocco or the villages in Ethiopia; here on the sidewalk outside the customs shed, the taxicab drivers competing for a fare to Jerusalem or Tel Aviv are the cousins we have not yet met. These drivers might try to communicate in English, French, or Spanish, but they are most comfortable in Hebrew; it is the language that Abraham and Sarah spoke with each other and in which King David wrote his psalms; it is the voice of their ancestors.

The State of Israel is very precious to all Jews. Its very existence is the supreme assertion that the Jewish people will always find the strength and the courage to begin over again. Contemporary Israel is more secular than religious, more modern than traditional, more factionalized than unified; and yet, it is the central repository of Jewish memories. Contemporary Israel takes Jews beyond their age-old factionalism to the bedrock of their innermost identity. It assures Jews that they are an eternal people.

CHAPTER 3

THE OUTSIDER

I understand Abraham and Sarah because I grew up in the home of my parents, Zvi Elimelech and Nechama. Their hospitality to the poor is a legend in Baltimore, where my father was rabbi for forty-two years, from 1929 to his death in 1971. The police knew that when they found someone wandering on the street looking for a meal or a word of kindness, they could bring him or her to my mother's kitchen, and this in the days when my parents themselves had very little. I do not recall a single meal without the presence of a stranger in need at our table. So, when I read the passages in the book of Genesis about the hospitality of the first Jewish family, these are not words about long ago and far away.

Like Abraham, my father was a breaker of idols. Franklin Delano Roosevelt was an idol among the Jews, for the political coalition that elected him four times to be president of the United States included 80 or 90 percent of the Jewish voters. Roosevelt's New Deal appealed to the moral sense of Jews—he was helping the poor. He ignored the anti-Semites by giving Jews an equal chance at jobs in the federal bureaucracies, and he appointed Jews to his cabinet and to the Supreme Court. But he made no effort to open the door of the United States wider to European Jews who were trying to escape the Nazis. The question became even more urgent in 1939, when the Germans invaded Poland and began to slaughter Jews. The news of these horrors reached America almost immediately, but Washington, which was still neutral until December 7, 1941, when the United States entered the war, did not protest what the Nazis were doing to Jews in Europe, and Jews who were trying to escape had ever greater difficulty obtaining a visa.

On Yom Kippur, the Day of Atonement, in 1941, my father said to his congregation, crying bitterly as he said it, that it was the duty of Jews in free America to protest this inaction. He called on every congregant and everyone else whom they could persuade to make their way to Washington the very next day and stand outside the White House to protest the silence and inaction of America. That evening, as we were breaking the fast, we heard a sound outside the door. My sister went to investigate and found an envelope that had been shoved underneath. When my father opened it, he found a brief note informing him that the board of the congregation had convened an emergency meeting immediately after the services and had decided to fire him for his disrespect to the president of the United States. My father was a breaker of idols, and he paid the price. The truth is that Jews have had the habit, since Abraham, of being willfully different and, yes, very often in opposition to the majority. In my parents' life, and even in my own, I have known that this flag is heavy.

∞   ∞   ∞

Everything we need to know about the Jew is already present in Abraham, the first Jew, and the archetypal Jewish character. As the leader of a small, dissenting minority living precariously on the margins of society, he defines the enduring role of the Jew as the outsider. The recurring themes of Jewish history—otherness, defiance, fragility, and morality—are all present in his life. The tale of Judaism's first family, as told in the Hebrew Bible and embellished in rabbinic legend, will be replayed over and over again in the long journey of the Jewish people. The mystery of the Jewish people lies on the border between myth and history.

Abraham breaks the idols of his father, Terach, and stands alone with the one God. He is the first Jew.

God tells Abraham to leave his birthplace to go with his wife Sarah to a distant land. There they dwell in tents like bedouin and tend their flocks and herds. They are strangers living among tribes of idol worshipers. Abraham tries to build bridges across this chasm. A man of immense charity, he opens his tent on all four sides. The hungry and miserable can come to him in a straight line, not wasting a step to look for the entrance.

In the arid land of Canaan, where water is the most precious of commodities and herders survive only if their flocks can drink, Abraham digs wells and takes the unprecedented step of making them available to everyone. He forms an alliance with one of the groups that fights in a local war but refuses to take any share in the booty. He is praised for his generosity.

When three angels announce that God is about to destroy Sodom and Gomorra for their wickedness, Abraham intervenes, pleading with God to spare these populations if a minimum number of righteous people can be found among them. In his appeal, Abraham dares to admonish God: "Shall not the Judge of all the earth do justice?" (Genesis 18:23–32) He is defending pagans and idol worshipers, even though he has broken with their ways, because they, too, are God's children.

Abraham thinks he is at home in Canaan. But at the hardest moment of his life he discovers that he has no friends among the Hittites. When God commands Abraham to sacrifice his son Isaac on Mount Moriah, none of those who had eaten in his open tent or had drawn water from his wells comes to comfort him. On the contrary, as Abraham and Isaac walk for three days to reach the mountaintop, his neighbors mock him from both sides of the road. Has not your God promised that a great nation will descend from your seed? Why then does he order you to uproot your people in its very infancy? These pagans have no quarrel with a god who demands human sacrifice, for that is their practice. Your God is no better than ours, they chide, so why do you believe that you are different? Some do not wait for the journey to end. They hasten back to Beersheba and tell Sarah that her husband has slain Isaac. Sarah dies of shock. She is the first victim of Jew-hatred.

Abraham and Isaac finally arrive on Mount Moriah. The father places his son on the altar. As Abraham raises his knife, a heavenly voice tells him to stop. A lamb caught in a thicket is sacrificed instead. They return home and find Sarah dead. At that moment Abraham must take stock of his life in the land of Canaan. He and his clan have been model citizens, but the pagans have never quite forgiven him for insisting on being different.

Sarah lies unburied before him. Abraham has no choice. He must go to the Hittite elders and obtain a burial site. Having refused to leave behind his otherness and adopt their ways, the patriarch is unable to possess any land. "I am a permanent dweller (toshav) among you," he says, "but I am also an alien (ger)" (Genesis 23:4). The assembly hears him out and responds with an elaborate show of courtesy. So honored a person, they say, can take his choice of the best of their land. Knowing that these are empty words, he asks for the Cave of Machpela in Hebron but insists on paying full price. The Hittite response comes quickly. Using rhetoric to suggest that they are really granting a favor, they ask for four hundred silver shekels. Abraham is being overcharged outrageously, and he knows it. But Abraham says not a word and pays.

As an alien, Abraham understood that he and his group could survive only by being unusually cautious and beneficent. He dared not say to the Hittite chiefs: You are at one with me and I with you; and yet we are not the same. You are pagans, and I affirm the one God, whom no image or statue can represent. I do not revere gods who are appeased by bloodshed; my God demands moral righteousness. In his grief, Abraham knew that he was the quintessential outsider: the lonely person of faith who stood with his family and followers on one side of a deep divide while the rest of society stood on the other.

The Jews entered history through a primal act of defiance. Abraham woke up one morning with the conviction that there is but one God and all idols are vain and empty. In the name of his new faith, Abraham smashed his father's stone icons. The point is made again and again in the Hebrew Bible that the God of Abraham is the true God and all the other deities are false. The Jewish liturgy, quoting from the book of Psalms, repeats the theme mockingly: "They have eyes and they see not, they have ears but they hear not" (Psalms 115:4–5).

Abraham may have been the leader of a small band of nomads, but he was no mere parochial figure. He transcended the image of a defensive and subservient alien by caring for strangers. He interceded with God to spare the innocent of Sodom and Gomorra, even though they were idol worshipers. He was a good citizen and a good neighbor, but he insisted on being different.

Abraham cut this groove, and his descendants deepened it. Jews in every era have struggled to reconcile two opposing inclinations. They have wanted to maintain a separate and special culture, even as they have wanted to be accepted by the majority. This desire to be both different and the same is the root of great turmoil on three levels: It is the source of tension within the souls of individual Jews who do not know to which culture they belong; Jewish factions keep quarreling with one another about how much of the majority culture is admissible before it compromises the Jewish character; and Jews are always trying to achieve equilibrium with the rest of society, balancing their otherness with their desire for inclusion.

Often one can find opposing responses to these tensions within the same family. Two thousand years ago in Alexandria, for example, the philosopher and theologian Philo spent much of his life arguing that biblical religion was superior to Greek culture. His nephew, Tiberius Julius Alexander, became a Roman general, a principal aide of Titus in the siege of Jerusalem. He participated in the council of war that decided to burn the Second Temple (he was in the minority, arguing that the shrine should be preserved). In the 1920s Lev Davidovich Bronstein, who became the Russian revolutionary leader Leon Trotsky, refused to bury his father in a Jewish cemetery. But the movement of Jews never has been in one direction—away from Jewishness and toward assimilation. Karl Marx's daughter Eleanor, who was the descendant of a long line of rabbis but, more immediately, of two generations of converts to the Lutheran faith, returned to the community of her ancestors in the 1880s through her admiration for the immigrants in the Yiddish-speaking labor unions in London's East End. And I have been told that Trotsky's only surviving descendant, a great-grandson, is today an Orthodox Jew living in Israel. And so the battles of Jews with one another and with the gentiles never leads to total defeat or total victory. Each generation of Jews confronts these struggles anew.

THE SAVING REMNANT

It should be understood that there are essentially two camps of Jews—those who have withstood great pressure and often unspeakable suffering to uphold their otherness, and those, often the majority, who have surrendered their Jewishness in pursuit of an easier life. The prophet Isaiah described the first group as the "saving remnant" (Isaiah 10:21). These Jewish loyalists are found not only among the Orthodox who cling to the holy covenant that their ancestors accepted in the wilderness at Sinai. The Conservative and Reform Jews, who now constitute the majority of the religious believers in the Diaspora, have joined with the Orthodox in insisting that Jews must continue as a separate community cultivating its own values and outlook. Nonbelievers, too, have found many reasons for refusing to assimilate into the majority culture. In the seventeenth century Baruch Spinoza, who denied the validity of biblical religion, nevertheless refused to convert because he could accept no other religion as more true than Judaism. Three centuries later, another philosopher of Jewish origin, Henri Bergson, was attracted to the teachings of Christianity, but he chose to remain a Jew because, in his view, leaving the community in the 1920s and 1930s, at a time when it was under bitter attack by Nazis and by French anti-Semites, would have been dishonorable and even treasonous. To this day many Jews remain within the Jewish community because some mysterious amalgam of honor, defiance, pride—and a faith they often cannot define—binds them to their ancestors.

Even as the saving remnant has preserved the Jewish people, in age after age large numbers of Jews have disappeared into the mainstream culture, whether pagan, Christian, or Muslim, or have adopted some version of universal values. In the worst of times and in the best of times, large-scale defection of Jews has been a fact of life. It has been estimated that if all the Jews by birth had remained Jewish through the centuries, we would be today a people of at least a hundred million, instead of just thirteen million. The big question is, will the saving remnant complete its journey and, in theological terms, witness the end of days—the coming of the Messiah, who will return the Jews to the Promised Land and bring peace to the world—or will the Jewish people wither and die? This question has been asked in every generation since the destruction of the First Temple twenty-six hundred years ago, and it is a subject of intense speculation today. I believe that the Jewish people will survive. It always has.

I am not offering this as a kind of bromide to make concerned people feel better about the prospect of Jewish viability. My estimate of the regenerative power of the Jews is based on the premise that Jewish history represents a series of periods of rise and decline. There are times of hope and times of despair, times of destruction and times of rebuilding. This is not a restatement of Ecclesiastes, that there is nothing new under the sun (Ecclesiastes 1:9). It is based on a theory of Jewish history proposed one hundred fifty years ago by Nachman Krochmal (1785–1840), a historian of religion who lived in southeastern Poland. In his book *A Guide of the Perplexed of This Time*, modeled after Maimonides's *Guide of the Perplexed,* Krochmal insisted that Jewish history has periodicity—it goes through cycles of birth (as at the time of Abraham); rises to a zenith (as at the time of Solomon when the First Temple was built); and falls into despair (as when that Temple was destroyed five hundred years later). At low points, some Jews say it is over—our God has been defeated. We are exiled from our land; let us forget Judaism and assimilate. Others say, we will not despair; we will not give up. They wait for a better time, for a sign of redemption.

Krochmal maintained that Jewish history is unique because it goes through this cycle of rise and decline again and again. Every other civilization (for example, ancient Egyptian, Greek, and Roman) goes through a single cycle—birth, apogee, and decline. The Jews never die; they just keep repeating the cycle. For Krochmal, this is proof of God's presence in Jewish history.

I want to add a corollary to Krochmal's observation. Not only do these cycles of rise and fall repeat, but certain dramas recur within them. Almost always, the Jews find themselves torn between those who want to continue the voyage through stormy seas and those who want to jump ship into calmer waters. When the Jews left Egypt, according to one rabbinic legend, four out of five remained behind as slaves; they preferred to enjoy their small share of the plenty harvested from the fertile banks of the Nile than risk the perils of the desert with Moses.

The same pattern has repeated in the modern era. After the defeat of Nazis, the Jewish survivors in the camps for "displaced persons" declared in Yiddish, *Mir Zeinen Do*—"We are here." Hitler was dead and his armies defeated; and these few survivors resolved to go on as Jews. But many Jews who escaped the Nazis, such as the parents of United States Secretary of State Madeleine Albright, could not wait to shed the burden of their Jewishness. We do not know the number of Holocaust escapees and survivors who disappeared from Judaism after the end of the Second World War, but I have heard an estimate that the number may have been as high as one in five.

In every age there have been those Cassandras who have declared that the Jews are on the edge of extinction. Such obituaries are always premature. Fifty years ago the historian Simon Rawidowicz mocked this recurrent prophecy when he said, "The Jews are the ever-dying people." Yes, Jews have lost vast numbers, but always the continuity of the Jewish people is guaranteed by those Jews who refuse to surrender either to despair or to the seductions of the surrounding culture. The saving remnant bears the burden, and the glory, of this people with unprecedented powers of rebirth.

THE HOLY ARK WITH THE STAVES STILL ATTACHED

The biblical promise that the descendants of Abraham and Sarah would settle down in their own land finally came to pass when the Hebrews conquered the land of Canaan more than three thousand years ago. King David united the twelve squabbling tribes into one kingdom, and his son Solomon built the Temple on a hill in Jerusalem. And so, the many years of wandering had come to an end, except for one curious incident. When the priests installed the Ark of the Covenant in the Holy of Holies, they did not remove the two long staves that had been used to transport it during the forty years in the desert after the exodus from Egypt. The rabbis of the Talmud explained that the staves remained with the ark because that simple, dusty box, which had held the tablets of the Ten Commandments, was destined to go with the Jews into all their exiles. At the moment of the Jews' greatest triumph, they kept the staves in the ark to remind them that, having begun as a wandering clan, they might one day be nomads again. But come what may, the Jews will never be separated from God's Law. The journey will continue until the day the Messiah comes; only then will the staves be removed, for the ark will have come to rest in a redeemed world, where sin and suffering are no more. Only then will the Temple be restored permanently and the Jews gathered to the Promised Land from all their exiles. And this glorious future will not be for Israel alone. In one talmudic passage, the holiness of Zion is seen as spreading out to include all the peoples of the earth, and Jerusalem "will be the metropolis of all the lands" (Exodus Rabba 23:10).

In the many ecstatic visions of the coming of the Messiah, Jews are always portrayed as returning to the land of Israel. The connection of the Jews to Jerusalem and Israel is reinforced by both Christianity and Islam. For Christians, the Second Coming of Jesus will occur only when the Jews accept his divinity. They will then return to the Holy Land and the "end of days" will begin. (That is why the United Jewish Appeal is receiving millions of dollars from evangelical Christians for the settlement of Jews in Israel.) Even the Koran acknowledges that the land of Israel belongs to the Jews. The prophet Muhammad said, "The Jews are living in the land which God gave them and which He has blessed" (Koran, Sura 17:1). The Jews have always rejected the scenario of return prescribed by Christians, that the final conversion of the Jews would bring the Second Coming of Jesus. They also have denied the Muslim assertion that the land of the Jews would be an enclave in a world controlled by the followers of Muhammad. For the Jews, Israel is their birthright, and the hope of eventual return has sustained them in all their exiles. But as we shall see, the relationship between the Jews and the Promised Land is much more complicated than it might seem from the many Jewish pronouncements of enduring love.

The tension of living in exile but longing for Israel has been and remains a central theme of Jewish history. The daily Jewish liturgy expresses a great yearning for Zion; Jews face toward Jerusalem when they pray; traditionally they leave a corner of their house incomplete to remind them of the impermanence of Diaspora life; the Passover seder ends with the words, "Next year in Jerusalem"; at Jewish weddings the groom customarily crushes a glass to temper joy with the memory of the destruction of the ancient Temple. When, at the end of days, the world is ultimately set right, the exile of the Jews will end and "They will live in the land of Israel each under his vine; each under his fig tree" (1 Kings 5:5).

This hope has been all the more powerful and all the more poignant because in their more than three thousand years of history before the creation of the State of Israel in 1948, the Jews had lived on their own land as a unified nation only twice—during the rule of David and Solomon for less than a hundred years in the tenth century B.C.E., and for another century (but only in part of the land of Israel) under the Maccabees in the second and first centuries B.C.E. Even in the glorious days of King Solomon's reign, significant numbers of Jews chose to settle in trading colonies outside the boundaries of the kingdom. The Jewish experience, therefore, can be described most accurately as a people's evolution in exile under foreign domination; it is to a much lesser degree the more familiar story of other nations—of a people developing a national culture on its own soil.

The first significant Jewish Diaspora took root in the Persian Empire following the conquest of Judea and the destruction of the First Temple in 586 B.C.E. Most of the Jews were taken into captivity. They cried out in despair, "How can we sing the song of the Lord on foreign soil?" (Psalms 137:4) The prophet Jeremiah told them that it is possible to remain a Jew anywhere on earth and that while waiting for God to restore them to their former glory, they should "seek the welfare of the city to which I have exiled you—and pray to the Lord in its behalf for in its prosperity, you shall prosper" (Jeremiah 29:7). Jeremiah had presumed that the exiles would soon return home at first opportunity; he did not foresee the emergence of an enduring Diaspora.

At the end of the sixth century B.C.E., King Cyrus issued a decree that the exiles could return to Jerusalem and rebuild the Temple. About thirty thousand returned, but the majority, many tens of thousands, remained in Persia. In the course of the next several centuries, the Jews spread far and wide throughout the realm. The largest numbers settled along the Tigris and Euphrates Rivers, where their descendants would compose the Babylonian Talmud, the authoritative rab-

binic compendium of law on almost every conceivable aspect of
Jewish living.

What is at the root of this propensity for Jews to prefer living in the
Diaspora? The Talmud explains that God did the Jews a great mercy
by scattering them among the peoples of the earth, so that on their
long wait for ultimate redemption they would not all live under one
regime, which might turn hostile and slaughter them all. But why
would the Jews have to be spread all over the earth, when God can
protect them in their own land? The majority of Jews have rationalized
their remaining in the Diaspora by asserting that they are the bearers
of a universal message for all of humanity (a claim also made by
Christians and Muslims). In the mythology of Judaism, Abraham converted the men and Sarah converted the women from paganism to the
one God, and so it was to continue to this day all over the world. This
was to be accomplished not by propaganda or by missions to the unbelievers but by example. And so Jews were enjoined to create in the
Holy Land an exemplary community populated by "a kingdom of
priests, a holy people" who would show the world that a whole society can reflect God's teaching. As we know, this vision has not yet
been achieved; the standards Jews set for themselves are beyond
human possibility, but Jews have tried to keep the prophetic ideal
within sight.

The self-justifications that Jews have used for remaining in the
Diaspora are too pat and high-toned. I am convinced that the great
majority of Jews did not choose to stay in exile because they had
appointed themselves missionaries to the world, especially not in the
long centuries of the Middle Ages, when such a mission was forbidden
on pain of death. The truer and more immediate reason was that,
almost always, travel to the Holy Land involved great risk and earning
a living there proved nearly impossible. It took heroism and deep religious conviction for Jews to live in the Holy Land. And yet throughout

the centuries some did, supported by Jews in the Diaspora. But the question remains: Why did the large majority of Jews stay in the Diaspora?

The deeper answer is to be found in the character of the Jews. The Five Books of Moses, the central text of Jewish religion, is about the journey of people who began as nomads, grew to a sizable population of slaves in Egypt, and roamed for forty years in the trackless desert of Sinai. Something of the wanderer has never left the soul of the Jew. One is most aware of this on the holiest of all days in the Jewish liturgical calendar, the Day of Atonement. One of the biblical lessons in the liturgy is from the prophet Jeremiah, who reports that the relationship of God to the Jewish people is that of a groom to his bride. God then adds that his fondest recollection of their "marriage," the high point of his relationship to the Jews is the memory "of the unfailing devotion of your youth, the true love of your bridal days, when you followed Me in the wilderness through a land unsown" (Jeremiah 2:2).

The Jews are sophisticated nomads. They have played a significant role in international trade and travel since antiquity. In this century, many have settled down again in their own land but continue to be curious about the world as a whole. They cannot rest until they have seen and experienced as much of it as possible. The rite of passage in contemporary Israel includes a year or so wandering around the world after military service. Ask these young men and women why they feel compelled to do this, and the answer is invariably the same: we have grown up in a small country, and we want to know the larger world. No single land is big enough to contain creative energy that bursts forth from this people.

The Jews have cared passionately for their ancestral homeland, have remembered it, and have remained connected to it longer than any people in history. And yet Jews are also the most cosmopolitan of all peoples. Again, this paradox began with Abraham and Sarah, who were born in Mesopotamia and wandered through much of the Near East and Egypt before settling down in a desert oasis near Beersheba. Jews speak almost all the languages of the world, and they are at home in almost every country. The Jew is, at once, a nomad, a nationalist, and a cosmopolitan. Tidy categories that may work for other peoples do not fit the profile of the Jews; that is what makes us so interesting, and so unsettling to others.

What, then, has kept the Jews from abandoning their tribal origins? How have they been able to resist the attractions and rewards of the dominant cultures in which they have lived since antiquity? The answer, simply, is that only the most ardent of the Jews have clung to the faith.

THE LURE OF GRECO-ROMAN CULTURE

The descendants of the Jewish tribes encountered many pagan societies, but none posed a greater challenge than Greek culture because of its intellectual and aesthetic allure. In the wake of the military conquests of Alexander the Great, Hellenism swept through western Asia and northern Egypt. The successors of Alexander established new settlements throughout the empire. One of the grandest was the seaport of Alexandria on the Mediterranean. Jews constituted half of the city's population, and their magnificent synagogue was even more splendid than the Temple in Jerusalem.

The Greek-speaking Jews soon needed to have the Hebrew Bible translated. Most could no longer comprehend the Bible in its own language, but they strove to be faithful to its laws. Equally important, Jewish leaders wanted to demonstrate to the Greek philosophers and political elite not only that the religion of the Bible was worthy of respect, but also that Judaism was at least equal, if not superior, to Hellenistic civilization. In defending their religion, Jewish intellectuals invented theology, the explanation of biblical religion in philosophical terms. The writings of Philo, the leading Jewish scholar in Alexandria in the first century C.E., would become central to Christian and Muslim theological studies in the Middle Ages.

Like most Diaspora Jews today, the Alexandrian Jews could no longer understand Hebrew, and so the Bible needed to be translated into the language of the majority. The Septuagint, the Greek translation, was the first rendering of the sacred writ into a foreign language, and many myths surround its creation. In a famous story, seventy scholars (in another version, the number is seventy-two) were locked into separate rooms, and each produced an independent translation. The finished works were indistinguishable. This story is the source of a friendly assessment by some rabbis in the Talmud that the identical translations of the seventy scholars (*Septuagint* in Greek meaning "seventy") was divinely inspired. The opposite opinion was represented in the Talmud by the observation that the day the Septuagint appeared "was as intolerable for Israel as the day the golden calf was made, because the Torah cannot be translated adequately" (Soferim 1). The rabbis who disapproved of the translation feared that unfriendly eyes would read the Bible without the benefit of Jewish commentary and that the enemies of Judaism would find passages to attack. The attitude of the ancient rabbis toward Hellenistic culture is best summed up in an oft-repeated dictum: "Be careful of Greek wisdom, which bears no fruit but only flowers"; that is, the culture of the Greeks produces beauty but not moral truth.

A number of myths about the early Jewish encounter with Hellenistic society appear in the Talmud. In one, the rabbis imagined Alexander the Great paying his respects to the high priest of the Temple in Jerusalem, Simon the Just. A variation of this talmudic legend has Alexander visualize in a dream an exact image of Simon the Just on the night before their meetings, and the emperor acknowledges that the

Jews are heir to a noble culture. Another favorite talmudic tale describes how the wise men of Athens come to ask the rabbis to explain difficult passages in the Bible. These stories represented the desire of the Jews to be accepted by the dominant world power. In reality, Alexander never set foot in Jerusalem, and the Hellenists viewed Judaism as inferior to Greek culture.

A hundred years later Rome emerged as the reigning world power, and Hellenistic paganism was pronounced the true universal culture. Greek became the second language of Rome. Cicero and other senators prided themselves on being learned in Greek philosophy. Anyone who did not adopt Greek culture was considered uncivilized. Judaism was the most striking intellectual, religious, and cultural tradition that refused to submit to the moral authority of the new order. Unlike barbarians, who could lose their inferior status by accepting Greek culture, the Jews (called Judeans) continued to believe in the one invisible God. In Greek and Roman literature, Jews were sometimes praised but more often condemned for their devotion to this strange God who had no form or image, but the Jews had to be taken seriously as the persistent and indomitable defenders of a counterculture that set them apart from the pervasive Hellenistic civilization. This state of affairs created the perfect climate for the invention of classic anti-Semitism.

One of the earliest depictions of this new formulation of Jew-hatred is found in a Jewish source: the biblical book of Esther, which was probably composed sometime in the third or second centuries B.C.E., at the height of the clash between Jewish and Greek civilizations. In the story, which is set several centuries earlier, the vizier Haman advises the king of Persia that there is a certain people scattered among the one hundred and twenty-seven nations of the realm whose customs and laws differ from those of all others. (This remark is a summary statement of Hellenistic anti-Semitism.) Haman accuses the Jews of ignoring royal edicts and counsels the king to destroy this subversive people. In the end, the Jews are saved by Queen Esther, who had kept her Jewish identity a secret, and Haman is hanged. To this day, this Jewish early victory over anti-Semitism is celebrated during the annual festival of Purim, a day when children come to the synagogue in costume, the Scroll of Esther is read aloud, and the congregation drowns out Haman's name with noisemakers.

A BAND OF LEPERS

The Jews did not make out as well in the writings of Manetho, a Greco-Egyptian priest who in the third century B.C.E. assailed the Jews for insisting on being different and remaining aloof from the rest of society. Manetho complained that the Jews do not eat or drink with us; they do not participate in our civic life; they marry only other Jews; and they believe their god is superior to ours. They will not display our gods in their Temple, even as we accept their god in our pantheon as a sign of peace between our communities. Manetho told the story of a renegade Egyptian priest, Osarsiph (this seems to be Manetho's version of the biblical Moses), who became the leader of a band of lepers and taught his followers not to consort with the rest of society.

Manetho's critique was restated in the first century B.C.E. in a book by Apion of Alexandria who argued that the Jews really did not revolt against Pharaoh, as written in the book of Exodus; the Jewish slaves were a horde of lepers whom the Egyptians had expelled. Apion, too, condemned the Jews for their uniqueness, for being the only people that disdained the pagan gods. He invented the absurdity that once a year Jews would seize a non-Jew, taste his entrails, and swear during the meal to hate the victim's people. This charge would become a prime source for the medieval Christian canard that Jews used the blood of murdered Christian children to season the Passover matzoh.

Apion's arguments were refuted in *Against Apion,* by Josephus Flavius, the Jewish military commander who had defected to the Roman side during the Jewish revolt of 66–70 C.E. Josephus's defense established the script for future debates on the Jewish question. He said, yes, we Jews are enormously loyal to the one God, but our unique faith does not keep us from being dutiful citizens of the Roman Empire, provided that we are accorded some tolerance and not compelled by the authorities to violate God's laws. He concluded that Apion's charge that Jews are really lepers and spreaders of disease was slanderous and vile. But once these ideas took root in the common imagination, they could not be dislodged by rational argument.

Apion's attitude was echoed in the writings of some of Rome's greatest writers, including the philosopher and statesman Seneca and the orator and essayist Cicero. Seneca thundered, "The customs of that most accursed nation [more exactly: most criminal nation, *sceleratissimae gentis*] have gained such strength that they have been now received in all lands; the conquered have given laws to the conquerors."[1] Cicero found the Jews equally offensive. He wrote, "Even while Jerusalem was standing and the Jews were at peace with us, the practice of their sacred rites was at variance with the glory of our empire, and the dignity of our name, the customs of our ancestors. But now it is even more so, when that nation by its armed resistance has shown what it thinks of our rule."[2]

Apion's portrait of the Jew as a carrier of disease was often repeated in the Middle Ages by Christians, who accused the Jews of poisoning wells and spreading the Black Death. It was repeated by Hitler and Goebbels, who portrayed Jews as bacillus; it was repeated by Stalin, who believed Jewish doctors were plotting to poison him; and it is repeated today by Black Muslims, who charge that Jews are infecting them with the HIV virus. Thus Apion's portrayal of the Jew as a leper, as a despised carrier of disease, as an enemy of the human race, became deeply embedded in Western tradition. It was a libel from which the Jews have never escaped.

Throughout the centuries many Jews have tried to free themselves from the curse of anti-Semitism by leaving the Jewish community. Often, those who shifted their allegiance have done so reluctantly, in pain and self-reproach, saying that they have made the sacrifice to ensure the safety of their children. Century after century, a saving remnant of the Jews have made the opposite decision. They have brought children into the world and passed on memories of expulsions, murderous persecutions, and pogroms—the very memories that drove the others out of the fold. Why? The simplest explanation is, of course, defiance. Bringing children into the world and raising them to be Jews is the assertion that "they can't do this to us." Whoever the "they" may be and whatever "they" may be doing.

But angry defiance alone does not account for the persistence of the Jews. Nor do they endure as a people in order to make an often unwilling world better. Jews choose to raise children to be Jews because we will not break the link with past generations of our kind. We will not deprive our children of their collective past. I pray every day that I may live long enough to tell my grandchildren about their grandparents. This will be their school of virtue.

We know, of course, that Jews will have to fight the risky battle to improve the world. As I said earlier, God seems to give us no choice, but that is not why Jews remain within the fold. By choice, we are ancestor worshipers.

The American philosopher and essayist Ralph Waldo Emerson once said that each person is a charabanc (that is, a public conveyance) on whom all his ancestors ride. That is a valid description of the essential and irreducible affirmation of the committed Jew. That is why the Talmud says that at the moment of God's revelation at Sinai, the souls of all Jews, the six hundred thousand witnesses and those yet unborn, were present together. Jews may argue with God and scream at one another with factional passion, but what keeps them together as a people is the conviction that they are the descendants of great ancestors. They want their children to continue the line.

We have now reached a turning point in the book. In the first three chapters we introduced the key components of the character of the Jews. The chapters that follow demonstrate the interplay of these elements in Jewish experience. We take the reader on a two-thousand-year journey from the period of the Jewish revolt against Rome and the birth of Christianity to the present time. We are not presenting a comprehensive history. Our goal is to show that the essential Jewish character has not changed much in good times or in bad, in the course of our many, and far-flung, dispersions. You will meet scholars and mystics, apostates and false messiahs, warriors and diplomats, writers and rebels. Age after age, these men and women, sometimes tragic and often heroic, have represented the soul of the Jewish people.

CHAPTER 4

THE WILD STREAK

A conquered or enslaved people has two obvious choices: it can obey its master, or it can revolt. In ancient times Jews tried both solutions, but neither worked. They were too rebellious to be pacified and not strong enough to withstand the Assyrians and the Babylonians who destroyed the First Temple in Jerusalem or their later conquerors, the Persians and the Greeks. So the Jews devised a third choice—martyrdom, the inner resistance of those who said, better to die in obedience to God's law than to live by the law of the pagans. Thus was born *kiddush Hashem*—to die for the sanctification of God's name.

Jewish martyrdom was defined in the second pre-Christian century by the Jewish pietists who resisted the imposition of Hellenistic culture in Palestine. Such tales as the story of Hannah and her seven sons, who sacrificed their lives rather than be forced to eat pork, originated in that era and have been retold by Jews ever since. This story was undoubtedly remembered by the besieged Jews on top of Masada in the year 73 C. E., when husbands killed their own children, and their wives and then themselves, rather than become captives and slaves of the Romans. The pattern recurred in 1096, when knights of the First Crusade murdered the Jews in the Rhineland towns of Mainz, Worms, and Speier. Some of the victims tried to resist. When that became hopeless, they committed mass suicide.

Wildness as a group characteristic usually has been identified with combativeness, and foolhardiness with short temper leading to self-destructive acts of aggression. This tendency certainly has shown itself among the Jews, especially in ancient and very modern times. Jews have had some armed power, but in the long centuries of living everywhere as a powerless minority, that wild streak expressed itself in martyrdom. Such deaths were the last resort of the weak and their supreme act of defiance.

The Jews of Alexandria, while comfortable with the outer trappings of Hellenistic culture, did not deviate from their abiding devotion to the God of Israel. They fought for and won the right of exemption from any civic exercise that included the worship of pagan gods. This aversion to idolatry was even stronger among the Jews in Judea, where Roman legions were proscribed from marching into the holy city of Jerusalem with their banners on display because the eagles adorning their staffs were worshiped as deities and therefore would incite the Jews. The most dramatic occasion of Jewish resistance to idolatry in this period was described by Philo. The emperor Caligula, the madman who had forced the senate to elect his horse as consul of Rome, proclaimed himself a deity and ordered that a statue of his image be placed in the Jewish Temple in Jerusalem. Here is Philo's account of the Jewish reaction:

> When the Jewish leaders heard what the Roman authorities planned to do, they broke down in tears and lamentation, and . . . vast crowds sped to where Petronius [the Roman legate] was located. When the huge congregation approached Petronius, they fell on their faces before him and shed tears. Then the elders stood before him and spoke: "We are unarmed, as you see, . . . [we] present our bodies as an easy target for the missiles of those who wish to kill us. We are evacuating our cities, withdrawing from our houses and lands; our furniture and money and cherished possessions and all other spoils we will willingly hand over. We should think ourselves gainers thereby, not givers. One thing only we ask in return [is] that no violent changes should be made in the Temple and that it be kept as we received it from our grandparents and ancestors. But if we cannot persuade you, we give up ourselves for destruction that we may not live to see a calamity worse than death. . . . We gladly put our throats at your disposal. . . ."

Petronius stalled, and Caligula in the meantime was assassinated, thus averting a disaster. No doubt these thousands who lay down in front of Petronius did not represent every Jew in Palestine under Roman rule. They were the ones who had the courage to come out and protest and who were willing to sacrifice their lives. They were demonstrating that Jews will go to the end in defending certain principles. Jews long ago learned how to be very cautious and adaptable in order to survive in alien cultures, but within them there is that streak of wildness that strikes with fury when a certain line is crossed.

The Caligula incident occurred during one of the most turbulent centuries in the history of the Jews. Within the Jewish communities all over the world, but especially in Israel, sectarian struggles took an angry and fateful turn under the harsh rule of Rome. The battle lines were drawn between those Jews who believed that the end of days would soon come through miracles and those who wanted to overthrow Roman rule by force of arms. The revolutionary fervor intensified during the festival of Passover, when the local population of Jerusalem swelled by many thousands, as pilgrims amassed in Jewish communities from all regions of the Holy Land and the Diaspora. They came to the holy city to remember the first liberation of the Jews, when God had led them out of Egypt. This festival was always a time of fervent hope that a new redemption would come on the annual anniversary of the biblical drama. Roman sentries were put on high alert to guard against any signs of unrest. Anyone who preached in the city or its surrounds was immediately suspected of plotting an insurrection. Jesus came to Jerusalem with his disciples to celebrate Passover; his "last supper" was a seder. But the Romans saw him as a rebel; all the proof they needed to condemn Jesus was his assertion "My kingdom is not of this world." Even a hint of messianist rhetoric was a capital offense.

What actually happened in Jerusalem during the trial and crucifixion of Jesus cannot be determined with any historical accuracy. The New Testament itself differs on several crucial matters, chief among them the degree of responsibility to be ascribed to the Jewish power elite—the Sadducees—which wanted to defend itself against any accusations of disloyalty; and the Romans, who wanted to suppress all dissent by Jewish sectarians. As Christianity ceased being a Jewish sect and moved into the wider world of the gentiles, Pontius Pilate (the Roman governor in Palestine who ordered the execution of Jesus) is made to look better in the retelling of the crucifixion, and the Jewish authorities are made to look worse.

In the last century or two, as critical Christian scholarship has sought to understand the historical Jesus, Jews have become comfortable with the assertion of many of these scholars that the religion *of* Jesus is Judaism and the religion *about* Jesus is Christianity. Jews are generally comfortable with the image of Jesus as a moral teacher within the seething world of the Jews of his day, and many Jews would have little problem with the more moderate declaration by Jesus that "in my father's house there are many mansions." That vision of different religious inspirations competing side by side to do good is consistent with Jewish thought. But overshadowing all these nuanced portraits of Jesus is the stark reality that for century after century since the crucifixion, Jews have been slandered, beaten, and murdered by Christians for supposedly killing the son of God.

Christians have wanted to know for a long time what Jews really think of their religion. This question has persisted because there is a fundamental lack of symmetry between Judaism and Christianity. Christianity is inconceivable without its relationship to Judaism. It has taken the Hebrew Bible for its own but calls it the Old Testament, for it is regarded as the first act of the divine drama, which came to climax and conclusion in the New Testament. On the other hand, there is absolutely nothing in Judaism, in its own terms, that requires it to have an opinion or a theology of Jesus. Judaism is no more obliged to produce an explanation of Jesus than Christianity is obliged to accommodate Muhammad in its theology. Nonetheless, living among the Christians, Jews have tried, on occasion, to give an assessment of Jesus. The normative Jewish answer has been, since medieval times, that he was a teacher of prophetic morality, a unique kind of rabbi, a spiritual figure of profound importance to the world. But this response has rarely eased the discomfort of Christians with Jews because central to their faith is the divine incarnation of Jesus. No amount of rhetoric can talk away this historic and fateful difference between Jews and Christians.

The truth is that in biblical religion each version insists that only its adherents know what God really wants of humanity. The problem is the degree to which each tradition tries to push or even force its faith on others. Jews, for one, have never expected Christians to agree that the correct understanding of the Bible is to be found in the Talmud. Believing Jews have been willing to wait for the end of days to prove who is right. The issue for Jews has always been Christendom, not Christianity—not the faith of the Christians but their wrath toward the "perfidious" and "faithless" Jews. For nineteen centuries Christians have been obsessed with the question: Why don't the Jews accept Jesus as the Messiah? Jews, in turn, have been obsessed with the question: Why do they keep persecuting us? To understand how a small Judean sect emerged as the dominant religion of the Roman Empire and the chief persecutors of the Jews, we need to go back to the year 66 C.E.—to the story of a supreme example of the wild streak in the character of the Jews.

THE REVOLT

Some thirty years after the execution of Jesus, a relatively small but determined group of Jewish rebels, the Zealots, launched a revolt against Rome. The hundreds of thousands of Jews who had inundated Jerusalem for Passover were trapped by the Roman legions that had laid siege to the city. These Jews had no choice but to fight. In his account of the fall of Jerusalem and the destruction of the Second Temple, Josephus glorified Titus, the Roman commander and future emperor, but he also described scenes of Jewish heroism—of Jewish defenders who hurled themselves into the flames consuming the Holy Temple rather than surrender. More than a million Jews perished in the revolt, and many more fell in its aftermath. Titus had given orders that all Jewish captives were to be taken alive, and he placed his friend Haterius Fronto in charge of the evacuation. Nonetheless, a "selection" took place. The Roman soldiers, though weary from the long campaign, were ordered to slaughter all the aged and infirm. Only "men in their prime" who could be sold into slavery or killed for sport in Roman arenas were to be kept alive. While Fronto was sorting out the prisoners, eleven thousand of them died of starvation.

Jewish perspectives on the Temple's destruction abound in talmudic literature. Why did God allow the Temple to be destroyed? The Talmud fixes blame on the Jews themselves. One rabbi said it happened "because during the time it stood, hatred without rightful cause prevailed. This [catastrophe] is to teach you that this sin is deemed as grave as . . . idolatry, immorality, and bloodshed combined" (Yoma 9b). The Jews were confronted not only with the destruction of the Temple, but also its desecration. The rabbis reached for the most lurid images to emphasize the horror and revulsion of witnessing the demise of Judaism's holiest shrine and the way of life that had surrounded it (Shir-Hashirim Rabba 1:5). The Talmud tells the improbable story that the Roman general Titus entered the Holy of Holies, spread out on its floor a scroll of the Torah, and used the parchment as the bedsheet on which he coupled with a harlot!

The divine will was accepted, but the anger that Jews directed at God was not muted. At the very moment when the Temple was being destroyed in flames (the story is told in two versions, about the destruction of both the First and the Second Temples), young priests climbed onto the roof and threw the keys to the sanctuary heavenward, and they cried out to God: "We have no further use of these keys to the Sanctuary . . . so You take them back." A hand reached down from heaven and took the keys. The priests then threw themselves into the flames (Taanit, 29a).

The revolt against Rome did not end with the fall of Jerusalem. It continued for three more years until the fall of Masada, where nearly a thousand Zealots resisted the Roman legions from a mountain stronghold on the edge of the Judean Desert near the Dead Sea. When Masada was about to be overrun, the Jewish commander Eleazar ben Jair called the defenders together and proposed a final act of defiance. In two impassioned speeches (as reported by Josephus) Eleazar insisted that the disasters that had befallen his people could not be attributed entirely to the revolt but were due also to the otherness of the Jews. The Jews in Caesarea, he reminded them, had been massacred by the mob while they "were engaged in observing their Sabbath festival." It had happened as well in Syria. "Thus the people of Damascus, though they could not even fake a plausible pretext, deluged their city with the most loathsome slaughter, butchering eighteen thousand Jews. . . ." And in Egypt, the toll was sixty thousand. Eleazar ben Jair explained that everywhere, their enemies did not forgive the Jews for being different: "These Jews perhaps died as they did because they were aliens and could not resist their enemies." As their last act of resistance at Masada, Eleazar urged his followers to take their own lives rather than to risk being sold into slavery. "I think it is God who has granted us this privilege," he said, "that it is in our power to die bravely in freedom. . . . It is evident that tomorrow we will be captured, but we are free to choose an honorable death together with those we love most."[2]

The choices faced by the defenders of Masada were repeated under equally desperate and tragic circumstances in April 1943, after the Nazis had decided to eliminate the last of the Jews in the Warsaw Ghetto. On the third day of the "great liquidation" the leaders of the various Jewish political parties in the ghetto held a strategy meeting.

One of those present, a Labor Zionist named Hirsch Berlinski, left behind a summary of the discussion, giving the reason why they had decided to fight with no chance of victory:

> In one way or another deportation means annihilation. It is therefore better to die with dignity and not like hunted animals. There is no other way out, all that remains to us is to fight. Even if we are capable of putting up a fight that only resembles real fighting, it will still be better than a passive acceptance of slaughter. . . . By acting in this manner we shall show the world that we stood up to the enemy, that we did not go passively to our slaughter.[3]

The stories of Masada and the Warsaw Ghetto Revolt became two of the great rallying cries of the modern State of Israel, a nation that had been established to end the powerlessness of the Jews in exile. Every Israeli child knows the slogan, "Masada shall not fall again." Climbing to the top of Masada is a rite of passage for the young, and the elite soldiers in Israel's armed forces are sworn in on the ground where Eleazar ben Jair made his fateful appeal almost two millennia earlier. And yet, these legendary episodes of Jewish heroism have a dark side, which cannot be denied. Jews, throughout the centuries, have found fault with themselves in the face of defeats. This note was sounded by Josephus in his introduction to *The Jewish War:* "For it so happened that of all the cities under Roman rule, our own reached the highest summit of prosperity, and in turn fell into the lowest depths of misery; the misfortunes of all other races since the beginning of history, compared to those of the Jews, seem small; and for our misfortunes we have only ourselves to blame." Josephus did not criticize the Romans as an expanding empire that needed to control Palestine as part of its strategic plan; he commented only the folly of Jewish resistance. Thus the Jewish tendency toward self-reproach rather than fixing blame on the real enemy has deep roots. Jews repeated this pattern after the destruction of both Temples, after the expulsion of the Jews from Spain, and in the aftermath of the Holocaust.

This attitude of Josephus foreshadows the liturgy of the traditional Jewish prayerbook. We have in every major festival service a prayer that begins "Because of our sins we have been exiled from the land." The notion of self-blame, that we are rebellious children who are punished by the displeased father, takes the edge off our anger with God and provides a framework in which we can make peace with the Almighty; it keeps the relationship intact. But the Jewish people never quite knows exactly for what sin it is being punished and why so severely. Even though Jews in prayer recite all the transgressions of which they might be possibly guilty, they know in their hearts that there is a serious imbalance between the sin and the punishment. What sin can the Jews possibly have committed that would necessitate the taking of six million Jewish lives, one and a half million of them children? This theological framework breaks down when measured on the scale of the Holocaust. Josephus called it into question at the time of the destruction of the Second Temple. Such events create an insoluble quandary. And so, believing Jews set theology aside and repeat after every tragedy: we mere humans cannot comprehend the ways of the Lord.

But Jews cannot let it go at that. After each great disaster, many Jews give up and disappear, but others strengthen their resolve to go on, often in defiance. The tale is told of a pious Jewish man who was driven from Spain during an anti-Jewish riot. After several years of wandering, he was cast upon some remote North African shore. His wife and his children had remained behind and were forcibly baptized. So there he sat, deprived of everything dear to him. And what was this man doing? He was writing a commentary on the Talmud. At one point he looked up and said, "Dear God, You have done everything imaginable to chase me away from You, but I will not let You. I will continue to believe in You; and I will continue to behave as part of Your chosen people. I do not know why You have sent all this pain and woe upon me, but if You are testing me as You once did Job, and expect that I might revile You, it will not happen." This Jew in all his misery was determined to uphold his part of the contract with God. He would remain faithful and obedient to the Holy One, but he insisted that God do the same, by protecting and delivering him or his descendants to the Promised Land.

The defiance of emperors and dictators and even of God is the Jewish assertion that surrender is the ultimate sin. The Jews have an unshakable will to go on, even when the rest of the world, and even God, seem to be against them. In the Bible God called the Jews a "stiff-necked" people; I call it the wild streak. Just when our enemies think we are defeated, the Jews strike back, sometimes with military force, sometimes by dying the death of martyrs, and sometimes by reinventing themselves.

THE "MESSIAH" ARMED

When Titus marched triumphantly into Rome displaying the Holy Menorah upon the backs of Jewish slaves, he thought that Rome had stamped out the last embers of Jewish armed resistance. He was wrong. A generation later, in the time of the emperor Trajan, minor uprisings erupted both in Palestine and in the Diaspora, but these were put down. The last major military action by Jews in ancient times was led by Bar Kokhba ("son of a star") in 132 C.E. At first, Bar Kokhba's forces pushed back the Romans, and for three years he led a Jewish government in Israel. Ultimately, the revolt was crushed and its supporters were either exiled or executed after torture. The Romans decreed the teaching of the Jewish religion to be a capital offense, but underground instruction continued. The rabbis who were caught accepted their deaths as the will of God. Among them was Rabbi Akiva, who had declared Bar Kokhba the Messiah. At age eighty-five, in the year 135 C.E., he was tortured to death by the flaying of his flesh with "iron combs."

One of the most famous talmudic stories tells of Rabbi Akiva, together with three colleagues, walking toward Rome in the aftermath of the Temple's destruction. As they approached the city, they heard the sounds of merrymaking crowds. His three colleagues began to weep, but not Rabbi Akiva. They asked him, "Why are you so cheerful?" He replied, "Why are you weeping? Look at these heathen, who bow and burn incense to idols; they live in safety and tranquillity. Yet we, the followers of the one true God, are defeated—our Temple has been destroyed. It is for that very reason that I am cheerful," Rabbi Akiva replied. "If they, who offend the Holy One, fare so well, how much better will fare those of us who please the Lord!" (Makkot 24a–b)

In his own life, Rabbi Akiva exemplified a central affirmation of the Jewish character: there is always another chance. He was illiterate until forty—but he became the greatest scholar of his age. He refused to bow to the Romans in defeat—so he joined the revolt by Bar Kokhba. After the revolt was stamped out, he defied the decree not to teach Torah. The spirit of Rabbi Akiva could not be crushed; even in the face of terrible death by torture, he was not defeated.

The fall of Bar Kokhba marked the end of any serious thought of continued armed Jewish resistance. The rabbis of succeeding generations turned to study and matters of the spirit to preserve the Jewish way of life. In time, relations between the Jews and Romans in Palestine improved. Tradition has it that Rabbi Judah the Prince, the spiritual and temporal leader of the Jews in Palestine in the second century, maintained a friendly correspondence with the Roman emperor.

A famous story in the Talmud reflects the ambivalence of the Jews in this period: Two rabbis are walking down the street discussing the nature of Roman rule. One says, "The Romans are doing a decent job. They are bringing order, structure, and a kind of civility and civilization to Palestine. They are building roads, bathhouses, and public works." The second rabbi says, "You fool, they are not doing this for you or me. They are building bathhouses for their own enjoyment. They are building roads in straight lines so they can march their legions quickly to any trouble spot—to control us!" (Shabbat 33b)

Jews continued for many centuries to be deeply ambivalent about the governments under which they lived. They looked to them for protection against hostile elements, but they also knew that the noblemen and kings who protected them sooner or later would confiscate all that the Jews owned and then expel them from the realm. Jews, therefore, acquired a healthy distrust of temporal powers.

A VICTORY OF THE HEART

In their failed military struggle against mighty Rome, the Jews nevertheless scored one victory of profound historical importance. They undermined the faith of the Romans in paganism. In the very times that the Jews were engaged in bitter warfare with the Romans, large numbers among the upper-class intelligentsia of the empire, in the outer provinces and in Rome itself, converted to Judaism, convinced that the true God is not an idol. The Jewish revolt conferred prestige and respect upon Jews and Judaism, for theirs was one of the two most bitter campaigns that Rome had ever fought (the other had been the war with Carthage, led by Hannibal). Many Romans were in awe of the Jews, who showed exceptional heroism in the war. They could not help but wonder about a religion and culture that moved this people to stand up to Rome with such determination and self-sacrifice. What kind of a god could inspire a degree of devotion and loyalty so much greater than any deity worshiped in Rome? The Jewish teachings of God, therefore, had to be taken seriously—and many were swayed by what they learned about the moral teachings of the Jews.

Roman women in much greater numbers than men became fully Jewish because their joining the faith required only immersion in some source of "living water" and acceptance of the rituals and laws prescribed in the Hebrew Bible. Men were more reluctant to undergo formal conversion. They did not want to subject themselves to the painful and often dangerous surgical ritual of circumcision; therefore, men who favored Judaism became sympathizers rather than proselytes. So widespread was this rush toward Judaism that the Roman satirist Juvenal (ca 60–130 C.E.) poked fun at the Judaizing Roman as one "who . . . worships nothing but the clouds and the divinity of the heavens . . . and who gives up every seventh day to idleness."[4] There is no reliable estimate of the number of converts and semiconverts to Judaism in the Roman Empire, but the historian Salo W. Baron calculated that Jews and sympathizers with Judaism numbered seven to eight million, one-tenth of the population of the Roman Empire in the first and second centuries![5]

The Jews conducted the religious war against Rome with the same intensity as the Zealots had fought in the armed revolts. Jews, on occasion, may compromise with the world and with one another, but at the root of the Jewish character lies a spirit of resistance to the imposition of false gods. Contemporary Jews are the descendants of stubborn people who resisted hostile cultures and powers for many centuries. Something of these ancestors lives within them. The lasting character of the Jews contains an element of defiance.

But it is more than an act of resistance to alien cultures and other gods, or even to persecution. The source of the Jews' determination to prevail is the fierce conviction that their values are the right ones.

CHAPTER 5

THE SYNAGOGUE
OF SATAN

One of the first books that I read about the Holocaust was *The Teaching of Contempt* by Jules Isaac, a French Jew who was the sole survivor of his family. Isaac had agonized over the question of how anti-Semitism could have poisoned European culture so deeply that Nazism became possible. His answer was that the Church had taught contempt for Jews from its beginnings, and therefore European culture had been fashioned with Jew-hatred as a central element. Isaac sent the book to Pope John XXIII, whom he had met before the war, when he had been the papal nuncio in Paris. The pope reacted by making this issue a central concern of the council that he called in the mid-1960s to reform the church.

Since then, the Roman Catholic Church has been moving toward the eradication of anti-Semitism. This process of shaping a new Christian understanding of Jews and Judaism has led to a number of historic firsts. In the fall of 1971, official representatives of the Vatican met with a delegation from Israel and the Diaspora (which I chaired) in a Paris synagogue. For three days, the bishops ate kosher meals together with rabbis. As I sat at those sessions, I was struck by the profound irony of the scene. In 1242 the Talmud had been burned publicly in Paris. Now, seven centuries later, bishops and rabbis were sitting face-to-face, not to dispute Judaism but to show it respect. We had come to Paris to set Jewish-Catholic relations on a new and conciliatory path. On both sides of the table, all of us knew that we could not simply set aside the burdens of past centuries. For healing to happen, history had to be confronted, openly and honestly. In this spirit we turn now to the question of the age-old conflict between Jews and Christians.

In *The Decline and Fall of the Roman Empire,* Edward Gibbon accused Christianity of destroying the Roman Empire. Christianity had flourished quickly because it offered an attractive option to Judaism. They would not be bound by the ritual laws "prescribed in the Old Testament"; they needed to obey only the moral laws as preached by Jesus and the apostles. Most important, the new religion guaranteed salvation in heaven for every individual who believed that God had appeared incarnate in Jesus and, through his suffering on earth, had redeemed humanity from its sins. Thus, a sect born in Judaism, the adherents of which Voltaire, the great skeptic of the eighteenth-century Enlightenment derided as a bunch of "reformed Jews," had retired the gods of Mount Olympus.

When the Roman emperor Constantine embraced Christianity in 313 C.E. and the new faith soon became the state religion, the Jews might have viewed this shift as their triumph over Roman idolatry. But the Jews could not savor this victory, for they were confronted now by a new nemesis—the imperial Church of Rome—which would declare itself the universal faith. The Jews were soon cast as the obdurate outsider in the vast empire now dominated by Christians, who became the chief custodians of the anti-Semitic tradition, which, as we have seen, had Greco-Roman roots. The Church denounced the Jewish religion as the "Synagogue of Satan," a concept that had appeared first in the New Testament (Revelations 2:9). The first Christians wondered why Jesus, the manifestation of God in human form, was rejected by his own people. The apostle Paul answered that the Jews were blind to this miracle before their very eyes because they clung obdurately to the old covenant, full of laws and rituals, which was "a dispensation of death carved in letters on stone . . . a dispensation of condemnation . . . [which] fadeth away, in comparison with a new covenant which is the 'dispensation of the spirit'" (2 Corinthians 3:6–11). The great Jewish sin was Christ rejection, not Christ killing (Christians believed that God had ordained the crucifixion drama). According to the Church the Jews, more than any other people, should have believed in Jesus as the Messiah because he was one of their own, but they refused.

For the Christians the destruction of the Temple was divine punishment for the sin of rejecting Jesus. The Jews could end their travail if only they would repent for having followed after Satan. In Christian doctrine, the Jews thus occupied both a uniquely negative and a uniquely positive role in the salvation drama. They were to be made miserable but not utterly destroyed; they had to be kept alive in order to play their theologically scripted role at the end of days. All of humanity would be redeemed, and the Jews would be converted to the true faith.

Christianity was a more formidable threat to Jews than paganism, which tended to be tolerant of other people's gods. The ancient Greeks and Romans harbored no theological hostility toward the Jews; they opposed the Jews on political grounds—for rebelling against the authority of the emperors. In the talmudic period, especially after the failed Bar Kokhba revolt, Jews learned to live in peace on the margins of pagan culture. But the situation of the Jews took a dramatic turn for the worse when the Church began to use state power to subjugate the Jews for refusing to accept the "new covenant."

The rabbis had no ready defense against Christianity as they had against idol worship, which was condemned over and over again by God in the Hebrew Bible. The Ten Commandments begin, "I am the Lord your God. Thou shalt not have other gods before Me," followed by the second commandment, "Make no graven image" (Exodus 20:2–4). Moses, in his final speech to the Jews, told them in awful detail what the punishment for idolatry would be: If you listen to my commandments, all will go well with you, but if you disobey the laws and follow after foreign gods, every possible curse will afflict you. At the end of this menacing speech, Moses admonished them: "And the Lord shall scatter these [idol worshipers] among all people, from the one end of the earth even unto the other, and there you will serve other gods of wood and stone.... Yet you will find no peace..." (Deuteronomy 28:64–65).

The Bible offers little direction or guidance on how to counter a breakaway sect claiming to be the "true Judaism." On the positive side, the Christians rejected pagan idols and accepted the divine revelation at Sinai, but their denunciation of the rabbis and deification of Jesus was heresy. In the face of this challenge, the only defense Jews could find in the Five Books of Moses was the passage in Deuteronomy (13:2–5), warning that if a prophet arises among you and teaches you things that are not written in this Torah, he is a false prophet. This argument was of little use in countering the Christians, who responded that Jesus does teach what is written in the Torah. At its root, this debate is about legitimacy: Which of the two biblical faiths was the true bearer of God's revelation to humankind? This argument cannot be resolved by rational argument. Fundamentalist Christians still insist that Jews will be saved only declaring their faith in Jesus, and believing Jews hold fast to their basic contention that God demands virtuous acts, not declarations of belief.

As the fortunes of the Church rose in the medieval period and Jewish conversion efforts were outlawed, the Jews conceded that their exile probably would not end anytime soon. A further blow came in the seventh century, when Islam arose and the Dome of the Rock was erected in Jerusalem on the very ground where the Second Temple had once stood. Christianity and Islam had become the dominant religions of almost all the lands in which Jews lived. The descendants of Abraham and Sarah had no choice but to settle down as outsiders in exile and wait for the miracles that would signal their redemption and repatriation to the Promised Land at the end of days.

Many Christians were made uneasy by their continuing persecution of Jews, but not because they doubted that the Jews deserved to be reviled; they feared that Jews were furious at their persecutors and wanted to take revenge, as Shylock did in Shakespeare's *The Merchant of Venice*. Such suspicions gave rise to a litany of wild accusations against the Jews, who supposedly were poisoning wells and spreading plague; draining the blood of Christian children to bake matzoh; breaking into churches at night and urinating on the sacramental wafers; and conspiring with the devil to sully everything that was sacred, clean, and virtuous. These false charges, which were believed widely among Christians, led to ever harsher outrages against Jews, who, in medieval Christian literature and art, were portrayed as ugly to behold and foul of smell; even their languages were deemed repulsive to the ear. Jew-hatred was thus transmuted from a theological argument to an anti-Semitic loathing of murderous potency.

POISONING THE WELLS

When the Black Death swept through Europe in the middle of the fourteenth century, killing an estimated twenty-five million people, the rumor quickly spread that Jews were engaged in a conspiracy to infect all the Christians. Never mind that Jews were not immune from the ravages of the plague; they were tortured until they "confessed" to crimes that they could not possibly have committed. In one such case, a man named Agimet was put on trial in Geneva on October 10, 1348. To spare himself further torment before his execution, Agimet was coerced to say that Rabbi Peyret of Chambery (near Geneva) had ordered him to poison the wells in Venice, Toulouse, and elsewhere. In the aftermath of Agimet's "confession," the Jews of Strasbourg were burned alive on February 14, 1349. The contemporary historian F. Closener, who did not believe that the Jews were poisoners of wells, made the following observation:

> The money was indeed the thing that killed the Jews. If they had been poor and if the feudal lords had not been in debt to them, they would not have been burnt. After this wealth was divided among the artisans some gave their share to the Cathedral or to the Church on the advice of their confessors. Thus were the Jews burnt at Strasbourg, and in the same year in all the cities of the Rhine, whether Free Cities or cities belonging to the lords. In some towns they burnt the Jews after a trial, in others, without a trial. In some cities the Jews themselves set fire to their houses and cremated them-selves.[1]

The economic exploitation of the Jew is a common expression of anti-Semitism, but it is not the cause. What gives particular impetus to this hatred is the perception that Jews are the enemies of conventional society, and therefore whatever they possess does not really belong to them; it has been stolen from the rightful owners of the land. When the Jews are perceived as having "too much," or when kings want to dispossess them, or when peasants want to avoid paying their bills, the obvious response is, "What, me, a Christian, pay that Jew?"

Thus Jews found themselves at risk both from above and below: if the nobility did not abuse them, the peasants would. As outsiders in Christian and Muslim societies, some court Jews might rise to positions of wealth and influence, but they lived in a constant state of insecurity.

THE KHAZARS

Amid increasing despair, one event gave the Jews hope that they might one day live freely in their own independent land. In about the year 740 C.E., the Khazars, a people who lived in the Volga-Caucasus near the Caspian Sea, formally converted to Judaism. Jews all over the world exulted in the news that a tribe numbering in the hundreds of thousands had adopted Judaism. They took solace in the fact that at least somewhere in the world, a people had recognized that the true religion is Judaism.

The story of the Khazars received special attention in Spain, where the Jews had achieved distinguished positions in the Muslim realms. In about 960 Hasdai Ibn Shaprut, who was the chief commercial and foreign affairs minister and physician to the caliphs of Córdoba, wrote a famous letter to Joseph, king of the Khazars, to inquire whether it was true that Jews exist somewhere in their own independent kingdom. If there is such a place, confided Ibn Shaprut, he would abandon his high estate, leave his family, and cross mountains and seas to where the king resides in order to behold his royal magnificence and the "tranquillity of the Israelites." Hasdai also wanted to know "whether there is among you any computation concerning the final redemption, which we have been awaiting so many years. . . . We have been cast down from our glory, so that we have nothing to reply when they say daily to us, 'Every other people has a kingdom, but of yours there is no memorial on the earth.'"

Hasdai's letter moved from hand to hand through what is now Hungary, Romania, and Bulgaria, finally reaching King Joseph in his capital of Itil, on the Volga River. A reply in Hebrew arrived about five years later. The king responded with great respect to Hasdai's questions and recalled the story of how his predecessor, King Bulan, had chosen Judaism over Christianity and Islam:

> Having assembled all his princes and ministers, and the whole of his people, he (King Bulan) said to them [the representatives of Christianity, Islam, and Judaism], "I ask you to choose for me the best and truest religion." They begin to speak without, however, arriving at any result. Thereupon the king said to the Christian priest, "Of the religions of the Israelites and Mohammedans, which is to be preferred?" The Christian priest answered, "The religion of the Israelites." He then asked the Mohammedan Kadi, "Is the religion of the Israelites, or that of the Christians better?" The Kadi answered, "The religion of the Israelites is preferable." Upon this, the king said, "You both confess that the religion of the Israelites is the best and the truest, wherefore I choose the religion of the Israelites, which is that of Abraham.". . . Henceforth Almighty God was his helper, and strengthened him, and he was circumcised, and all his servants.[2]

Early in the eleventh century a Spanish-Jewish rabbi and theologian, Yehuda Halevi, wrote the *Khuzari*, a book inspired by the Khazar king's letter to Hasdai (which may not have been authentic). Halevi, who wanted to prove that the Jews were the people through whom God connected with all of humanity, wrote, "Were it not for the children of Israel there would be no divine teaching in the world." Using the conversion of the Khazars in his polemic, Halevi turned the tables on the dominant religions of his day. He argued that the New Testament and the Koran were simply clashing sectarian additions to the Hebrew Bible. The true faith, as the Khazar king had recognized, was Judaism. Yehuda Halevi's chauvinism was a reaction to the growing power and influence of the Muslims and Christians. The Jews, already in exile for nine hundred years, had become a lesser power, and nothing was happening in their favor. To maintain hope, the Jews insisted that the power and the glory of the Christians and Muslims are temporary but that the truth of the Jews is permanent.

THE GOLDEN AGE IN SPAIN

The Jewish infatuation with the Khazars indicates that even in the best of times in the history of the Diaspora, the lavish "Golden Age in Spain," the Jews felt a profound sense of alienation. Hasdai Ibn Shaprut, who commanded great influence in his own generation, was, as we have seen, consumed with longing to live in a Jewish kingdom where power was held by his own people. The same discontent was present two centuries later in Moses Maimonides (1135–1204), known as the Rambam, who rose to the very height both of Jewish knowledge and of contemporary culture. He had mastered all the texts, ancient and modern, that could be read in Arabic, but he was distrustful of the Muslim majority. Soon after his bar mitzvah in the year 1148, a fanatical Islamic sect, the Almohads, conquered Córdoba, the city of

Maimonides's birth, forcing the family to wander for ten years through Spain before finding an uneasy refuge in Fez, Morocco. The family finally settled in Egypt, after a brief stay in the Holy Land, then in Christian hands. Maimonides joined his brother in the trading of precious stones, but he turned to the practice of medicine after his brother was drowned in the Indian Ocean while traveling abroad on a trading expedition. Maimonides eventually became a physician in the court of the sultan Saladin.

His years as a refugee under unrelenting religious pressure (the Almohads did not hesitate to kill Jews in forcing them to convert) created much bitterness in his heart. This anger came to the surface on the occasions when Maimonides permitted himself some personal remarks. In the epilogue to his *Commentary on the Mishnah,* the central text of the Talmud, Maimonides apologized for any imperfections or errors in this work. The task itself was difficult, he wrote, but "In addition, I was agitated by the distress of our time, the exile which God had decreed upon us, the fact that we are being driven from one end of the world to the other." A few years later, he wrote in the prologue to his *Epistle to Yemen:* "How could we study the law when we were being exiled from city to city, and from country to country?"[3] In the text of that letter to the Jews of Yemen (they were being forced into apostasy by Muslim fanatics), Maimonides wrote with great bitterness about both the Christians and the Muslims who continued to persecute Jews, but he assured the Jews of Yemen that the believers would survive: "Put your trust in the true promises of Scripture, brethren, and be not dismayed at the series of persecutions or the enemy's ascendancy over us, or the weakness of our people."

Our understanding of Hasdai and Maimonides casts doubt on the common depiction of Jewish life in Muslim Spain as a Golden Age. To be sure, some of the Jews did think that they were at home in Islamic culture. They traveled easily between Jewish and Arabic cultures, even while affirming the superiority of the Jewish faith. The rich among the Jews in Islamic Spain thought of themselves as fully the equals of Arab nobility. The Jews learned from the Arabs to be philosophers and poets, scientists and astronomers. They wrote in Hebrew or Arabic on every subject of intellectual discourse. But rarely were Jewish authors or thinkers cited in Arabic literature. Apparently, the Muslims felt they had nothing to learn from the Jewish culture, which they considered inferior. This so-called Golden Age was largely a one-sided affair. It signified little more than the tolerance of Islamic rulers for Jews who brought them economic advantage and helped them in their wars with the Christians.

ASSAULT ON THE TALMUD

In the High Middle Ages, beginning in the thirteenth century, the Christian attack on Judaism took a radical and most threatening turn. Church leaders decided that when the rabbis had rejected the New Testament, they were really saying that the Talmud was the true interpretation of the Hebrew Bible. Therefore, if the Talmud was the source of the refusal of the Jews to acknowledge that the Hebrew Bible had predicted Jesus, then its authority needed to be destroyed. This new tactic was invented by a Jewish convert to Christianity, Nicholas Donin, who had been a disciple of a famous rabbinic scholar, Jehiel of Paris. He constructed a list of thirty-five accusations against the Talmud, charging its rabbinic authors with blasphemies and obscenities directed against the figures of Jesus and Mary, and Christians as a whole. This attack prompted a disputation in Paris in 1240, in which Donin debated his former teacher, Rabbi Jehiel. In this confrontation the Talmud was put "on trial" for the first time. The outcome was predictable: the Talmud was condemned to be burned. This sentence was carried out two years later when twenty-three cartloads of rabbinic texts were put to the torch in a public ceremony. But this tactic did not succeed in stopping Jews from studying the Talmud, because the bailiffs who were sent out to collect these forbidden texts could not find all the copies, and even if they had, the learned among the Jews had committed all the sixty-three tractates to memory.

The most famous medieval disputation was held in Barcelona, Spain, in 1263 before the Christian monarch, Jaime I of Aragon. The Jewish protagonist, Moses ben Nachman (1194–1270), known as Nachmanides, was the greatest rabbi of the time and one of the towering Jewish religious and intellectual figures of the medieval period. He consented to this disputation because the king had guaranteed his personal safety. His opponents were Raymond Penaforte and the apostate Pablo Christiani, who had received a rabbinic education and knew some Talmud. Again, the Christians enlisted a converted Jew to prove the Talmud had foreshadowed Christianity and to show that this truth had been distorted in rabbinic interpretations. It was asserted by Christian polemicists that Pablo Christiani would be able to "refute the Jews' malice and errors, since . . . [they] could no longer audaciously deny, as they did before, the genuine text and glosses of their own ancient sages whenever they agree with our own saints in matters pertaining to the Catholic faith."[4]

This challenge was met by Nachmanides. Without debating the talmudic text passage by passage (which would have undermined Pablo Christiani in the presence of the king and the high prelates whom he had come to serve), Nachmanides reminded the audience that Christiani had made previous conversionist preaching tours of the Jewish communities in the Provence. Each time he had failed to convince any learned Jews that the Talmud had recognized Jesus to be the Messiah. If the Talmud had said such a thing, Nachmanides said, why would the Jews persist in rejecting Christianity and remaining faithful to their own understanding of Scripture? Nachmanides did not dare to deny, directly and openly, the divinity of Jesus, for such a statement would make him guilty of blasphemy. He limited himself to the argument that by continuing to make wars, the Christians were betraying Jesus, the prince of peace.

On the Sabbath after the opening of the debate, the king visited the synagogue in Barcelona, and he let Nachmanides go on his way. And so the disputation ended inconclusively. Any other outcome was essentially impossible. The Jew could not be declared the victor by a believing Christian king, and he could not be pronounced the loser by an honorable king who would have to go back on his word and force the rabbi's conversion.

Nachmanides soon published a book in Hebrew in which he recounted his great victory in the debate. It included the very critique of Christianity that he could not make in public. The Christians published their own summation of the debate in Latin, in which Nachmanides was portrayed as having been tongue-tied and totally ineffective. Unfortunately for Nachmanides, the Hebrew-literate converts obtained a copy of his polemic. His life in Spain was now untenable. Despite the king's assurances that he would not be punished for his role in the debate, Nachmanides did what Yehuda Halevi had done before him; he escaped to the Holy Land. His decision was not surprising in light of the fact that he had been the major authority among the medieval rabbis who ruled that under any and all circumstances— no matter what the dangers—every Jew was obligated by religious law to move to the land of Israel.

Nachmanides had overstepped the bounds of a Jewish public figure of that day. Jewish leaders had to keep a public silence when their religion was denigrated by Christians. But it was the responsibility of these leaders not to let their side down, for they had to give their people hope and courage. The Jews had become adept at this form of inner resistance; it was the only weapon at their command.

CHAPTER 6
THE TERRIBLE CHOICE

In June 1940 I was graduating from college in the very week that France fell to the Wehrmacht. Suddenly the Atlantic Ocean was not wide enough to make me feel secure in Baltimore. This fear showed in the conversations I had that week, as I made the rounds to thank the teachers who had been particularly kind to me. I told one of them about my fears and asked him directly what he would do if the Nazis came to Johns Hopkins and installed a Gauleiter in the office of the president. He thought a moment and decided to give me a frank answer: "You would have no choice because you are a Jew; I would be able to lie low and stay out of harm's way." He would remain at his post, hoping to do his best to protect and preserve the ideas and values of the university. The conversation seemed to be at an end, so I got up and thanked him, as best as I could, for all that he had done for me through my years at college. He knew, however, that I had heard his unspoken message, and something within impelled him to make it explicit. As I was heading for the door, he said to me, "Arthur, if the Nazis come, don't expect me to risk my family to hide you."

In the next five years the European majority did look away as the Jews were being murdered, but a million or more did survive. Many owed their lives to Christians who took grave risks to help them. Jews continue to be deeply grateful and extraordinarily moved by these stories of bravery and compassion, and we have done everything within our power to express our admiration and our indebtedness. Nonetheless, for me and for every Jew who has been affected by those horrors, the question arises whenever we draw close to someone who is not Jewish: If, God forbid, the Nazis ever appear again, is this the kind of person who would take the risk of hiding Jews?

This terrible question became embedded in the soul of Jews long before the Holocaust; it has existed, certainly, since the destruction and exile of the Jews from Spain five centuries ago. Jewish communities had been expelled before, from England, France, and other European realms, but in these places Jews existed in small numbers, in communities with limited influence. The Jews of Spain numbered more than five hundred fifty thousand, well over half of the Jewish population in all of Europe. The Jews of Spain had been in that land since antiquity, and they had achieved prominence in every sphere of society, from the affairs of state and commerce to art and science. The summary expulsion of so prosperous and integrated a community came as a great shock to all the Jews of that time. If this could happen in Spain, Jews were not secure anywhere. The fall of German Jewry repeated this history. Once again the Jews learned that in times of political or economic upheaval, a cultured nation in the forefront of science, art, and learning could not be trusted.

Jews are freer today at the end of the twentieth century and seemingly better protected all over the world than ever before, but they take note of every incident of anti-Semitism with exaggerated fears. The trauma of Spain, reenacted in Germany and much of Europe, has left many Jews with a deep-seated fear that their friends are far too few.

In the thirteenth to the fifteenth centuries in Spain, as the Christians reconquered the land from the Muslims, Jews were repeatedly confronted with a terrible choice. So long as they remained Jews, they would be harassed and, sooner or later, attacked by the mob. Their enemies made it unmistakably clear that Jews would find no peace.

Under such relentless pressure, the continuing exile of the Jews became increasingly unbearable. Simply to continue in the ancestral Jewish path of obedience to the inherited law no longer satisfied the mind or uplifted the heart. In this despair, some Spanish Jews rediscovered the Kabbalah, the ancient tradition of "secret wisdom" that nourished the individual's soul with the secrets beneath the surface of the sacred texts. It was believed that this knowledge had the power to lift individuals beyond their circumstances and enable them to experience the direct and immediate presence of God. The most important contemporary text on Kabbalah was the *Zohar (The Book of Splendor)*, which its author, the thirteenth-century Spanish kabbalist Moses de Leon, based largely on older mystical sources.

Kabbalah was expounded in those days by many other writers, who did not always agree on specific teachings, but together they moved Jewish religious practice toward inwardness and individualism. The kabbalists obeyed the rules of the Bible and Talmud, which they regarded as necessary in the unredeemed world of the present. But these laws would be abrogated at the end of days, when the still-hidden, deepest meanings of Scripture would be revealed to all the world. It was a short step from such an assertion to the notion that the kabbalist who understood these hidden meanings might already be exempted from obeying the holy commandments. The distance from this assertion to the further notion that there might be some truth in Christianity, which had dispensed with these rules long ago, was suddenly not as wide it had once seemed. Some Jews had even begun to hate the faith for which they were suffering. Inevitably, many Jewish authorities, both rabbis and lay leaders, viewed the kabbalists with suspicion. The greatest fear was that younger students, who were not deeply rooted in the inherited Jewish tradition, might be led by kabbalistic studies toward apostasy. They knew that the Kabbalah was making it possible for some Jews, and not only young beginners, to convert to Christianity out of religious conviction.

For twenty-five years, Abner of Burgos (1270–1340), a physician and kabbalist, pondered the sufferings of the Jews in exile, and he could find no answer in any of the Jewish doctrines or texts that satisfied him. At about the age of fifty, Abner converted to Christianity. He then spent the rest of his life writing books in Hebrew aimed at converting the Jews of his native Spain. Abner was not content with merely proposing the truths of Christianity out of Jewish sources; he added terrible charges against Jews and Jewish teachings. Most curiously, an anonymous book exists, written in Hebrew, in which all of Abner's arguments against Judaism are refuted. Modern stylistic analysis of this work shows that it is possible, even probable, that this work was written by Abner himself. This may be only speculation, but in those difficult centuries, the Spanish Jewish intellectuals, and especially the mystics among them, were divided souls.

The beginning of the end of Spanish Jewry came in 1378, when the archdeacon of Ecija, Ferrant Martinez, incited the people of Seville to destroy the city's twenty-three synagogues. He forced a complete separation of Jews from Christians. The royal court took measures to curb Martinez, but it could not prevent the riots that swept through Spain in June 1391. In Seville the mob murdered most of the Jews of the city and forced the survivors to convert. The synagogues and other properties belonging to the Jews, including homes and workshops, became church property.

Throughout most of Spain Jews were compelled to choose between death and conversion. Most Jews converted, creating for the first time a large number of *conversos,* or "new Christians." Some *conversos,* in fact, did become devout Catholics and even turned against the Jews, but others tried to maintain their original faith in secret. The "new Christians" were under suspicion from both sides. The old Christians did not believe their sincerity, and Jews doubted the *conversos* retained any loyalty to the faith of their ancestors. Many families were bitterly divided. The complexities of these relationships are evident in a letter written in 1391 to a man who had only one immediate Jewish relative left, his mother. His father and brother had converted.

> Regard the misfortune of your [brother who] has left the fold never to return! . . . Look about you! Everywhere brother is divided against brother and kin against kin. . . . As for your poor, regal mother, I can inform you that she is living in bitterness in her husband's house and continues to abide by the [Jewish] Law and act decorously; and although many are her tormentors and would-be converters, her one reply is that she would die before going over.[1]

Despite these terrible disruptions of Jewish life and intermittent persecutions in the next century, the Jewish population in fourteenth-century Spain constituted a large proportion of the middle class, the courtiers, and the financiers. Many of these rich Jews lived like noble-men and traveled with large retinues of assistants and servants. Even under attack and in decline in the 1400s, the Jews of Spain were regarded as a success story among other Diaspora Jews, who looked upon them with awe.

THE EXPULSION

On March 31, 1492, the Jews in Spain were given four months to make a terrible choice—they could convert to Christianity or get out of the country and leave all their possessions behind. About half of the Jews chose exile, and the rest became *conversos*. Those who converted but practiced Judaism in secret, the crypto-Jews, were called *marranos,* meaning swine. The poorer Jews generally chose to leave, but the elite was divided. Its two leading personalities, Abraham Seneor and Don Isaac Abrabanel, were expected to go into exile with their people, but they did not stand together.

Abraham Seneor (1412–1493) served as titular rabbi and supreme judge of the Jews in Castile; in practical terms he acted as chief Jewish tax collector for the royal court. To his credit, Seneor did protect the Jews within his jurisdiction, who held him in high esteem and even referred to him as "exilarch," a term used for the leader of the Jews in Babylonia (the other great Jewish center in the Diaspora). It is said of Seneor's personal wealth that "he rode together with thirty mules . . . and wore a golden necklace . . . [and] all the dignitaries of the king-dom accompanied him." On the eve of the expulsion, Seneor offered the monarchy a vast fortune to rescind the edict. Ferdinand and Isabella refused. Seneor was forced to make the terrible choice. On June 15, 1492, at Guadalupe, Abraham Seneor and his family converted in a grand public ceremony, attended by the king and queen in their role as godparents for the baptism. Seneor took the name Fernando

Nuñez Coronel and was promptly elevated to the royal council of the realm. A year later, this old man of eighty-two was dead. Perhaps the years had become too many for him, or perhaps he could not bear his dishonor.

Don Isaac Abrabanel (1437–1508) held an even more exalted position than Seneor in the court of Ferdinand and Isabella. At the time of the expulsion, this great scholar of Judaism served as minister of finance of Spain and as head and principal protector of the Jewish communities. The king and queen offered to keep Abrabanel in his post if he would agree to convert. He refused. Don Isaac abandoned his titles and his great wealth and sailed with the other Jewish refugees in search of a new home. He would live his final days in Venice, Italy.

A year before his death, ailing and almost blind, Abrabanel wrote a confessional letter to Rabbi Saul Hakohen Ashkenazi, a young Jewish scholar living on the island of Crete. Abrabanel looked back on his life with great sorrow, bemoaning the years he had wasted:

> All the time I was in the courts and palaces of kings, I had no leisure for study and looked at no book, but spent my days in vanity, and my years . . . in getting riches and honor; and now those very riches have perished, by evil adventure. . . . It was only after I had become a fugitive, and a wanderer on earth, from one kingdom to another, and without money, that I sought out the Book of the Lord. . . . I confess my guilt that in the vanity of my youth I spent much time on the natural sciences and on philosophy. Now, however . . . I say to myself, why devote so much time and attention to Greek literature and other such matters foreign to me. Therefore, I have limited myself to the contemplation of the *Guide of the Perplexed* and to the exposition of the Bible. These are the sources of all

knowledge and in their wisdom all doubts and perplexities are dissolved. . . .²

It is not surprising that Abrabanel would devote himself to studying the writings of Maimonides. These two masters of Jewish learning had lived parallel lives. The very regrets that Abrabanel was expressing in his letter had been expressed three centuries earlier by Maimonides. In a letter to Samuel ben Judah Ibn Tibbon (the translator of the *Guide of the Perplexed* into Hebrew from Arabic), Maimonides had asked Ibn Tibbon not to come to see him in Egypt because his daily schedule was such that "you would not derive any advantage from your visit." Maimonides then described his daily schedule:

My duties to the Sultan are very heavy. I am obliged to visit him every day, early in the morning; and when he or any of his children, or any of the inmates of his harem, are indisposed . . . I must attend to their healing. Hence, as a rule, I repair to Kahira [Cairo] very early in the day . . . and do not return [home] to Mizr [Fostat] until the afternoon. Then I am almost dying with hunger. . . . I find the antechambers filled with people, both Jews and gentiles, nobles and common people, judges and bailiffs, friends and foes—a mixed multitude who await the time of my return. I dismount from my animal, wash my hands, go forth to my patients, and entreat them to bear with me while I partake of some slight refreshment, the only meal I take in the twenty-four hours. Then I go forth to attend to my patients and write prescriptions and directions for their various ailments. Patients go in and out until nightfall. . . . I converse with and prescribe for them while lying down from sheer fatigue. . . . In consequence of this, no Israelite can have any private interview with me, except on the

Sabbath. On that day the whole congregation, or at least the majority of the members, come to me after the morning service, when I instruct them as to their proceedings during the whole week. . . . In this manner I spend that day. I have here related to you only a part of what you would see if you were to visit me.[3]

Moses Maimonides and Isaac Abrabanel had put themselves into positions of influence in order to protect Jews, but their deepest desire was to study, which has been the age-old affirmation and solace of Jewish believers. Centuries later, in the late 1940s, the aging Rabbi Stephen S. Wise, who had been for many years the public face and political leader of the Zionist and liberal wings of the Jews in America, said to me late one night in a nearly deserted waiting room at the railroad station in Philadelphia that he deeply regretted having spent most of his life in the public arena. He wished he had studied Torah instead. Why this persistent lament? Jews such as Stephen Wise were raised within the classic Jewish tradition. In its scale of values, the highest expression of being Jewish is not to be busy with the affairs of the Jewish community. Such efforts are necessary and laudable, but activism is not the fundamental Jewish virtue. Maimonides and Abrabanel, and even the very contemporary Stephen Wise, knew that they were on loan to the Jewish community from their true calling, to commune with God by studying the holy books.

THE SUPREME HOLINESS OF STUDY

Jews throughout the ages have known that the study of the Word is their most authentic Jewish link with eternity. Most of them have been raised on the talmudic myth that in heaven, the righteous sit in the academy on high and busy themselves throughout all eternity with explicating the meaning of sacred writ. In this myth, God appears occasionally to give the intended meaning of a certain verse in the Torah; sometimes the scholars disagree with God's own interpretation! On occasion Moses shows up to hear Rabbi Akiva expound the Torah, and Moses says to God, You gave the Jews the Torah through me, yet I never imagined such meanings as Akiva has found in it. God replies that these meanings surely must have been hidden in the text for future scholars to uncover. In the heavenly academy there is no past or future; here Moses, Akiva, Maimonides, Abrabanel, and all Jews who are lovers of the Word are continuing a discussion they began in their own lifetimes.

It is no accident that old Jewish manuscripts typically have notes written in the margins. Sometimes these notes represent the original author's second thoughts; more often, they are the comments of later scholars or students who continue the discussion that the master began. Such conversations are as close as one can get in this world to the academy on high.

Even as the debates continue among ancestors and descendants, there is in the classic study of Torah a culture of respect and humility. Those who write comments on the margins of books readily concede that they might be disagreeing with the text because they did not properly understand what the older worthy meant. But inherent in this notion of study is the right to hold an independent or dissenting point of view. Thus the study of Torah is a school that teaches both courage and civility. In the middle of the nineteenth century, a brilliant young talmudist was ushered into the presence of the Hasidic rebbe Menachem Mendel of Kotzk. The young man very proudly announced to the rebbe that "he had been through" seven hundred folios of the Talmud. The rebbe was not impressed. He asked the proud young scholar, "And how many of these seven hundred folios have been through you?" The rebbe of Kotzk was teaching the arrogant young scholar the Jewish concept of study. It is a form of surrender, of self-annihilation, which enables the student to truly hear God's Word and the teachings of those of past ages who have wrestled with its meaning.

The Jewish community at its most authentic views itself as a school, a place where young and old commune with God through learning, a place where everyone—including Maimonides in the twelfth century and Abrabanel in the fifteenth and the Gaon of Vilna in the eighteenth—knew that they had not yet learned enough.

Let there be no misunderstanding: for Jews, study is not an elite enterprise limited to rabbinic intellectuals and professional scholars. The commandment to study the holy books was largely obeyed by all Jews. Those who were not learned enough to understand the Talmud met together regularly to read the psalms, which spoke to their hearts and to their pain. The weak took comfort in knowing that their own despair had been felt even by King David, who is regarded as author of these lyrical poems.

In every Jewish community throughout the world, people met their peers daily to study together. In Warsaw, until the Nazis destroyed the Jewish community, some of the Jewish coachmen would tether their horses at the gate of the synagogue and enter to study together for an hour after a short prayer service. In Vilna the great synagogue was surrounded by many smaller conventicles, each with its own specialized constituency, such as "the congregation of those who study the Talmud" and "the congregation of those who study the psalms." The women in the "women's gallery" were not passive observers of the service on the main floor of the sanctuary; they too were studying. On Sabbath morning throughout Europe the most learned of the women (usually the wives of the rabbis) would read a translation and commentary in Yiddish on the weekly Torah reading. Invariably, questions were asked of the learned leader, and a spirited discussion would follow.

Learning Torah is the ultimate Jewish value because at that moment the Jew is as close as one can ever be to God's revelation. Study is the point at which Jews stop hearing themselves, their needs, and their vanities. Study is the point at which Jews again stand, with all the other souls born and not yet born, at the foot of the mountain in the desert of Sinai.

Study supersedes prayer. Therefore, it should not be surprising that the Talmud ruled that a synagogue may be sold if the money is needed to build a school. The talmudic master, Rava, once found his disciple Hamnuna deep in prayer. So great was Hamnuna's concentration that he seemed lost within himself. Rava interrupted him and said to his disciple, "Woe to him who concentrates on his own concerns and neglects the concerns of eternity." To pray excessively is to be overly concerned with the self. Rava admonished his disciple because the correct Jewish attitude is to rise beyond the self through study, and thus to converse with God and all the Jewish generations (Shabbat 10a).

THE NEW KABBALAH

In the immediate aftermath of the great disaster of 1492, two responses emerged, and each would have a profound impact on Jewish thought and character for many generations. One was the apocalyptic Kabbalah, which taught the belief that after this catastrophe the end must be near and the return to Zion imminent. The second response, born of the *marrano* experience, set Jews on the road to the secular age of modernity.

The apocalyptic response appeared immediately. Exiled Jewish mystics began to redefine the Kabbalah. What in the past had been a way by which the *individual* Jew strove to come closer to God now became an instrument of messianic redemption for the whole of the

Jewish people. The new kabbalists focused on bringing about *national* redemption by supernatural means. The Spanish kabbalist Joseph della Reina, for example, wanted to force the hand of the Messiah by trying to predict the exact date of the redemption, though such speculations were forbidden in the Talmud. Even Don Isaac Abrabanel turned his attention to this task and figured out that the end of days would fall sometime between 1503 and 1541. The primary impetus for all this kabbalistic agitation was a desperate attempt to end the torment of Jewish otherness by lifting the Jewish people out of their exile and into the Promised Land.

This effort came to climax in the next generation, in the work of the single most important kabbalist of the sixteenth century, Isaac Luria (1534–1572). Luria's father was of Ashkenazi (Yiddish-speaking, central European) background; his mother was the daughter of an exiled Spanish Jewish family. In his final years, Luria settled in the Galilean town of Zefat (Safed), where he emerged as the most charismatic figure among the town's kabbalists, some of whom regarded him as the forerunner of the Messiah.

Luria invented the idea of *tikkun olam,* the repair of the world. When God created the world, some of the divine light became trapped by *klippot*—shells or husks of matter—which encased these sparks of the spirit and hid their light. It therefore became the function of humans to break the husks so that these hidden sparks of light could be released. This notion of *tikkun olam* moved the kabbalists from a concern with one's own soul to concern with the world as a whole. When the *tikkun* takes place, the Jews, who are hemmed in by the force of evil, will be restored to their proper shining beauty and gathered into the Holy Land. Thus, Lurianic Kabbalah became a radical prescription to redeem the Jewish people from its exile. The redemption of the Jew was part of repairing the world.

URIEL DA COSTA, THE MARGINAL *MARRANO*

The second continuing response to the expulsion was symbolized by Uriel Da Costa (1585–1640), who was born to a *marrano* family in Portugal and was raised as a devout Catholic. He later rejected Christianity but could not identify with mainstream Judaism. Marginal to both traditions, he made his way to Amsterdam, where he invented a romanticized version of Judaism that denied both the New Testament and rabbinic teachings. He published a book attacking the Pharisees as misreaders of the Bible, and he criticized the "pride and arrogance" of the city's rabbis, calling them "the Pharisees of the Amsterdam synagogue." A rabbinic tribunal responded with a decree of excommunication. Da Costa was fined and briefly imprisoned, and his book was burned. After living in Amsterdam as a pariah for fourteen years, Da Costa rejoined the Jewish community. But he could not restrain his antipathy for the religion of his ancestors. He declared the Law of Moses to be of human origin, and he ceased all Jewish practice. When he tried to discourage people from converting to Judaism, Da Costa was excommunicated a second time. He remained cut off from the Jewish community for another seven years. Uriel Da Costa believed in neither Judaism nor Christianity, but he could not live in isolation; he desperately needed to be part of a community. Unable to endure the separation any longer, he agreed to subject himself to public penance, a humiliating ritual of abjuring his errors. At the end of the ceremony he received thirty-nine lashes of the whip and was forced to prostrate himself on the threshold of the Portuguese synagogue as hundreds of departing congregants strode over his body and spat at him. Devastated by this ordeal, Da Costa returned home, wrote a few pages of his autobiography, and shot himself.

Like Luria, Uriel Da Costa had proposed a radical solution to end the otherness of the Jews. Luria wanted to effect national redemption through Kabbalah; Da Costa wanted to move toward a universal religion. Luria lived within Jewish law; Da Costa was excommunicated because he had moved out and beyond Judaism. Both appeared on the scene because the Jewish Diaspora had been so deeply shaken by the tragic events in Spain and Portugal.

CHAPTER 7

THE LADY VS. THE POPE

On the eve of the expulsion from Spain, Abraham Seneor had offered Ferdinand and Isabella more than a king's fortune to induce them to rescind the decree. This tactic had been used many times throughout the Middle Ages to ward off such evil decrees; it was the only one that had ever worked. This time it failed. The forces arrayed against the Jews were too powerful and intransigent.

The low point came at the very end of July 1492, when the last of the Jews boarded the ships that would take them into exile. They had lost everything, and they had no assurance that they would be allowed to land anywhere. Columbus passed some of these refugee ships as he left harbor on his journey westward, and he must have thought that these exiles were a defeated and despairing people. No doubt most of the men and women on these ships thought so themselves. They did not yet know that they were about to change the course of Jewish history. On the journey away from Spain, the exiles knew that appeasement had not worked. Henceforth, they would have to find the means to fight back. They would have to acquire power and learn to use it to deter and even punish their enemies.

The exiles, and especially the *conversos* who got out of Spain to reclaim their Jewishness, soon became an international economic power. There were bankers and international businessmen among them. The economic well-being of the major port cities of Europe depended to a large degree on the activities of the Jews. By the middle of the sixteenth century an extraordinary figure appeared, Doña Gracia Nasi. She commanded a large fortune, and she used it to defy and to try to humble so powerful a figure as the pope himself. Abraham Seneor might have sent Pope Paul IV a very large gift to try to persuade him to act more kindly toward the Jews; Doña Gracia attacked his economic interests as temporal ruler of the papal states. In days to come Jews would sometimes fall back on the older techniques of appeasement, but Doña Gracia represented a turning toward resistance.

The dramatic story of Christopher Columbus (1451–1506) sailing to discover the new world has been told countless times, but though he was born and died a Christian, his life and career are also part of the tragic history of the Jews in Spain. There is a near consensus among scholars that the ancestors of Columbus had converted to Christianity following the anti-Jewish riots in Spain about a century before the expulsion of 1492. As is well known, the family settled in Genoa, Italy, where Columbus was born; he became a seaman there at a young age and joined his brother in Lisbon after being shipwrecked off the coast of

Portugal. In 1492 Columbus appeared before Ferdinand and Isabella, in the very midst of the stormy discussions about the banishment of the Jews, to propose a voyage westward, a supposedly shorter sea route to the riches of the Orient. Until the last minute, it was far from certain that Ferdinand and Isabella would actually expel their Jewish subjects. Their most trusted advisers were Jews, or *conversos,* with strong familial and business ties in the Jewish community. To be sure, the Jews did everything in their power to resist the decree. They were confident of winning at least a reprieve, so they conducted business as usual.

Columbus had strong Jewish support. His principal allies and financial backers were Abraham Seneor, Don Isaac Abrabanel, and Luis de Santangel, a *converso* who was comptroller-general of the realm. The foremost astronomers of the day, Abraham ben Samuel Zacuto and his student Joseph Vecinho (who became a *converso*), invented the nautical instruments and worked out the tables that Columbus used to guide his fleet. The crew of the three-vessel fleet included several *conversos,* among them the interpreter, the physician, the surgeon, and two sailors.

The evidence strongly suggests that Columbus retained an emotional connection to the Jews and took special interest in their destiny. He began his account of the voyage with a reference to the expulsion of the Jews from Spain, which reached its terrible climax on July 31, 1492, only three days before he set sail. In another document Columbus referred to the Second Temple as the "Second House" *(Bayit Sheini),* a term used only in Jewish sources. And he seemed to have timed the beginning of his voyage to coincide with the Ninth of Av, the solemn day of fasting to commemorate the destruction of both the First and Second Temples and the exiles that had followed. He certainly had close contact with the leaders of Spanish Jewry, and it is even likely that some of his own relatives were practicing Jews. Columbus, thus, was fully aware that the expulsion from Spain signified a defining event in the history of the people in which his own family had roots.

Neither Columbus nor any of the *conversos* among his crew planted a crypto-Jewish settlement in the New World. His interpreter, the *converso* Luis de Torres, remained in Cuba, but there is no record of his having established a secret synagogue somewhere on the island. Many of the *conversos* who remained on the Iberian Peninsula, even those who decided to break with their Jewish past and become true Christians, found themselves closely watched for any signs of "relapsing." To keep them out of positions of influence, the authorities invented the idea of *limpieza de sangre:* Jews would be discriminated against because of their impure blood. These new Christians who in private and very much in secret maintained as much of Jewish observance as they could, lived in mortal danger of the Spanish Inquisition, which had been established in 1478 to purge the Church of heretics. Among the *conversos*—the sincere, the waverers, and the secretly defiant—many had good reason to get as far away from the Iberian Peninsula as possible, even if it meant crossing the Atlantic. The Inquisition, so they thought, would not reach the colonies, at least not quickly. They were wrong.

In the early decades of the sixteenth century, crypto-Jews migrated in large numbers to Mexico (New Spain), Brazil, and other South American territories. They become so prominent in Mexico that the Inquisition was formally established there in 1571, but the first autos-da-fé, public burnings of heretics, had occurred there already forty-three years earlier. The victims were two *conversos* who had sailed with Hernando Cortez to New Spain in 1519. One of them, Alonzo de Avila, the former bookkeeper of the conquistador, was the first mayor of Veracruz until someone denounced him as a "Judaizer." His accuser testified that de Avila kept a crucifix under his writing desk and took joy in stepping on it, a typical false accusation to "prove" contempt of

Christianity. De Avila was burned alive for his alleged sinfulness, but his real crime seems to have been success itself. Prominent Jews were particularly susceptible to such accusations. A leading Jewish merchant in Mexico, Tomás Trevino de Sobremonte, was tried in 1649 and condemned to death for hosting a secret synagogue in his home. He told the inquisitors that he had been denounced not for his religious deviations but because "I have supplied . . . goods at lower prices than the other traders, my motto being small profits and quick returns."

So prominent were crypto-Jews in Lima, the capital city of the Spanish viceroyalty of Peru, that the city as a whole was referred to mockingly as "la Judería," the Jewish ghetto. Everywhere in Spain and Portugal and in the Americas, the crypto-Jews were sufficiently prosperous to incite aggression born of jealousy. On January 23, 1639, eleven "Judaizers" were burned at the stake, including Manuel Bautista Perez, the wealthiest merchant in Lima. Thus the unrelenting search for crypto-Jews, both in Europe and in the new colonies, was motivated as much by economic competition as by the need to defend Christian orthodoxy.

That the charge of Judaizing was most often leveled against people of means proved to be a mixed blessing from the point of view of state interests. The rulers of sixteenth-century Spain varied in their piety, but they were all loyal Catholics who had a strong aversion to "relapsed" Jews. In the short term, they profited from the burning of heretics, whose wealth was confiscated by the crown. But the war against the *marranos* disturbed the inner peace of the realm. The enmity against the *conversos* created a bitter division within Spanish society, driving the embattled former Jews to foreign lands. The departure of Jews deprived Spain not only of capital but also of valuable trading and banking connections throughout the world.

Those who fled Spain did so in anger, usually after having fought off a denunciation or two and buying their release from prison. They could no longer tolerate the indignities of pretending to eat pork or doing business on Yom Kippur in order to prove that they had abandoned the old faith. There was enough of Don Quixote in these *conversos* (the creator of this hero, Miguel de Cervantes, was believed to be of Jewish ancestry) to excite a spirited, indignant defense of their honor. Even as the most unfortunate among them were offered the opportunity of an easier death, if only they renounced their errors— that is, they would be strangled rather than be put on the pyre alive— many refused. They insisted on keeping their dignity before the spectators who seemed to want them to beg for mercy. These *marranos* were doubly defiant; they had inherited the stiff-neckedness of Jews, and they had acquired the quick-tempered dignity of the Spanish nobility.

Among the new Christians who did get out, some began to strike back at their tormentors. This militant response represented a new chapter in the Jewish Diaspora experience. No longer would they ask for favors; no longer would they buy their way in and buy their way out. These Jews were prepared to fight openly for their rights and to inflict pain on those who persecuted them. They used the one weapon available to them—severing all business with the enemies of their people.

DOÑA GRACIA, THE MILITANT *MARRANO*

The turn into the new era hinged on one of the most fascinating and heroic figures in all of Jewish history, Doña Gracia Nasi. She was born Beatriz de Luna in 1510 to a wealthy and distinguished Portuguese crypto-Jewish family. At the age of eighteen she married the banker Francisco Mendes, who died eight years later. Shortly after her husband's death, Doña Gracia Nasi closed the Lisbon branch of the family business and moved with her daughter to Antwerp, the commercial capital of northern Europe. There she joined her brother-in-law Diogo

Mendes, an international trader of exceptional skill who had cornered the pepper trade and had become known as the "spice king of Europe." Diogo, too, died young and left to Doña Gracia, and not to his own wife, control of one the greatest fortunes in Europe, the assets and businesses of the House of Mendes. Diogo had grown to admire the talent, courage, and judgment of his sister-in-law.

In Spanish-ruled Antwerp, Doña Gracia attended mass regularly and gave generously to the Roman Catholic Church. In private she was a devout Jew; the kitchens in her home were kosher, and her family ate matzoh on Passover, fasted on Yom Kippur, and took part in secret meetings for Jewish prayer. In the lifetime of Diogo and after his death, under the sole direction of Doña Gracia, the House of Mendes financed and operated an underground railroad all over Europe to aid and resettle crypto-Jews who had escaped the "iron cauldron" of the Iberian Peninsula. These activities could not be kept totally secret. In 1532, four years before the arrival of his sister-in-law, Diogo had been arrested and charged with heresy and helping fugitive *marranos*. He bought his release after two months in prison. The discomforts and dangers of living as very rich crypto-Jews in Antwerp became intolerable, so Doña Gracia moved her family to Italy, first to Venice and then, under the protection of the duke, to Ferrara. For the first time in her life, she was not immediately threatened by the Inquisition. But the respite in Ferrara was short-lived; the Counter-Reformation, the battle of the Catholic Church against all heresy, soon swept through the papal states. Cardinal Giovanni Pietro Caraffa (later to become Pope Paul IV) led the assault. He vowed to destroy the Protestant heretics, and he moved with a vengeance against "relapsed" Jewish *conversos*.

In 1553 Doña Gracia relocated her household and business to Constantinople, the capital of the Ottoman Empire. One contemporary observer, Andres Laguna, recorded in his memoir the scene of her arrival:

One day a Portuguese lady who called herself Doña Beatriz Mendes, who was very rich, entered Constantinople with forty horsemen and four triumphal chariots filled with Spanish ladies and serving-women. The household that she had with her was not less than that of a Spanish duke; and she could afford it, for she is very rich. She had her respects paid for her at Court. . . .[1]

Having the center of the Mendes family business empire in his realm delighted the Ottoman Sultan, Suleiman I. Doña Gracia quickly became a formidable presence within the Jewish community of the Ottoman Empire. Her charities were on a princely scale. She established and funded synagogues and academies of Jewish learning, financed a Spanish translation of the Bible for former *marranos,* and set a place at her table for anyone in need. Her praises were sung in *A Consolation for the Tribulation of Israel,* a book by Samuel Usque to offer hope amidst all the disasters that had befallen the Jewish people. A direct beneficiary of Doña Gracia's beneficences, Usque praised her for "succoring the multitude of necessitous and miserable poor . . . a bank where the weary rest; a fountain of clear water where the parched drink; a fruit-laden shady tree where the hungry eat and the desolate find rest. . . ."[2]

As an acknowledged leader of the *marranos* of her generation, Doña Gracia prefigured the central role that the Rothschilds would play in the worldwide Jewish community in the nineteenth and early twentieth centuries. But Doña Gracia was more than a pious Jewish woman with a penchant for good deeds. She possessed a political mind and a militancy of the kind that had not been seen among Jews in fourteen centuries of exile.

The trouble began in July 1555 when Pope Paul IV sent an apostolic commissioner to Ancona to take action against the *conversos* who had reverted to Judaism. The papal representative ordered the arrest of one hundred persons, of whom half escaped through bribery. So the pope dispatched a second enforcer who could not be swayed by the temptations of gold and jewels. The prisoners were shackled and tortured until they "confessed." Upon receiving the first reports of the Ancona outrage, Doña Gracia interceded with the sultan of the Ottoman Empire, who, in early March 1556, sent a message to the Vatican demanding the release of all prisoners who were Ottoman subjects. The pope refused. In April 1556, the victims were paraded to a public square before a jeering crowd. Among the first to die were the aged Doña Majora, the only woman in the group, and Jacob Masso, one of Doña Gracia's local agents. The executioner strangled them before disposing of their bodies on the Inquisitional pyre. Another of the victims, Solomon Jachia, refused the mercy of strangulation. He recited the traditional Hebrew benediction before martyrdom and leaped into the flames.

Judah Faraj, one of the Ancona prisoners and an agent of Doña Gracia, escaped to the Ottoman Empire. He carried with him a letter from the prisoners describing the tragedy in Ancona and calling for a boycott of the "city of blood." An emergency meeting was convened in Constantinople, attended by the most distinguished rabbinical and lay leaders in the Ottoman Empire, including, of course, Doña Gracia Nasi. They agreed to impose an eight-month boycott of Ancona, the leading port of the papal states; any Jewish trader who disobeyed would be subject to excommunication. For a short time, the boycott succeeded and Ancona was pushed to the edge of bankruptcy, but the effort could not be sustained because of divisiveness in the Jewish ranks. Those Jews who broke the boycott argued that its continuation would threaten their livelihoods and would only further enrage an already hostile pope. Imperious by temperament, Doña Gracia had no patience for such arguments. She took immediate action against those Jews who opposed her. In one case, she withdrew her subvention to the talmudic academy of Rabbi Joseph Ashkenazi because he dared to defy her by trading with Ancona.

Both the pro- and antiboycott camps solicited rabbinic opinions, but no consensus was reached. Rabbi Joshua Soncino, rabbi of the great synagogue in Constantinople, opposed the action on the basis of the talmudic principle that self-preservation should not be pursued at someone else's expense. The boycott, he insisted, would ruin non-*marrano* Jews in Ancona and subject them to harsh retaliation at the hands of Christians. Doña Gracia solicited the opinion of the eminent Rabbi Joseph Caro of Safed, author of the authoritative code of Jewish religious law, the *Shulkhan Arukh* ("prepared table"), who ruled in favor of the boycott.

Doña Gracia insisted that economic self-interest had to yield to principle. The torture and burning of Jews could not go unpunished. To retreat now, she argued, would make a mockery of Jewish power for generations to come. But, in the end, the boycott failed. Doña Gracia took it as a personal defeat.

Such a drama would play out again in the 1930s, after the Nazis came to power in Germany. Rabbi Stephen S. Wise, the founder and president of the American Jewish Congress, proposed a worldwide boycott of German goods. American Jewish opinion was divided. Opponents gave it little chance of success and warned that it would further enrage the Nazis. Fearing the wrath of Hitler, the leaders of the Jews in Germany asked Stephen Wise to back off. He did not. But weakened by factionalism, the effort failed just as Doña Gracia's campaign had to be aborted in the 1550s. Doña Gracia's failure was honorable and heroic. Even in defeat, she emerged as the first truly modern Jewish political leader; not until Golda Meir became prime minister of the State of Israel did another Jewish woman achieve her stature.

CHAPTER 8

MESSIANIC MANIA

Doña Gracia had the economic clout with which to declare war on a pope. Her near contemporary, the greatest rabbinic figure among the Jews of central Europe, the fabled Maharal—the "high rabbi" Judah Loew of Prague (1525–1609)—had only the power of his vast learning and his brilliant mind with which to defend his people. But Jewish lore endowed him with mystical powers. It is said that he created the Golem, a superhuman creature of clay, by inserting into its head a parchment bearing the ineffable name of God. The Golem's task was to guard the inhabitants of the Jewish ghetto against the Jew haters from the outside. At first, the Golem performed this task admirably, but ultimately it attacked everyone in sight. Fearing a catastrophe, the

Maharal decommissioned the Golem by removing the Hebrew parchment. The creature collapsed into a heap of dust, and its remains were supposedly stored in the attic of Prague's Alteneuschul, the "old-new" synagogue. Tourists are still spellbound when their guide points up the staircase of the medieval synagogue and recounts the famous legend.

The Maharal and his successors would not have dared to lead their people into battles with Christians. Most central European Jews were poor, or very poor, and they lived throughout Europe largely on sufferance. The slightest provocation might easily result in their expulsion or worse. Yet the Maharal demanded religious tolerance for the Jews. In 1598 he opposed the censorship of Jewish books by the Church and argued that religious fanaticism splits the unity of nations and therefore that each people should be allowed to preserve its own faith. The Maharal went on to plead, eloquently and remarkably, for religious freedom for all; he even made the argument for civil disobedience: "For if a king of flesh and blood decrees something against religion, his decree is to be disregarded, and only the King of Kings is to be obeyed; and this is a rejection of the decree of his royal authority." The Maharal took this position as a defender of his people because he knew very well that kings had long been in the habit of making decrees that Jews were obligated by religious law to disobey. If ordered to work on the Sabbath, the Jews would refuse. If ordered to take religious instruction in the dominant faith, the Jews would invent ways of malingering. Only if the state would sanction the otherness of the Jew could such conflicts be avoided.

The Maharal did not isolate himself within the ghetto. Living in Prague, one of the great cultural centers of Europe, he was aware of the intellectual life around him. He befriended the famous astronomer Johannes Kepler, and he studied mathematics as an aid in elucidating talmudic points that require precise measurements and calculations.

Learning of the indigenous cultures in the "new world," he expressed the hope that the explorers who were opening these remote regions might discover the whereabouts of the lost tribes of Israel. The Maharal related everything new to classic Jewish themes: exile, otherness, and the chosenness of the Jews. Above all, he defended the old values and inherited truths of his ancestors, especially the assertion that Jews are better than their tormentors.

The Maharal continued in the tradition of Judah Halevi, who had insisted that the division between Jacob and Esau (that is, between Judaism and Christianity) is as natural "as between water or fire." Esau is in command, at present, but his success is possible only because the existing world is defective. Jacob will achieve his victory when the world is repaired and becomes worthy of God's people. In the meanwhile, the Jews live in the unnatural state of exile, but ultimately Israel will be restored to its proper domain because, so the Maharal wrote,

> exile is a change and departure from the natural order. . . . The place they [the Jews] deserved according to the order of existence was to be independent in Eretz Yisrael [the Land of Israel]. . . . Furthermore, according to the order of being, it is not fitting . . . for Israel to be under the rule of others.[1]

Doña Gracia defied the pope because she refused to surrender to the oppressive rule of others. The formidable rabbi of Prague talked back to Christendom in the same spirit of defiance (which may explain why the Golem myth is part of his legacy). Until the time of Doña Gracia and the Maharal, the Jews had almost always stood before gentile powers as supplicants asking for a favor or trying to buy goodwill. The new militancy of Doña Gracia and the Maharal expressed growing impatience and irritation with Jewish powerlessness, but they could not alter the situation; Jews remained everywhere vulnerable.

The Inquisition continued in Spain and its possessions. In the Ukraine, the peasants, led by Bogdan Chmielnicki, rose up against their Polish rulers and slaughtered Jews by the tens of thousands. What greater proof could there be that the situation of the Jews was abnormal and dangerous? The stage was now set for radical, even apocalyptic, attempts by Jews to end their otherness. The two solutions proposed represented a revolt against the Jewish past.

THE RISE AND FALL OF SHABBETAI ZVI

In the 1660s a scholar and kabbalist from Smyrna (Ismir) in the Ottoman Empire inspired a messianic movement in Judaism not seen since the fall of Bar Kokhba some fifteen hundred years earlier. At least half of the world's Jews, from bankers to beggars, embraced Shabbetai Zvi as the Messiah after he was announced to the world by his prophet, Nathan of Gaza. The two had met in 1665 while Shabbetai was on a pilgrimage to Jerusalem. Shabbetai, who suffered from alternating bouts of ecstatic delusions and debilitating depressions, sought out Nathan, a kabbalist who was reputed to be a healer. But instead of bringing peace to Shabbetai's troubled soul, Nathan convinced the man from Smyrna that he truly was the long-awaited redeemer of Israel. Nathan, who had a gift for persuasive writing, sent out a circular letter announcing to his brethren in Israel "that our Messiah is come to life in the city of Ismir and his name is Shabbetai Zvi." Nathan wrote:

> Soon he will show forth his kingdom to all and will take the royal crown from the head of the Sultan and place it on his own. Like a Canaanite slave shall the King of the Turks walk behind him, for Shabbetai is the power and the glory. . . . And when he is entered into Jerusalem, God will send down a

temple of gold and precious stones from heaven, and it shall fill the city with its brilliance, and in it shall the Messiah offer up sacrifice as High Priest. And on that day shall the dead throughout the world rise from their graves. . . .[2]

Nathan's letters became a sensation throughout the Jewish world, stirring people to great excitation. In her memoir, Gluckel of Hameln reported on the effect these letters had on the Jews in Hamburg, Germany:

The joy, when letters arrived, is not to be described. Most of the letters were received by the Portuguese. They took them to their synagogue and read them aloud there. The Germans, young and old, went into the Portuguese synagogue to hear them. The young Portuguese on these occasions all wore their best clothes and each tied a broad green silk ribbon round his waist—this was Shabbetai Zvi's color. So all, "with kettle-drums and round dance" went with joy . . . to hear the letters read. Many people sold home, hearth and everything they possessed, awaiting the redemption.[3]

During his manic periods, Shabbetai carried on in a most provocative manner. In Jerusalem, he once circled the walled city seven times on horseback, as if he were the Messiah. The rabbis of the Holy City reacted by excommunicating him. In Smyrna, he led a large crowd to the synagogue of the Portuguese, the headquarters of those who opposed him, and began to break down the locked doors with an ax. Upon gaining entry into the sanctuary, he commandeered the service and scorned the rabbis of the congregation by comparing them to unkosher animals. He took a holy scroll from the ark and sang an ancient Castilian love song about the emperor's daughter, into which he read kabbalistic mysteries. Shabbetai then announced himself to be the "anointed of the God of Jacob," the redeemer of Israel, and proclaimed June 18, 1666, as the date of the redemption.

When that promised day arrived, the would-be messiah was locked up in a Turkish prison. There, on September 15, 1666, he was offered a choice: death or conversion to Islam. Shabbetai Zvi chose conversion and took the name Aziz Mehmed Effendi. As an eminent convert, he was given the honorary title "Keeper of the Palace Gates" and granted a royal pension. In the aftermath of his apostasy, Shabbetai fell into a deep depression. Nathan of Gaza and the other apologists for the messianic pretender explained that their master had descended into the "forty-nine gates of impurity" in order to recover the holy sparks trapped in the *klippot* (husks), which were now concentrated in Islam. Only Shabbetai, the Messiah, could perform this formidable task of repairing the world *(tikkun olam)*. Only he could effect universal redemption.

Shabbetai Zvi's appeal in the Jewish world was unprecedented. Jewish merchants, bankers, and other hard-headed business people sung his praises even in Amsterdam and Hamburg, where they could practice their religion in relative peace. Why did these Jews pack up their bags and wait to be wafted by the Messiah to the Holy Land? For the Jews of that day, no Diaspora, however benevolent, could compare with the prophetic vision of living a normal life in one's own vineyard and under one's own olive tree. Shabbetai Zvi wanted to end the long and bitter exile of the Jews by leading them back to the Promised Land. His solution followed the classic Jewish script of redemption: the Messiah (played by Shabbetai) would restore the Jews to God's favor, and they would be returned to Zion. But the miracles did not come. Life for the Jews remained unchanged, and so the dream shattered. Other messianic pretenders would arise in almost every generation and gain a devoted following, but the promised redemption never came. When will we know when the true Messiah comes? Perhaps the most Jewish answer to this question was given by the colorful and controversial Israeli scholar, Yeshayahu Leibowitz. He said, the messiah who actually appears, and announces himself, is always the false messiah.

My grandfather and his father before him slept every night in their clothes so that when the Messiah appeared, they could get up immediately and greet him. And they rose at midnight for *tikkun hatzot*, special prayers to remind God that the Messiah had tarried too long.

Historically, when disasters struck, the Jews became especially impatient and their longing for the Messiah grew more intense. After the expulsion from Spain, the leading Jewish mystic of the next century, Isaac Luria, wanted to use the kabbalah to bring the Messiah and thus restore power to the Jews. A century later, even though the Spanish-Jewish Diaspora had achieved substantial economic clout, the hope for the Messiah burned within them. This emotion was driven even further by the Christian belief, especially among Protestants, that the end of days was imminent. And so, when a Jewish Messiah announced himself in the person of Shabbetai Zvi and gave the year 1666 as the time of redemption, well over half of the Jews in the world were seized with enthusiasm. The Messiah was about to come, and the Jews would become the dominant power in the world. What a heady dream!

The redeemer of the Jews did not come in the seventeenth century, but the dream did not die. It reappeared again and again, even in our own day in Brooklyn, where the charismatic Hasidic leader Menachem Mendel Schneerson, the Lubavitcher Rebbe, was proclaimed by some of his followers to be the Messiah. Many of his disciples believe that their rebbe, who died in 1994, will yet reappear as the Messiah. I am convinced that even those Hasidim who do not admit that they believe that the rebbe will return to life still keep that hope in some corner of their hearts. It does not really matter how many people are waiting for the rebbe to rise again and remake the world. What matters is that sober, religious, observant Jews nonetheless see themselves as the vanguard of a great dramatic climax of history. Every time I see a Lubavitcher Hasid driving by in his car with bumper stickers reading, "I want Moshiach (messiah) now!" I think of my grandfather and great-grandfather sleeping in their clothes.

CHAPTER 9

THE AGE OF DISSENT

One summer day in the early 1980s, I was taken to the library of Jesus College at Oxford, to a section that had been blocked off for centuries. My host was a senior fellow at the college who had told me the long-guarded secret that the college library possessed a copy of the first complete edition of the Talmud, which had been printed in Venice between 1520 and 1523. He had the key to the case in which the treasure was housed. I opened the volumes to find that, more than four and a half centuries after the set had been brought to England, the pages had never been cut. I asked the librarian how these priceless books had come to the college and why the volumes had remained untouched. He told me that they played a role in the drama of the battle in the

1530s between Henry VIII and his lawful wedded wife, Catherine of Aragon. He wanted a divorce so he could marry Anne Boleyn, but the pope refused; divorce was absolutely forbidden by Catholic teaching. Henry VIII decided that he would prove the pope wrong by invoking the much more permissive law of the Hebrew Bible, as interpreted by the Talmud, so he asked his ambassador in Venice to get him the necessary texts. By the time this pristine copy of the Talmud arrived in England, the issue was moot. Henry had banished his wife, forcing a schism with Rome. The king of England, I was told, gave the set of the Talmud to the archbishop of Canterbury, and the volumes eventually were transferred to the library of Jesus College.

I knew that these books were of great historical significance, even if they had not been used directly by Henry VIII. He had recognized their authority in his effort to prove that divorce was permitted in the law of the Bible and its Jewish commentaries. A king of England had sanctioned the sacred literature of the Jews in his dispute with the pope. He had even asked the opinion of some Italian rabbis, and one of them had dared to side with the king of England. Henry VIII was invoking Jewish precedents at a time when the Jews, who had been expelled in 1290, were still forbidden to set foot in England. The first-edition Talmud before my eyes signified a profound historic turning.

In those very days, Judaism was being taken more seriously than it had been since ancient times. The revival of learning in Greek and Latin during the Renaissance rekindled interest in the language of the Bible. Protestant Hebraists were especially drawn to the Kabbalah because they thought it contained proofs of the truth of Christianity unavailable anywhere else. The greatest among the Italian Hebraists in the last decade of the fifteenth century, Pico della Mirandola, wrote an instantly famous book asserting that he had found such proof in the Kabbalah. No Jew accepted his interpretation of the texts. But Italy did not remain for very long the home of Christian Hebraism. The

German scholar Johannes Reuchlin (1455–1522), the most learned Hebraist of his generation, had a lifelong interest in the Kabbalah. The more he learned about Jewish mysticism, the more sympathetic he became to Jews and to Judaism. Reuchlin, a Catholic, defended the Talmud against attacks by Johannes Pfefferkorn, a Jewish convert to Christianity, who defamed his former religion by asserting that the Talmud contained many slurs on Christianity and on the character of its founder and his mother. Reuchlin replied, "The Talmud was not composed for every blackguard to trample with unwashed feet and then to say that he knew all of it." Johannes Reuchlin will always be remembered for his courageous insistence that Jews and Judaism had to be understood as they really are and that Christians had to treat them justly. His immediate contemporaries, the founders of Protestantism, took special interest in Jews, hoping that a reformed Christianity would bring them into the true church. The Protestant revolution began in 1517, when a German priest, Martin Luther (1483–1546), denied that the pope and those whom he had ordained held the keys to salvation. Luther insisted that every believer was autonomous and that the only valid authority was God's will as revealed in the Bible. To understand what God desired, each believer had to search the holy words of Scripture individually and without intermediaries.

Inevitably, Judaism came into play at the very beginnings of this battle between the Catholic Church and Protestantism because the "Old Testament" was invoked by the reformers in their theological polemics. They studied the original Hebrew to establish that they, and not the followers of the pope, held the correct understanding of God's revelation as recorded in both the testaments. But without exception, these Protestant Hebraists were convinced Christians, and they believed that the Jews would hasten to convert if only Christianity were properly presented.

At first Martin Luther attributed the Jews' rejection of Jesus to the "papal paganism" of the Catholic hierarchy. He wrote in 1523,

> If I had been a Jew and had seen such idiots and blockheads rul-
> ing and teaching the Christian religion, I would rather have
> been a sow than a Christian. For they have dealt with the Jews
> as if they were dogs and not human beings. They have done
> nothing for them but curse them and seize their wealth. . . . I
> would advise and beg everybody to deal kindly with the Jews
> and to instruct them in the Scriptures; in such a case we could
> expect them to come over to us. . . .[1]

When the Jews rejected Luther's advances, he condemned them with a ferocity that left a deep imprint on both Protestant Christianity and modern German culture, upon which he, as translator of the Bible into German, had a profound influence. In 1543, he wrote,

> What then shall we Christians do with this damned, rejected
> race of Jews? . . . Since they live among us and we know about
> their lying and blasphemy and cursing, we cannot tolerate
> them if we do not wish to share in their lies, curses, and blas-
> phemy. . . . First, their synagogues or churches should be set
> on fire, and whatever does not burn up should be covered or
> spread over with dirt so that no one may ever be able to see a
> cinder or stone of it. . . . Secondly, their homes should likewise
> be broken down and destroyed. . . . Thirdly, they should be
> deprived of their prayerbooks and Talmud in which such idol-
> atry, lies, cursing and blasphemy are taught. Fourthly, their
> rabbis must be forbidden under threat of death to teach any-
> more. . . .[2]

Jews took comfort in the fact that other Protestants countered Luther's attacks. Some of the leading thinkers of the Reformation, most notably the Swiss Heinrich Bullinger and the German Hebraist Andreas Osiander, denounced Luther's slanders and incitements against the Jews. One of Luther's closest friends and colleagues among the first reformers, Philip Melanchthon (he was a nephew and disciple of Reuchlin), also disagreed with Luther's insistence that the Jews should be persecuted. In a letter to a gathering of the princes of Germany, he defended the Jews against the charge that they think of nothing else but desecrating the holy symbols of Christianity. "It is always easier to accuse others," he declared, "when it would be better for us to indict our own. . . ."[3]

This intense debate about the place of the Jews in God's plan for humanity was inconclusive, but it began to redefine the Christian attitude toward the Jewish people. Despite Luther's incitements, the older presumption that Jews ought to be kept subservient and subjected to attacks and expulsions was no longer taken for granted. In this debate no one was saying yet that the Jews ought to be left alone to be themselves. Judaism was still depicted by both Catholics and Protestants as a religion that had been superseded by Christianity; the Jews still needed to be converted, but a first step had been taken to put an end to the violence against Jews and the slanders against their teachings.

The next turn in the religious discussion of the Jews took place two generations later, in the 1630s, in the far-off Massachusetts Bay Colony. Roger Williams, the Protestant divine and first voice for religious freedom in Puritan New England, insisted that religious conscience should not be coerced and that all people—Jews, Muslims, and infidels—had the right to worship according to their conscience. Williams was forced out into the wilderness, where he founded Rhode Island. But let it not be imagined that even Williams really accepted the permanence of Judaism. Christians, he said, have been trying to convert the Jews by persecuting them; the way to effect their conversion is to give them freedom and to treat them with kindness. It would take several more centuries, to our own time, before Christianity in any of its versions began to imagine that Judaism was legitimate and here to stay on its own terms.

Christianity was thus moving toward more sympathy for the Jews in the sixteenth and seventeenth centuries, largely as a repercussion of internal Christian struggle. After a century of religious war, the Roman Catholic and Protestant powers, weary of the fight, agreed in the Treaties of Westphalia (1648) to live with the fact of a fractured Christianity. The Jews were no longer the only group that had to depend on the law of the state for protection against the tyranny of the majority, and the laws that allowed some tolerance of Christian dissenters implied that Jews, too, might be treated with more civility.

As Christians became more sympathetic to Jews, there was a shift among many Jews toward friendship with Christians. Jewish scholars and members of the upper bourgeoisie who were doing business with Christians wanted to debunk the notion that Judaism was inherently hostile to Christianity. Some of the most distinguished rabbis of the age, men who could not be suspected of deviating in the slightest from the ancient Jewish faith, began to formulate positions more amenable to Christianity. Rabbi Moses Rivkes of Vilna, who had lived for some years in Amsterdam, argued that the term *gentiles* refers in rabbinic literature to the ancient pagans and not to "the peoples in whose shade we, the people of Israel, are exiled and amongst whom we are dispersed." Contemporary gentiles, he insisted, believe "in the main principles of religion and their whole aim and intent is to [glorify] the Maker of heaven and earth." We Jews, therefore, are "obliged to pray for their welfare . . . and the success of the kingdom . . . over which they rule. . . ." In support of his position, Rivkes quoted Maimonides's ruling that the "pious of the gentile nations, too, have a portion in the world to come."[4]

Rabbi Jacob Emden (1697–1776), one of the towering rabbinic personalities of his time, went even further in absolving Christianity. He insisted that Jesus had intended not to free the Jews from observing the Torah, but to spread the moral principles of Judaism among the non-Jews. Therefore, the root of Christian-Jewish enmity was predicated on a misreading of history.[5] What was driving Emden? The Jewish businessmen of Hamburg and Altona, including Emden himself, needed an acceptable answer when their gentile associates inquired about the Jewish attitude toward Christianity. Rabbis Rivkes and Emden were stretching an old Jewish idea to its limit. They were finding ways of saying that Christianity was not idolatry but a version of monotheism, which raised the moral levels of gentiles though it had no relevance for Jews.

These attempts at rapprochement may have made, on the surface, some of the high Jewish bourgeois, the people with connections at court and in international business circles, feel less alien. But the mass of the Jews in Europe experienced only the darker side of the Jewish-Christian encounter. For them, the story of the execution in Vilna in 1749 of the *ger tzedek,* "righteous convert" to Judaism, represented the dominant Christian attitude toward Judaism. The story became a legend in eastern Europe. Count Valentin Potocki, a Polish nobleman, converted to Judaism in Amsterdam. Upon returning to Poland, he wandered from place to place until he was arrested and tortured for the heinous sin of abandoning Christianity for Judaism, a capital offense. His mother and friends pleaded with Valentin to save his life by returning to Christ. He refused. On May 24, 1749, Valentin Potocki was burned alive in Vilna. Some of his ashes, secured by a Jew through bribery, were buried in the Jewish cemetery. His grave became a pilgrimage site, and for generations

of Polish Jews the mention of his name inspired courage in times of pain
and sorrow.

THE POWER OF MONEY

Christians and Jews were being pushed toward each other not only
because of changes in religion but also by economic expediency. In the
seventeenth century, some of the major powers of Europe, and especially the Dutch, were moving away from the notion that the state
existed as the servant of religion; the main purpose of the state would
become the economic well-being of its citizens. In accordance with
this new doctrine of mercantilism, the most advanced economies of
Europe began to welcome people who brought economic advantages
to the state, regardless of what religion they might profess. The door
was now open far wider than it had ever been for Jews, at least for the
wealthy, who brought with them money and business connections.

The two forces shaping the European outlook—the Reformation
and mercantilism—were at play in the 1650s, when Rabbi Manasseh
ben Israel of Amsterdam journeyed to London in an attempt to persuade Oliver Cromwell to readmit Jews into Great Britain. They had
been banned for more than three hundred years. The rabbi presented
two arguments, one economic and the other religious. He reminded
the statesman that Jews were making enormous contributions to the
prosperity of Amsterdam, so why deprive England of similar riches?
The rabbi then offered a theological consideration. As a passionate
Puritan, Cromwell believed that the end of days could come only
when the Jews finally accepted Jesus as their savior. The rabbi
reminded him that this drama required that the Jews be scattered to all
four corners of the earth, from which they would be ingathered to the
Holy Land by the triumphant Christ at his Second Coming. As
England was considered one of the corners of the earth, the continued

ban against Jews, so the rabbi argued, was impeding the coming of the Christian Messiah. Cromwell issued no formal decree readmitting the Jews to England; the government simply looked away as Spanish *marranos* who had drifted into London came up from underground, and illegal Jewish immigrants entered the country in ones and twos. By the time the monarchy was restored in 1660 with the return of Charles II, a synagogue was already functioning in London.

With the increase in commercial interaction between Jews and Christians in western Europe came changes in the lifestyle of Jewish bourgeoisie. The Sephardim, who had shaved their beards and worn Western clothes during their *marrano* years, continued these practices in Amsterdam, London, Hamburg, Bordeaux, and wherever else they had settled. This external Westernization spread to the Jews in Germany, first among the rich and gradually throughout the entire Jewish community. By the end of the eighteenth century, it had become well established in Yiddish, the language still spoken by the Jews from Alsace to the Ukraine, that a *"deutch"* was a Jew who imitated the dress and manners of German gentiles.

These changes were noticed, and condemned, by the defenders of the older way of life, who insisted that Jews were secure in their identity only so long as they spoke a "Jewish" language and wore distinctive clothes. In the 1760s one of the founders of the Hasidic movement, Rabbi Pinhas of Korzec, deplored these assimilationist tendencies and made the following observation:

> The Jews [in Germany] are indistinguishable from the gentiles in their dress and speech. The exile in the land of Ishmael [Turkey] is not as bitter as in Germany because Jews, at least, are distinguished by language, though not by dress. However in Poland, where both their clothing and language are different, the exile is less bitter than anywhere else.[6]

At about this time, Rabbi Jonathan Eybeschutz preached a bitter sermon in which he railed against the customs practiced by the upper class of his community in the Rhineland town of Metz. Like their rich gentile neighbors, these Jews rode out in their coaches bedecked in all their finery, with picnic baskets and servants, to watch from a hill while the French and Austrian armies fought each other in a set battle during the Seven Years' War. Eybeschutz thundered from the pulpit that their behavior was an offense against all the basic values of Judaism and an offense against God. Such spectacles, where questions of political power are being decided, do not concern us, he insisted. We Jews are put in the world to study God's holy commandments and to wait for our redemption by the Messiah. In the interim, we must make a living to survive, but we have nothing else in common with non-Jews. The Jewish bourgeoisie of Metz listened politely, but they did not surrender their fashionable coaches, discard their picnic baskets, or discharge their children's French tutors.

So in the eighteenth century the rich Jews in central Europe were beginning to find a common ground with their Christian neighbors, but these relationships were superficial. By day, Jews and non-Jews operated in business in the same world, but in the evening most of them had little contact socially. They differed by religion, custom, and culture. The Jews were still other, though less so than previously.

Another profound change in European consciousness was the first stirrings of freedom to dissent from all religious dogmas. People were still being burned at the stake or excommunicated for blasphemy, and witches were still being hanged, but philosophers were beginning to question the divine authorship of the Bible and even the existence of a personal God. In this new intellectual environment, the Jewish religion became one of several expressions of religious faith, and it soon could be discussed, even by some Jews, as no more true or false than any other that claimed to be the revealed word of God. This view had been expressed late in the sixteenth century by Jean Bodin, the progressive French social and political philosopher, who maintained that the major religions of the world essentially taught the same moral outlook. Bodin had dared to suggest even that Judaism was a more natural and proper faith for all of humanity than was Christianity.

As we have seen, Uriel Da Costa had tormented himself by battling against the specific religions, including Judaism, in the name of a universal faith. He had not given his religious philosophy a name, but in the years in which he was having his ill-fated altercation with the rabbis in Amsterdam, a group of "free thinkers" defined a new belief—Deism. The Deists saw God in the laws of nature, not in supernatural revelations as described in the Bible. The ground had been prepared for the boldest of all the critics of biblical religion, Baruch Spinoza (1632–1677). More than any other philosopher, he was the hinge on which European society turned to a new, postreligious age.

It was almost predictable that Spinoza would appear in Amsterdam, the freest city in Europe, the major commercial and cultural center of the revolutionary republic that had declared its independence from Spain in 1581. Soon after the creation of the Dutch republic, *marranos* from Spain and Portugal began to find their way to Amsterdam, where they were permitted to return openly to Judaism. In 1675 the ex-*marranos* and their descendants erected the beautiful Spanish-Portuguese synagogue, which is still in use. The Jews of Amsterdam were notable for their cultural attainments, such as plays and theological tractates composed in Spanish, the language that the *marranos* had brought with them. Several of the rabbis of the community became scholars of considerable renown. One of them, Rabbi Manasseh ben Israel, was sufficiently at home in the learned world of Europe to write pamphlets in defense of Judaism in Latin. Significantly, however, the Jews did not produce serious literary works in Dutch. The two cultures had not yet interpenetrated in the seventeenth century.

There were enough picturesque types in Amsterdam's Jewish quarter to attract the interest of the great Dutch master Rembrandt Harmenszoon van Rijn (1606–1669), who painted portraits of some notable Jews, including one of Rabbi Manasseh ben Israel. The artist regarded Jews as a welcome part of the human scene in this unique city. Here the Jew seemed less other because Amsterdam conducted trade and commerce with Japanese, Indonesians, Native Americans, and many other peoples in both the eastern and western hemispheres. Jewish businessmen made a comfortable life for themselves in such a society. They held shares in Dutch companies and seats on the stock exchange, and occasionally they entertained royal visitors in the synagogue. In 1654, when Peter Stuyvesant, the governor of New Amsterdam, wanted to expel a boatload of Jewish refugees who had arrived from Recife, Brazil, to escape the Inquisition, the Jewish stockholders in the Dutch West Indies Company had enough clout to override him. Thus began the history of the Jewish community in America. Some restrictions still applied to Jews in the predominantly Protestant Dutch Republic, including a ban on proselytizing, but in Amsterdam they could breathe more easily and speak more openly than anywhere else in the world.

THE HERESY OF SPINOZA

Baruch Spinoza was the son of a *marrano* family that had fled from Portugal. Baruch received a first-rate education in classic Jewish texts at the Jewish high school of the Spanish-Portuguese community of Amsterdam. His first printed work, an essay on Hebrew grammar, appeared in the school's journal. The young Spinoza showed great promise as a Jewish scholar, but that would change dramatically when he came to question and then reject the divinity of the Bible.

Spinoza's famous book on religion and society, *A Theologico-Political Tractate,* written in Latin, demolished the foundations of biblical religion, championing instead the idea of universal morality. Breaking with the tradition of Philo of Alexandria and Maimonides, who believed that faith was always superior to reason, Spinoza asserted that all religious texts are human creations; therefore, reason is the judge of faith. Spinoza became the ultimate skeptic, but he made no move to leave the Jewish community. On the contrary, he continued to pay the assessments levied by the Spanish-Portuguese community in Amsterdam. In 1654, the synagogue was raising money to help Jews on two fronts—those from the Ukraine who were fleeing from Chmielnicki's Cossacks, and those escaping from Recife, in Brazil, which the Portuguese had reconquered from the Dutch. In that same year a rabbinic tribunal in Amsterdam convicted the twenty-four-year-old Spinoza of heresy. The community elders confirmed this judgment with sadness, but firmly:

> The chiefs of the council make known to you that having long known of the evil opinions and acts of Baruch de Spinoza, they have endeavored by various means and promises to turn him from evil ways. Not being able to find any remedy, but on the contrary receiving every day more information about the abominable heresies practiced and taught by him, and about the monstrous acts committed by him, having this from many trustworthy witnesses who have deposed and borne witness on all this in the presence of said Spinoza, who has been convicted; all this having been examined in the presence of the rabbis, the council decided, with the advice of the rabbis, that the said Spinoza would be excommunicated and cut off from the Nation of Israel.

Three hundred years after the banishing of Spinoza, Israel's first prime minister, David Ben-Gurion, called for the reversal of that ruling. No rabbi took up the cause because, in its own terms, the original tribunal had been correct. These rabbis had compassion for this brilliant young man (two of them had been his former teachers), but how could Orthodox believers who were devoting their lives to teaching the authority of God's revelation in Holy Scripture countenance his heresies? And how might the powerful Calvinist Church fathers have reacted if no sanction had been taken against a learned young Jew who declared the text of the Bible to be an imperfect human work that was no more authoritative than Homer's *Iliad*? Even in the relative freedom of the Netherlands, a frontal assault by one Jew on established religion might backfire on the entire community.

Spinoza himself had accepted that judgment as a fact of life. He knew very well that he had revolted against and denied the very foundations of the inherited Jewish faith. To be sure, he was not to publish his *Theologico-Political Tractate* until 1670, and then only anonymously, but he had long held the views that he expressed in that radical work.

At the end of chapter three of this treatise, Spinoza took on frontally the doctrine of the chosenness of the Jews. He quoted a number of passages from the Bible and especially from the prophets that state variously that "the seed of Israel shall ever remain the nation of God" (Jeremiah 31:36). Spinoza then counterposed these passages with statements from the prophets suggesting that God's election of the Jews is dependent on their behavior, that is, on their displaying "true virtue." As human beings are essentially the same, virtue can and does arise among all peoples: "Therefore there is absolutely nothing that Jews can arrogate to themselves beyond other people." For Spinoza, the only standard of judgment is reason, and reason commanded him to believe that all humanity is one, both in its vices and in its capacity for virtue. The chosen, therefore, are the virtuous, independent of their group origins.

How then did Spinoza account for the survival of the Jews? Their continued existence, Spinoza maintained, is not proof "that God had chosen for Himself the Jews forever," nor is there anything "marvelous in it." The Jews are still here because they have lived separately from all the other peoples by their religious rites and "by the sign of circumcision which they must scrupulously observe." This separation has brought down upon the Jews the hatred of others, and that hatred has kept them as a separate community. Spinoza added that the religious separatism of the Jews is "so important that I could persuade myself that it alone would preserve the nation forever." Then, with some evident unhappiness, he conceded that the otherness of the Jews cannot be erased because enough Jews will continue to insist on being different and will continue to practice their separate customs as an act of choice. With stunning insight, Spinoza raised the critical questions that modern Jews would ask repeatedly in the next three centuries: Why should the Jews insist on being different? What is that difference? How is it to be defined and cultivated?

Spinoza offered two alternatives. Many Jews, like the bulk of those who converted to Christianity in Spain before the expulsion in 1492, would soon disappear into the majority. Having left the Jewish religion, they would have no reason to remain different. Some of those ex-Jews would fail to assimilate because the Jew haters would not let them, but assimilation remained, for Spinoza, the logical result of the loss of faith in God's specific election of the Jews. But Spinoza added that it was still possible that Jews might be able to gather together again in the land of their ancestors and reconstitute their own commonwealth. "Nay, I would go so far as to believe that if the foundations of their religion have not emasculated their minds they may even, if occasion offers, so changeable are human affairs, raise up their empire afresh. . . ."[7] As we shall see, these were the very conclusions that Theodor Herzl reached more than two hundred years later: faced with persistent anti-Semitism, the Jews will either assimilate into European society or will create a state of their own in Palestine.

In the past sixty years I have read and reread those pages of *Theologico-Political Tractate* in which Spinoza discusses the future of the Jews, and each time I return to the text my awe increases. In three pages Spinoza foresees and defines the main outline of Jewish modernity—its problems and the possibilities. I am less impressed with Spinoza's overt message, that logic dictates the end of the Jewish people and that its claim to a unique relationship with the God of Sinai is a myth. Reading between the lines, I now understand that Spinoza is sending an unprecedented message: he is giving Jews license to leave Judaism in good conscience. In earlier times many Jews had abandoned their faith to convert to Islam or to Christianity, but conversion out of Judaism was rarely a calm passage. The converts had taken this step usually amid inner turmoil and, more often than not, with regret. Others had left Judaism in anger, heaping scorn on their past. Spinoza provided a justification for assimilation based on philosophical rationalism and universalism. He made it possible for Jews and Christians alike to abandon their inherited religions with the quiet assurance that they are moving toward a philosophically secure universalist morality.

I find no visible anger in his discussion of biblical religion, even though Spinoza experienced the humiliation of excommunication. He was simply suggesting that biblical religion is an early prephilosophical stage of human consciousness and that philosophers rise beyond this level as they raise themselves to a higher truth. It is thus possible to leave Judaism with rueful respect for one's childhood, while announcing oneself as having reached philosophical maturity. This attitude would reappear in future centuries, as the bearers of new ideologies felt obliged to discard the past, which not only had outlived its usefulness but also had become an affliction. Karl Marx and Sigmund Freud would do exactly that when each in his own way suggested that the separate existence of the Jews and their antiquated traditions were nothing more than impediments to a healthy society.

What intrigues me most about these three pages is what Spinoza leaves unstated. He could not bring himself to state explicitly that the Jews will persist as an act of sheer will or because they believe with a mystical certainty that their existence has special meaning in the world. But what else can he be telling us when he writes, "These Jews might cease to believe in God but will cling to circumcision and all their separatist rituals"? This rationalist is saying that the Jews will defy logic, and he is right. Generations of modern nonbelieving Jews have adhered to their Jewishness for reasons they themselves cannot articulate.

Spinoza's most astonishing remark is his forecasting of a time when the Jews might reconstitute their nation. He asserts that the Jews will be able to become a political power again if their spirit has not been weakened by centuries of living under the strictures of their religion. Here he foreshadows the central criticism of the modern Zionists—that Jews in the Diaspora would have to reject their ghetto mentality before they could live as free men and women in their own land.

In these three pages Spinoza makes yet another intellectual revolution: he redefines chosenness. Only those who live virtuous lives, he insists, have earned this special distinction. Spinoza knew very well that such an argument had once been advanced by the early Christians, who maintained that the "election of Israel" had moved from Israel according "to the flesh" to Israel according "to the spirit"; the new chosen people, therefore, were those who had elected to join the believers in Jesus. But Spinoza does not define his new elect as those philosophers who simply understand universal morality. On the contrary, he lays the accent on a life of virtue; what matters is not what people think, but how they behave. In his *Ethics* Spinoza called for action that will lead humanity "to greater perfection." The motto of all of creation is to "act well and to rejoice." I hear in what Spinoza is saying more than a little of what he learned in his Jewish studies as a youth. Surely Spinoza knew the kabbalist doctrines of Isaac Luria, which portrays the world as a place of struggle in which we must redeem the hidden, holy sparks so that the world might be perfected. I suspect that long after Spinoza had ceased saying his daily prayers, he remembered the progression in the morning liturgy that urges the worshiper "to learn, to teach, to obey [God's word], *and to act*." And long after his banishment, Spinoza retained the moral sensibilities that became ingrained in his earliest years as an Orthodox believer.

Spinoza's estrangement from Judaism left him in near solitude. He lived the rest of his life apart from his family and from all the people he had known in his childhood. Even though his originality as a thinker was recognized by some of the leading spirits of his time, such as Gottfried Wilhelm Leibnitz, his influence spread slowly. In the eighteenth century, anybody of any intellectual consequence read him, but most did not admit it or at least pretended that they had been horrified at the writings of this atheist (which Spinoza was not; he identified God with the discernible laws of physics and morality). Those who did read Spinoza seriously knew that their own religious faith had been subjected to devastating criticism, and anyone who wanted to continue to be a believer would have to answer Spinoza for himself or herself.

The first attempt to dispute Spinoza was made in Amsterdam in 1687 by a physician and essayist, Isaac Orobio de Castro, who argued against what he regarded as the overt atheism of Spinoza. But Orobio was essentially a defender of the classic biblical doctrines of a personal God. A much more serious critique appeared early in the eighteenth century in Naples, Italy. The Italian lawyer and philosopher

Giambattista Vico argued that the universal values that Spinoza had deduced by reason were, in reality, mediated through culture and history. Spinoza was denying something very basic to human experience: people do not identify themselves with all of humanity; that is an abstraction. Each of us belongs to an immediate family, to an extended family, to a people and its history. Each community meets and wrestles with the problems and possibilities of human existence in its own way.

Why have I not embraced Spinoza? It should be obvious that I admire his towering intellect and take his views seriously. My deepest answer is that I agree with the hints that Spinoza has left between the lines to explain the persistence of the Jews, the very hints that he cannot fit into his rational system. He has taught me that it is difficult to believe the image that God sat on Mount Sinai and dictated to Moses, who then acted as scribe and messenger. Spinoza has made his argument all the more powerful by insisting that God could not possibly have commanded, literally and verbatim, some of the cruelties that have been committed "in His name." And yet, I persist in believing that something unexplainable and mystical has guided our passage through history. Our existence is not merely the sum of our rational choices; it is rooted in the most hidden recesses of the Jewish soul.

The other nonrational hint in Spinoza is the suggestion, to put it in my own terms, that Jews have continued to exist by a defiant act of will. He is right but for the wrong reason. It is not the belief that God chose the Jews that has kept us going. Abraham did not begin his journey because God suddenly appeared and said to him, I have chosen you and your descendants to be my special messengers on earth. On the contrary, Abraham first chose God by breaking the idols of his father, Terah; that is the driving impulse of Jewish existence.

We long ago ceased believing that God speaks to us directly. When the Hasidim revived this idea in the eighteenth century, they were immediately engulfed, as we shall soon see, in a titanic battle with the established Jewish order. What the Jews—religious believers and doubters alike—do know about themselves is that in every age they have looked at the world with their own different eyes. Jews continue to choose to break idols, and we know that we cannot help ourselves. It is our destiny. I think of Spinoza, the excommunicated Jew who is "cut off from his people," as slaying the sacred cows of Western society. I think of this irritating questioner of the accepted verities accepting his lonely path because, like Abraham, he could not constrain himself.

CHAPTER 10

THE HASIDIC
REVOLUTION

Yitzhak Leib Peretz (1852–1915), one of the founders of modern Yiddish literature, wrote a short story a century ago that captured something of the essence of the clash between the *Hasidim* (pious ones), the ecstatic and mystical pietists who appeared in the middle of the eighteenth century, and their opponents, the *misnagdim*, those who scoffed at the antics of the Hasidim and their wonder-working rebbes or tzaddikim ("holy men"). In Peretz's story, "If Not Higher," the rebbe of Nemirov would disappear every morning during the *slichos* prayers, the penitential services on the days immediately before Rosh

Hashanah, the Jewish New Year. The rebbe's followers knew exactly where their master went—he ascended to heaven. Where else could the holy man be if not in communion with God, pleading the cause of his persecuted people before the heavenly court? But a newcomer to town, a "Litvak," refused to believe that the rebbe could simply vanish. (*Litvak* or Lithuanian is synonymous with *misnaged,* because the most famous opponent of the Hasidim was the Gaon of Vilna, the capital of Lithuania.) The Litvak, a hardheaded talmudist, could quote chapter and verse to prove that humans could no longer go to heaven to talk with God; that had ended with the last of the biblical prophets, Malachi. Rebbes disappear into heaven only in the minds of their foolish and gullible disciples.

The Litvak, so the story goes, resolved to expose this trickery, so he hid under the rebbe's bed and kept him under surveillance. To stay awake, the Litvak recited long talmudic passages from memory. Just before dawn, the rebbe got out of bed and walked across the room to a closet. He put on the clothes of a peasant and tucked a woodsman's ax under his leather belt. The disguised rebbe then walked into the forest at the edge of town, chopped some firewood, tied the pieces into a bundle, and carried it back to a ramshackle hut in town. The rebbe knocked at the window and announced himself in Russian as Vassil. The old bedridden woman inside asked in a frightened voice what he wanted. In a gruff voice, the rebbe replied that he had wood for sale at almost no cost. The woman protested that she had no money. "Vassil" said he would trust her to pay when she could. He then entered the hut and placed the wood on the hearth. As he lit the fire, the rebbe chanted the *slichot* prayers. Having witnessed all this, the Litvak declared himself to be a disciple of the rebbe of Nemirov. And ever since that day, whenever anyone said the rebbe has ascended to heaven, the Litvak would add, "If not higher."

An enlightened Jew with socialist learnings, Peretz romanticized the Hasidim and found something to admire in their way of life. More than anywhere else in the Jewish world of the nineteenth century, the poor Hasid had claim on the rich Hasid because both were adherents of the same rebbe. In theory, and even often in practice, they were equal in the sight of their leader, as they were in the sight of God. Peretz even found virtue in the Litvak, who recognized that an act of righteousness is the highest of all Jewish values, even higher than the mastery of holy texts.

The Hasidim portrayed by Peretz and those often found in literature or polemics were not the Hasidim among whom I lived in my parents' home or encountered in the Hasidic synagogue that my father led. They did bear some resemblance. My father cared about the poor and the defenseless at least as much as Peretz's mythic rebbe of Nemirov, and my mother would never rest at the end of the day until she was sure that every needy person of whom she was aware had been helped. But the hero of Peretz's story seemed to be more of a labor leader than a rebbe. (No Hasid, and certainly no rebbe, would enter the hut of a woman unaccompanied, but this is what Peretz had the rebbe of Nemirov do.) I have never found in any real Hasidic text the idea that the spiritual descendants of the Baal Shem Tov were really crypto-Socialists in black caftans. I did find, page after page, the demand for compassion, for love of every individual. My father taught me that the biblical commandment "Thou shalt love thy neighbor as thyself" was unnecessary in the case of people we like; it is necessary because it demands that we care for those we find disagreeable. We are all God's children, the obnoxious no less than the gracious. But the religious duty to love your neighbor is not a call for socialist revolution, though the children of some Hasidim did leave the faith of their parents to head for the barricades.

My discomfort with the partisan and usually polemical usurpation of the Hasidim became all the more pointed one day in 1949. I was in

Jerusalem for the first time, in the guise of a journalist. I asked the chief press officer of Israel's new government to arrange an interview with Martin Buber, the most famous modern interpreter of Hasidism. Buber was a cultural celebrity because of the importance of his philosophical and theological work, at the center of which was a famous concept that human values arise out of true encounters between individuals, the "I-Thou" relationship. I came to Dr. Buber's home at the appointed time, and I saw through the open door to his study that he was deeply immersed in a text spread out before him. He let me wait for a few minutes, then he looked up and asked me, "What unanswered question has brought you to me?" For a moment the young man of twenty-eight standing before this legend (in the 1890s Buber, at nineteen, began his career as an assistant to Theodor Herzl, the founder of modern Zionism) was nonplussed. I had come to discuss Hasidism with him, but did I dare tell him what had brought me to him? Did I dare try to enter into a true I-Thou relationship with Martin Buber?

I decided he would know if I faked it for the sake of peace, so I told him what was bothering me. He had written in the *Tales of the Hasidim* about ancestors of mine, but they did not look like the descriptions of their character and teaching that had been handed down by the family or that I had found in their writings. Buber was, of course, a careful scholar, and his renderings of the stories were correct, but his portraits of the Hasidic masters seemed distorted. They reminded me of exotic, Eastern sages whom European writers were in the habit of conjuring up to criticize, either directly or by inference, the materialism and lack of spirituality of Western society. For all the spiritual depth that he correctly ascribed to them, I was disturbed that Buber paid scant attention to the profound and absolute obedience of the Hasidim to the religious practices and laws in the Talmud.

After an hour of conversation about how the Hasidim were to be understood, I referred to Buber, provocatively, as a "neo-Hasid." The implication was obvious; I did not consider him a Hasid. Buber was instantly angry. "I am not a neo-Hasid," he insisted, "I am a Hasid." I took up the challenge, and I said to him, in his own house, "Dr. Buber, an ancestor of mine, Elimelech of Lizhansk, was one of the disciples at the table of Dov Ber of Mezritch, the first great disciple of the Baal Shem Tov (the first Hasidic holy man). You, Dr. Buber, are a deeply religious person, but you avowedly do not live within the discipline of Jewish law and practice. Does that make you a Hasid in the line of Elimelech and my father? Or are you a neo-Hasid?" Buber repeated, "I am a Hasid," and our conversation ended.

Several years later, while on a visit to New York, Buber seemed to have forgiven me for my youthful impertinence, for he asked me to translate some of his essays from German into English for publication in the United States. I was drawn, in particular, to the second of "Three Speeches About Judaism," which he had given before and during the First World War to various audiences of Jewish intellectuals who were trying to find their way from assimilation to some understanding of how they might affirm themselves within the wide spectrum of Judaism. In that speech Buber had named his own spiritual paternity, citing as his Jewish ancestors such figures as Jesus and Paul, Shabbetai Zvi, and the Baal Shem Tov. All of these, so Buber had asserted then, represented a heretical strain in Judaism; they had been bold enough to confront the inherited tradition and to shake it to its very foundations. When I called Dr. Buber's attention to this passage, he suggested that he now would want to delete it from the new American edition. I somehow felt that he was telling me that he had moved away from thinking of himself as heir to Jewish heretics and, especially, that he no longer thought of the Baal Shem Tov as a rebel who could be mentioned together with Paul and Shabbetai Zvi.

My encounter with Martin Buber was the first of three with leading interpreters of Hasidism in Israel. In 1949 I also met the central figure among the modern Jewish historians at the Hebrew University, Benzion Dinur. No one could be more official, more the historian laureate of the Zionist enterprise, than Professor Dinur. His central theory was that Jewish history had been moving for centuries toward the climactic moment of reestablishing statehood in the ancestral homeland. As part of his analysis, Dinur kept insisting that the Hasidim came into being in order to bring to the surface the dormant messianic longing for the return to the Holy Land and that the main thrust of Hasidism was to lead the Jewish masses away from Diaspora existence and toward Zion. He was aflame with enthusiasm that summer in 1949. I was in the audience when he spoke to some of those who had volunteered from America during Israel's War of Independence. Dinur told us that we had a task to complete: to realize the end of Jewish history by getting even American Jews to join the "ascent" to Israel.

Some years later, I met and became friendly with an even greater scholar, Gershom Scholem, the creator of the modern discipline of studies in the history and thought of the Kabbalah. Scholem knew an enormous amount about Hasidism, so I hesitated to take issue with him, not least because he was a most formidable controversialist. Scholem insisted vehemently that Buber and Dinur were both wrong. Scholem denied that the Hasidim had come into being to make revolutions against inherited religious practices or to be proto-Zionists. They had appeared, he said, at a time when Jews were losing hope; they wanted to rekindle the feeling that God was near at hand and to teach the masses of Jews that even in awful poverty they were a family, belonging to one another and to God. For Scholem, Hasidism represented a climactic stage in the influence of the Kabbalah in Jewish life. The essential teaching of the new movement was that with the proper attitude, anyone anywhere could experience God. I did not dare say to Scholem that he, too, was annexing the Hasidim to bolster the thesis of his life's work: that the Kabbalah had been the great counterforce to talmudic law, which taught patient and unswerving obedience to religious law. I had almost found the chutzpah to raise my objection when Scholem began to attack the Marxist interpretation of the Hasidim by the historian Raphael Mahler, who had described the Hasidic movement as a rebellion of the masses against the coalition of the magnates and the rabbis who controlled the official Jewish communities in eastern Europe. Scholem countered Mahler by pointing out that at the very beginning the Hasidim were poor, but that situation did not last long because some of the rich and learned were attracted to wonder-working rebbes in whose miracles they believed and whose advice they followed.

So who indeed were the Hasidim? Despite Scholem's authority, the major point of contention among scholars remained, and still is, the question of whether the Hasidic movement was essentially messianic. Did the Hasidim come into being as a direct attempt to hasten the Messiah's coming? This question was complicated by the fact that the Hasidim did not cast, at least not publicly, any of their early leaders as the Messiah waiting to reveal himself. In its formative years, the Hasidic movement was constrained not to go beyond muted hints and allusions of messianism because the Jewish world was still deeply wounded by the convulsion of a century earlier, when the meteor Shabbetai Zvi had blazed across the horizon and crashed into apostasy.

In the very years that Hasidism was emerging in eastern Europe, a new pretender to the role of the messiah, Jacob Frank, appeared. Frank was even more offensive than Shabbetai Zvi had been because he fought his rabbinic enemies by enlisting the aid of Christian clerics and he gave credence to the anti-Semitic canard that the Talmud requires Jews to use of the blood of Christian children in the baking of the unleavened bread for Passover. Even worse, Jacob Frank and his followers had defied not only the ritual but the moral laws of Judaism; they engaged in sexual orgies and incest. So when Hasidism arose, there was great fear among the rabbis that it was another manifestation of the Shabbetean heresy. This suspicion was regarded as all the more likely because, in those very days, the rabbis of central and eastern Europe were bitterly divided over the charge leveled by Rabbi Jacob Emden that an even more celebrated scholar, Rabbi Jonathan Eybeschutz, was a secret adherent of Shabbetai Zvi and that he distributed amulets encoding the "messiah's" name and prayed for his blessing. The truth of the charge was less important than the fact that it was believable because, in fact, crypto-Shabbeteans, including some rabbis, existed in every major Jewish community. Therefore, even if the early Hasidim were messianists, they had to disguise it and to take great pains to distinguish the new movement from any suggestion of Shabbetean influence.

Taken together, several Hasidic tales dating back to those formative days make this point with great clarity. The most picturesque is the story that the soul of Shabbetai Zvi had been unable to find a permanent resting place either in heaven or hell, so it was wandering about the world in great torment. When the Baal Shem Tov revealed himself as "the master of the name"—that he knew the very name of God and with this knowledge he could effect great cures—the roving soul of Shabbetai Zvi came to the Baal Shem Tov and asked the Hasidic master for a *tikkun,* a redemptive healing. The Baal Shem Tov agreed, and he struggled mightily to raise the soul from the impurities into which it had fallen during Shabbetai's final descent into apostasy. The Baal Shem Tov explained that he was engaged in this labor because the fact that Shabbetai Zvi's soul had come to him proved that this messianic pretender was still attached to the body of the Jewish people, and so long as a limb is attached to the body by even a single sinew, there is still some hope of its being totally reattached; the moment it is severed, the hope is gone. But one day the Baal Shem Tov, so the tale goes, cast the soul of Shabbetai Zvi away, permanently and forever, into the deepest pit. The holy man had discovered that Shabbetai's soul had come to him not for a *tikkun* but to try to mislead the Baal Shem Tov into heresy and apostasy. Clearly, this tale was constructed to explain why some of the early Hasidim did, evidently, have contact with crypto-Shabbeteans—to bring them back from their evil ways—and that when this attempt failed, the Hasidim would have nothing more to do with them.

That the messianic impulse was present in Hasidism, muted but real, is unmistakable in two other stories, both of which are based on a kernel of historic truth. The Baal Shem Tov tried to make the journey to the Holy Land, but he could not complete it because his ship sank en route. He was cast up on some island in the Mediterranean, where his daughter Odel, who had accompanied him, had to teach him the Hebrew alphabet because he had forgotten all his learning. It all came back to him when he realized that he should not continue his journey. The moral of the story has always been given as follows: if the Baal Shem Tov, the holiest man of his time, had encountered the Holy Land, the light created by that encounter would have been so brilliant that it would have compelled heaven to reveal the messiah, and "the time was not yet ripe."

The Baal Shem Tov's great-grandson, Nachman of Bratzlav, repeated this drama a half century later. He did reach the Holy Land, but the Hasidic tale places him there for only a few hours. The holy man had come to perform some mysterious *tikkun,* and we do not know whether he had completed it or whether he had discovered it could not be done because "the time was not ripe." In any event, so the tale goes, he left immediately. We now know that Nachman of Bratzlav stayed in the Holy Land for a few months. He tried without success to find a permanent home, all the while giving many hints that his encounter with the Holy Land would hasten the end of days and suggesting obliquely that he might be harboring the soul of the Messiah within his body. But in the end, Nachman of Bratzlav did not remain, and the end of days did not come.

THE OPPONENTS

The Baal Shem Tov and the Gaon of Vilna are the last great religious figures to arise within Judaism before the world of the ghetto crumbled. Near the end of the premodern era, in the middle of the eighteenth century, these two towering figures offered conflicting solutions to help the Jews of eastern Europe bear the endless sorrow of their exile.

Elijah ben Shlomo Zalman was born in 1720 to a family of talmudic scholars in Selets near Grodno. By age six he was recognized as a prodigy of rabbinic learning. Before his tenth birthday he had studied all of the Bible and Talmud and many of the commentaries on these basic works, as well as some texts of the Kabbalah. He even found time to study mathematics. In a very few years, the Jewish world came to recognize him as a *Gaon,* an "excellency" and a "genius" on a level not known for centuries, probably not since the time of Maimonides. His reputation was so great that the Jewish community in Vilna regarded it as an honor to help support him and his family; henceforth, he could devote himself entirely to study. The authority of the Gaon of Vilna derived from his personal modesty, his unbounded charity to the poor, and his asceticism. By precept and example he taught that Jews had only the study of God's word as their refuge. Any attempt to break the mold of obedient waiting for the Messiah was heresy. Such efforts had to be suppressed, by excommunication if necessary.

The Gaon was uncompromisingly strict with himself. He once jumped out of a wagon, instantly, when he became aware that its canopy had been crafted from flax and wool together. (He was obey-

ing punctiliously the biblical law that forbids the combination of animal and natural fibers.) The story is told that a scholar once came to
him and dared to suggest that Rashi, the revered eleventh-century
commentator on the Bible and the Talmud, had erred on occasion by
straying from the plain meaning of a particular text. The Gaon of Vilna
said nothing at the moment, but he arranged for the Jewish authorities
in Vilna to humiliate this man in the courtyard of the synagogue by
administering thirty-nine lashes and having the congregation pass by
and spit in his face.

The Gaon was widely revered, especially in Vilna and in all of
Lithuania, where rabbinic learning was deep and widespread, but even
in this region Jews were becoming terribly weary of waiting for the
Messiah. Obedience to the letter of the law was scant consolation to
the wounded heart. They yearned for a more direct way to experience
God's presence. If the time of the Jewish prolonged exile is indefinite,
then let it be transformed. Let the Jews, especially the poor and persecuted among them, find within their souls a radiance to lift them
beyond the drab and tragic present. Once again, the Jews would search
for an answer in their mystical tradition.

Hasidism was the last religious movement to be born within the
older world of Jewish piety, that is, before the Jews entered the world
of modernity. Its founder, Israel ben Eliezer was born c. 1700 in the village of Okup on the eastern border of the Polish province of Podolya.
Few facts about his life are known. In some legends, he is reported to
have been not very learned, and in others he is described as a man who
possessed the totality of Jewish knowledge. He is believed to have
lived for many years in near solitude, making his living in various
menial occupations. It is said that at the age of thirty-six he revealed his
miraculous powers of healing and prophetic foresight, and became
known as the Baal Shem Tov (Master of the Good Name). He taught
his disciples that God is present everywhere and that all Jews can

connect with the Holy One through joyful prayer and unbound enthusiasm. The Baal Shem Tov and his disciples infused all the inherited
pieties with spontaneity and cheerfulness. Many a Hasidic master has
taught that one who recites the daily morning prayers with the same
degree of emotion as the day before is committing idolatry; the words
must be recreated each time with unique passion and devotion. In
their outer, everyday existence most of the Hasidim lived in bleak
poverty, but in their inner life they saw themselves as God's beloved
children, basking in the light of divine presence.

After the Baal Shem's death in 1760, the mantle of leadership
passed to his disciple Dov Ber, known as the Maggid (preacher) of
Mezritch. Dov Ber surrounded himself with dozens of charismatic figures who brought the teachings of Hasidism to all the Jewish communities of eastern Europe. These Hasidic masters came to be known as
tzaddikim, or rebbes, and they were thought by their disciples to be
the mediators between heaven and earth—not themselves divine, but
something of divinity graced their presence.

The revolutionary doctrine of the tzaddik contravened a long-held
rabbinic axiom. The Hasidim boldly claimed for the Baal Shem Tov
and his followers the power of prophecy, ignoring the pronouncement
in the Talmud that prophecy was restricted to the Holy Land and that,
in any case, it had ended with Malachi, the last prophet, in the Bible. In
the Hasidic mind, every shtetl in eastern Europe was part of the Holy
Land because in these places prophets (the rebbes) were again com-
muning with God. Spiritual perfection, the Hasidim insisted, can be
achieved anywhere, even by the most unlearned person, if he or she
only truly bends mind and heart to God's service. We do not have to
wait for the Messiah to taste the end of days; it can happen in our own
time. To be in the presence of the tzaddik is to be in the Holy Temple
in Jerusalem. The tzaddik is the high priest, and his table is the very
altar of God. The rabbinic opponents of Hasidism attacked such

notions as idolatry, and the "enlightened" Jews mocked them as fool-ish—but the Hasidim clung to their rebbes with adoration.

The Gaon of Vilna and his followers did not need to study Hasidic doctrine to condemn this incipient movement. In the two Hasidic syn-agogues in Vilna they watched ecstatic Hasidim turning somersaults during prayer and improvising the prescribed Hebrew liturgy with spontaneous blessings and meditations in Yiddish. Worst of all, the Hasidim followed after the Baal Shem Tov in rejecting the long-established Ashkenazi prayerbook and replacing it with their version of the one that had been arranged by the revolutionary mystic of Safed, Isaac Luria. This substitution alarmed the Gaon because it was Lurianic Kabbalah that had set the stage for the Shabbetean heresy. The Hasidim, therefore, were very much under suspicion of being secret followers of the apostate messiah. In the denunciations of the Hasidim, the followers of the Gaon, the misnagdim, applied the term accursed sect, which had been used to condemn the Shabbeteans.

Dov Ber of Mezritch sent two of his most learned disciples, Shneur Zalman of Lyady and Menachem Mendel of Vitebsk, to Vilna to try to persuade the Gaon Elijah that the Hasidim were not rebels against the inherited religious tradition. Dov Ber hoped that the Gaon would rec-ognize in his disciples their devotion to the very values about which he cared, for these two were very learned in the Talmud. Elijah refused to see them, giving as his reason that it is forbidden even to behold the countenance of a heretic. No doubt Elijah thought that learning and even meticulous piety could be a cover for secret belief in Shabbetai Zvi or, even worse, Jacob Frank. He could not know that the Hasidim were engaged at that time in neutralizing the very poison that these false messiahs had injected into the body of the Jewish community.

This battle raged to the very end of the Gaon's life in 1797. Several excommunications were pronounced against the Hasidim, and messengers were dispatched near and far to denounce these "heretics." The very first of these excommunications, signed by seventeen rabbis, including the Gaon himself, was issued in 1791:

> Our brethren in Israel, you are certainly already informed of the tidings whereof our fathers never dreamed, that a sect . . . has been formed . . . who meet together in separate groups and deviate in their prayers from the text valid for the whole people. . . . The study of the Torah is neglected by them entirely, and they do not hesitate constantly to emphasize that one should devote oneself as little as possible to learning and not grieve too much over a sin committed. . . . Every day is for them a holiday. . . . When they pray according to falsified texts, they raise such a din that the walls quake . . . and they turn over like wheels, with the head below and the legs above . . . . So long as they do not make full atonement of their own accord, they should be scattered and driven away so that no two heretics remain together, for the disbanding of their associations is a boon for the world. . . .'

The misnagdim would not eat in the homes of Hasidim, nor would they permit their sons and daughters to marry into Hasidic families. But the misnagdim did not succeed in suppressing the "accursed sect." The enmity eventually softened when the misnagdim ceased believing that the Hasidim wanted to break away from orthodoxy and when the Hasidim ceased believing that their opponents were nothing but dry legalists, devoid of spirituality. They have fought with equal passion to preserve the otherness of the Jew by keeping the faithful behind ideological barriers.

The most persuasive evidence that messianism is inherent, indeed central, to at least major elements among the Hasidim is to be found in the writings of Shneur Zalman, the progenitor of the powerful sect that derived its name from the center of its activities, the town of Lubavitch. Shneur Zalman was the only founding figure in Hasidism who wrote a systematic account of his religious teachings. The book is commonly known as the *Tanya*, and it is studied to this day by Lubavitcher Hasidim in order to see divine truth through the eyes of this holy guide. The climactic doctrine of the *Tanya* is Shneur Zalman's teaching about the Messiah. He rejects the notion that God will send the Messiah as compensation for the suffering of Jews after they have finally expiated their sins (whatever they may be). In this classic Jewish conception, the Messiah will come to an exhausted people to lift it beyond long centuries of despair. The *Tanya* teaches a radically different doctrine: the image of the Messiah is extraordinarily, even cosmically, optimistic. The Messiah will come soon to bring the world to perfection. God has created the world to be his dwelling place, but first all the "garments," the vessels that impede his finding a home in this world, must be removed. How can that be effected? The answer lies in what each Jew does. The human body itself is such a garment, and it can be removed as an impediment only if the individual purifies it by proper and joyous observance of each of God's commandments, for each one of them corresponds to a specific part of the human anatomy. So it is with the world as a whole. Jewish acts of piety remove the material husks that keep the divine sparks imprisoned; it is within the power of each individual to bring the redemption closer by the godliness of his or her life. Thus there is only one road to bringing the Messiah: to get all Jews to observe more of the tradition willingly and with joyful hearts. The world as a whole will then be redeemed for Jews and for all of humanity.

Shneur Zalman is teaching in the *Tanya* a good bit of what he, admittedly, had learned from the revolutionary kabbalist of the sixteenth century, Isaac Luria: Jews need not wait patiently for the

Messiah; they can hasten his advent. What is new in Shneur Zalman is that he has democratized the Lurianic Kabbalah by giving every Jew a necessary role to play in the messianic drama. The Messiah will not be hastened by the kabbalistic exercises and meditations of the few who are capable of such ascents toward the infinite. All Jews, from the most ignorant and the most alienated to the most learned and most pious, must join in bringing the Messiah closer by what each does in moving toward more observance of God's commandments or mitzvot.

Shneur Zalman's thoughts about the Messiah have been studied in the *Tanya* with regularity by generations of Lubavitcher Hasidim. They hold as a sacred command these words in the thirty-seventh chapter: "Now this ultimate perfection of the messianic era and [the time of] the resurrection of the dead, meaning the revelation of Ein Sof-light [the infinite] in this physical world, is dependent on our actions and [divine] service throughout the period of exile." If this is achieved, so Shneur Zalman writes, "the totality of the vital soul of the community of Israel will become a holy chariot for God." He adds that "the general vitality of this world," which is now obstructed by the dark force of impurity, "will also emerge from its impurity and sickness and will ascend to holiness, to become a chariot for God. . . . Then all flesh will behold godliness together."[2]

Shneur Zalman insisted that the Messiah could proceed only on a road that was paved with Jewish piety, obedience, and learning. He was also teaching that the destiny of the Jewish people, and the world as a whole, was in everybody's hands; it was not a matter for elites. Above all, he was telling all those who would join him that each individual had an indispensable and active share in bringing about the cosmic redemption. It could be now or very soon, if all Jews willed it.

The author of the *Tanya* declared boldly that the "Sabbath of the world" will come in the seventh millennium according to the traditional Hebrew calendar (he lived in the middle of the sixth millennium). No wonder that his seventh-generation descendant, Menachem Mendel Schneerson, who had lived and died as the seventh millennium was approaching, was so intoxicated with the expectation that the Messiah was poised to appear.

I know that in recent decades many people, and not only Jews, have marveled at the strange sight of emissaries of Menachem Mendel Schneerson appearing around the globe to try to induce Jewish individuals to say a prayer or partake in a ritual or make a promise to adopt one more religious practice as part of their daily lives. Often these emissaries step out of a "Mitzvah Mobile," and always this vehicle has a sign on it announcing that its occupants "want the Messiah now." In this generation, many—even most—of the Lubavitcher Hasidim believed that their rebbe was the Messiah waiting to reveal himself. If this sounds like a sudden case of messianic mania, one must realize that this impulse was set into motion seven generations ago by Shneur Zalman of Lyady.

Did the Lubavitcher rebbe, Menachem Mendel Schneerson, think that he might be the incarnation of the Messiah? I can only wonder why he would not visit the Holy Land. He never made that journey from Brooklyn, but I think not for the reason that was usually given publicly—that if he arrived there, he would be bound by the ancient rabbinic ruling that one should never leave its sacred soil. I am inclined instead to accept the whispered, deeply Hasidic reason: the seventh Lubavitcher rebbe, like the Baal Shem Tov and Nachman of Bratzlav, could not encounter the Holy Land unless it was the moment of the revelation of the Messiah, and Menachem Mendel Schneerson knew "that the time was not ripe." So he remained in Brooklyn. He even allowed his disciples to build a replica of his synagogue and headquarters in their community in Israel, a home that would be familiar to the rebbe when he did arrive in the Holy Land as the Messiah or, at least, as his precursor. Menachem Mendel Schneerson hoped that this generation could be made worthy of the coming of the Messiah, and his Hasidim kept asking out loud, Is there a more worthy candidate than our rebbe? The fires that were lit in eastern Europe over two centuries ago by the first Hasidim still burn for some Jews everywhere in the world.

CHAPTER 11

UNREQUITED LOVE

In 1762 Isaac de Pinto, a Jew of Spanish-Portuguese descent, wrote an open letter of protest to the leading literary figure in France and of all Europe, Marie Arouet de Voltaire. Six years earlier Voltaire had published a historical article stating that since ancient times, the Jews had been the scourge of humanity. Isaac de Pinto challenged Voltaire's assertion. He was making the case that people like himself were no less part of the contemporary and enlightened world than Voltaire himself. But de Pinto did not defend all Jews. "A Portuguese Jew from Bordeaux and a German Jew from Metz," he wrote, "appear to be two entirely different beings." The Portuguese Jews "do not wear beards and are not different from other men in their clothing; the rich among them are devoted to learning, elegance and manners to the same degree as the other peoples of Europe, from whom they differ only in religion." The Portuguese are honest businessmen, almost never usurers, and have been of great use to the economies of the countries that have admitted them. They have the vices that go with such virtues—a taste for luxury, prodigality, laziness, and "womanizing," the vices of "great spirits."

De Pinto added that "because of the delicacy of their emotions," modern Jews like himself would not trade away their religion, even though they had become Deists in their inner hearts. Indeed, such Jews should be admired for their "greatness of soul" in clinging to "a religion that is proscribed and held in contempt." De Pinto was saying to Voltaire that Jews ought to live up to the standards of "enlightened" behavior and belief, but he, and others like him, would remain other out of some deep sense of communal solidarity. They would not abandon their less fortunate brothers and sisters.

Voltaire responded with "an apology," in which he granted de Pinto the right to be anything he pleased, even a Jew, so long as he was a "philosophe," that is, a man of the Enlightenment. Had Voltaire been candid with de Pinto in his "apology," he would have confessed his anti-Semitism. Eleven years later, in 1773, Voltaire was very frank, and nasty, in a letter to a friend. Voltaire agreed that in the English colonies some Jews seemed to be behaving like other businessmen, but it was a charade:

These marranos go wherever there is money to be made. . . . But that these circumcised Jews who sell old clothes to the savages claim that they are of the tribe of Naphtali or Issachar is not of the slightest importance. They are, nonetheless, the greatest scoundrels who have ever sullied the face of the globe.[1]

Isaac de Pinto's boldness in challenging so formidable a figure as Voltaire owed something to his *marrano* heritage. His forebears had acquired in Spain and Portugal something of the hidalgos' sensitivity to slights on their honor. But he was no Doña Gracia defying the pope. There was something new and cringing in de Pinto's open letter to Voltaire. He was begging the literary high priest of the Enlightenment to be nice to him and his kind because some of them had already become "enlightened" and others were on the way. De Pinto's response to Voltaire marked an important turning point. Until the middle of the eighteenth century, all Jews who remained within the Jewish community had no doubt that their judge was God. De Pinto, by contrast, essentially ordained the gentile intelligentsia as his judge and jury. This was happening for the first time since Hellenistic times, when Jewish young men in Jerusalem and Alexandria and in many other places surgically obscured their circumcision so that they could compete naked in the Greek gymnasia without looking different. They no longer wanted the approval of the Jewish God; they wanted to be accepted by Hellenistic society. This was beginning to happen again in the eighteenth century. De Pinto, who had become a Deist, wrote elegant French, and he believed that the benighted majority of the Jews would soon shed everything that kept them from being welcomed by the philosophes. He was wrong. The Jewish mainstream would never give up its otherness, and the modern anti-Semites would never agree that any Jew, even the most assimilated, could become a true German or Frenchman or Englishman. So much of the history of the Jews in the modern era is the story of unrequited love.

The encounter between modernist Jews and the Enlightenment ushered in the era of Jewish self-contempt, which has persisted to this day. Many Jews found it embarrassing to be identified with the religion and the faith of their ancestors. There was a near consensus among the philosophes that the Jewish character had been corrupted by the many centuries of living apart in the ghetto and that Jews' obsessive study of the Talmud and other Hebraic texts had seriously impaired their intellectual development. Voltaire maintained that the Jews were hopeless and that society would be best served by defending itself against them. The mainstream of the Enlightenment was more charitable. It believed that the Jews could be "regenerated" by being permitted, or even forced, to leave the ghetto and to live a healthier life in the open air of the larger society.

The fashionable economic theory of those days, which had been formulated by the Physiocrats, added to the negative assessment of the Jews. The Physiocrats insisted that the only productive occupations were working the land or fashioning raw materials into finished goods. Most Jews, who at best were middlemen and at worst petty moneylenders, were condemned as unproductive. The influence of the Physiocrats was so great that Queen Marie Antoinette felt compelled to dress herself and her ladies-in-waiting as milkmaids and engage in the "productive occupation" of tending cows in an elegant pseudobarn on the grounds of her palace at Trianon. In the same spirit, rich Jews, all of whom made their money in business and banking, started in the 1780s to found philanthropic institutions to transform Jews into productive craftsmen and farmers. Thus the culture and the economic pursuits of Jews in past centuries underwent a major devaluation so that the Jews might be acceptable to the new cultural currency of the Enlightenment and become more like everybody else.

Jewish self-contempt was based on two propositions: that the inherited Jewish culture was inferior and that Jews had been for generations *luftmenschen*, people who "lived on air" and had contributed nothing of value to society. This estimate of the intellectual and spiritual creativity of the Jews after the Bible is born of either prejudice or ignorance. I have never been able to understand why a high school teacher of mine, who was reputed to read Homer and Plato in the original Greek, was regarded as a man of high culture, but my father, who studied the Talmud, the Kabbalah, and the works of the Hasidic masters in Hebrew and Aramaic, was simply a quaint figure from the new ghetto, the east side of Baltimore. I knew that my father's mind was by far the more acute and his moral and intellectual standards more exacting than any I encountered outside his house. I also cannot understand why these Jewish bankers and businessmen of the eighteenth century, who were pioneering money and trade connections on a worldwide scale, did not simply reject the propaganda of the Physiocrats. Isaac de Pinto, who was a substantial economist in his own right, defended the importance of the stock exchange, but he agreed with the Physiocrats that poor peddlers were useless. Such an assertion was nonsense even in its own day. The Jewish peddlers were bringing goods to farms and villages that no one else could reach, and they were extending credit to people to whom no one else would advance a few miserable francs. In the next century some of these Jewish peddlers moved to Berlin or Paris, where they were allowed the freedom to open retail businesses that grew to become Europe's first department stores. Similarly, in the mid–nineteenth century, Jewish peddlers would find their way to every sizable town in America and in the center of every one of them plant the seeds of Sears, Bloomingdales, Lord and Taylor, and the Levi Strauss Company. To deny that these pioneers contributed to the economy is to accept the simplistic idea that milkmaids matter but those who distribute dairy products to stores are parasites. In the middle of the nineteenth century Karl Marx revived the ideology of the Physiocrats when he insisted that the workers who engaged in "primary production" were producing real value, and the bourgeoisie, personified by the Jews, got rich off the labor of the proletariat. But I am getting ahead of the story. Let us get back to the last decades of the eighteenth century when modern Jews, in the image of Isaac de Pinto, were finding the courage to fight for their rights but losing respect for their own heritage.

In 1774 the highly assimilated leaders of the Jewish community in the port city of Bordeaux, France, made a radical decision: they excluded instruction in Talmud from their school. These rabbinic texts, the Jewish elders said, taught ideas that were contrary to the laws of universal reason. French and arithmetic were taught instead. Bible study continued "because it is the sole means of discovering the true commandments which God has enjoined upon us." In other words, it expressed universal values that both Jews and Christians could accept. Rabbi Hayyim Yosef David Azulai of Hebron visited the school in 1777 and was repulsed by what he observed:

> They teach only the Bible, and they even forbid the teaching of the commentary of Rashi because it contains many quotations and interpretations from the Talmud. They do not even allow Maimonides. Woe to the eyes who have seen such things. May there be an end to this sin!

The leading families of Bordeaux were international merchants who lived in villas on the outskirts of the city and commuted to their offices in splendid carriages. The most glittering of these families, the Gradis, maintained business outposts in the Caribbean and in North America. When French Canada was falling to the British in the late 1750s, the Gradis firm was the last shipowner willing to take the risk of running the British blockade. Every other trading merchant had abandoned the cause, so the last French ship to sail into Quebec Harbor to supply General Montcalm for the final battle, which he lost, was a ship that carried the Gradis colors. During the American Revolution, when some merchants in Bordeaux tried to raise the money by subscription to supply the French navy with a ship of war for its campaign in support of the colonists, the bulk of the donations came from the Jewish shipowners. They were demonstrating their special loyalty to the

French Crown. These Jewish men of means spent their time with one another and with some of the more liberal high bourgeois and even nobility. Inevitably, they became more like their class and less like their poorer coreligionists. Consequently, a succession of Bordeaux synagogue presidents were avowed Deists, Jews who no longer believed in the divine revelation of the Bible. It is therefore not surprising that the Jewish community's schools took so radical a turn.

In London the committee in charge of the school of the Sephardi (Spanish-Portuguese) Jews reported in 1779, with regret and anger, that among its sixty students one could find only seven or eight who had even slight comprehension of the Hebrew texts that they had supposedly been studying for years. In the next year, the new rabbi for the community of Ashkenazi Jews in London, David Tevele Schiff, complained in a letter to his brother, "I find myself here as someone stuck in the desert. I have no colleagues; I have no friends, no students to teach, and not a single person with whom I can talk about the fine points of Jewish religious laws." The Jews in Bordeaux and London were not yet emancipated in civil law, but they were already moving away from Jewish learning and from Jewish otherness to become more like their gentile neighbors.

Perhaps the single most influential Jewish educational reformer of the day was Naphtali Herz Wessely (1725–1805), an "enlightened" Jew who lived in Berlin. In 1782 he published a book in Hebrew entitled *Words of Peace and Truth,* in which he argued that the curriculum taught to Jewish children should no longer be limited to Bible and Talmud; it must also include the language and literature of the majority, arithmetic, and crafts that can free Jews from the occupations of peddling and petty moneylending. Wessely defended his plea by misquoting a passage in the Talmud to say: a traditional Torah scholar who has no knowledge of the *way of the world (derekh eretz)* is inferior to the carcass of an animal. The term *derekh eretz* actually means *manners* or *respect*. Wessely fired an opening shot in the war for modernity by calling for a bicultural education, making it possible for Jews to belong to both worlds. His idea would become the basis for the modern Jewish day schools, which appeared in the first decades of the next century. But in his own day, he was denounced by the Gaon of Vilna and Rabbi Ezekiel Landau of Prague for having proposed an educational program that they believed threatened the substance and method of Jewish learning as it had been practiced for generations; they held that Wessely was undermining the Jewish way of life.

Wessely's theory of education posed a serious dilemma as Jews stood on the threshold of modernity. Which world is superior: the old world ghetto or the emerging society of the Enlightenment? He had finessed this question by asserting that the new Jewish education would do justice to both the old and the new. The study of contemporary learning and practical crafts formed well-rounded Jews, but always religion would remain at the core of instruction. This "solution," of living in two worlds, Wessely had learned from his mentor, the most influential Jew of the age, Moses Mendelssohn.

MOSES MENDELSSOHN, "THE JEWISH PLATO" OF BERLIN

Moses Mendelssohn (1729–1786) was the first punctiliously observant Jew to become a major philosophical and literary figure in German letters. The son of a scribe, Mendelssohn received a traditional Orthodox Jewish education in Dessau, in Germany. The leading Jew in the town was Moses Benjamin Wulff, the "court Jew" of the duchy of Anhalt Dessau. Wulff had acquired some secular education and had developed a great interest in medieval Jewish philosophy. He established a press and printed Maimonides's *Guide of the Perplexed,* the first edition ever to be printed by and for the Yiddish-speaking Jews of central and eastern Europe. One of the few pieces of self-deprecation that has come down to us from Moses Mendelssohn is his remark that he had forced his spine to curve by sitting for untold hours over the *Guide*. In his early teens, Mendelssohn began to imagine himself as a latter-day Maimonides, a believing, talmudically schooled Jew who is as accomplished in the general culture as society's best and brightest.

Mendelssohn's early life was marked just as indelibly by the fact that he had taught himself perfect German. After moving to Berlin at age fourteen, he added Greek, French, Italian, and English to his linguistic repertoire plus mathematics, science, and other disciplines. At age thirty-four, Mendelssohn achieved distinction as a philosopher by winning first prize in an essay contest sponsored by the Prussian Royal Academy of Sciences; Immanuel Kant, who was soon recognized as the great philosopher of that age, took second place. So Mendelssohn became part of the intellectual elite of Berlin, the very city that long denied him permanent residence because he was a Jew. The society of Jewish Berlin to which he had come was headed by a few banking and merchant families, which had gained the right to live in the city by royal decree. Mendelssohn was permitted to stay in the Prussian capital as a bookkeeper to one of these worthies. He was granted the right of permanent residence only after becoming a celebrated intellectual.

Mendelssohn proved that one could be an Orthodox Jew and still be a prominent figure in the larger society. Even in the drawing rooms of his most highly placed non-Jewish friends, Mendelssohn would excuse himself in the late afternoon in the middle of philosophical discussion and go off to a corner and say the prescribed afternoon prayers with devotion and concentration. The food he ate, even in the most elegant salons, had to be impeccably kosher. He continued to study the Talmud, and he exchanged letters on fine points of Jewish law with some of the leading rabbinic authorities of his day.

Mendelssohn attracted to his study all kinds of European intellectuals who, it seems, could not quite believe that this Orthodox hunchback could be a luminary of the Enlightenment; they came to see if this curious man lived up to the legend. The prevailing image of the Jews in "Enlightened" Europe was that of an inferior people, due either to their biological inheritance or their having been debased in the stagnant ghetto. Mendelssohn aroused consternation among those intellectuals who did not believe it was possible for a man so brilliant and enlightened to remain a believing Jew, to stand apart from the best of what advanced culture had to offer. Mendelssohn, after all, had accepted Spinoza's doctrine of universal morality. If all religions exist on the same moral plane, why remain a Jew?

All these motives were at play in the most famous incident in Mendelssohn's life: the challenge, in 1769, from Johann Casper Lavater, a Swiss Protestant clergyman who had once visited Mendelssohn and had been pondering the seeming contradiction of Mendelssohn's life ever since. Lavater advocated a version of the Enlightenment that considered Christianity to be the religion best exemplifying the principles of universal morality. He concluded, therefore, that Mendelssohn should become a Christian, and he challenged Mendelssohn either to defend the superiority of Judaism or convert. Mendelssohn rebuffed the minister's provocation and refused, "as a member of an oppressed people," to be dragged into a public disputation. Mendelssohn feared that such a debate would likely put all the Jews of Berlin at risk.

Lavater's challenge brought Mendelssohn to the brink of a nervous breakdown; for the next eight years he retreated from serious intellectual pursuits. Lavater had made clear to him that even an enlightened Christian could not tolerate an Orthodox Jew. Even Mendelssohn's friend Gotthold Ephraim Lessing, the most popular German writer of the day, did not really accept him as a believing Jew. Lessing used Mendelssohn as the model and inspiration for the hero of his play *Nathan the Sage,* about a wise man who pronounced all three of the biblical faiths to be equally the word of God, so that no religion had any greater claim on an individual than any of the others. Mendelssohn rejected this characterization of himself and spent the last years of his life trying to find his balance in a world that wanted to see him, the most famous modern Jew, as having transcended the religion of his ancestors.

In the aftermath of the Lavater affair, Mendelssohn turned his attention to the plight of his persecuted and maligned people. In Alsace the populist rabble-rouser, François Hell, was flooding the province with thousands of false receipts for the petty debts that Alsatian peasants owed to Jewish moneylenders. As a result, these Jews, who themselves were poor, faced immediate bankruptcy. Mendelssohn persuaded an upper-level bureaucrat in the Prussian government, Christian Wilhelm Dohm, to write a book defending the Jews. Dohm explained that Jews had been forced into petty moneylending and other disreputable occupations not out of avarice but because they were the victims of anti-Semitic exclusion. The "affair of false receipts" ended inconclusively; the courts and public opinion agreed that François Hell was guilty of fraud, but the thousands of petty debts were never collected. However, Dohm's book was an important step in the movement for improving the situation of the Jews in western and central Europe.

In 1783, three years before his death, Mendelssohn wrote *Jerusalem*, his explication of the Jewish religion. God had chosen the Jewish people to live according to a particularly strict regimen of religious laws, wrote Mendelssohn, so that they might become a beacon of righteousness. He based this argument on the classic biblical, and talmudic, idea that the Jews are a kingdom of priests, a holy people. Jews, therefore, are obliged to obey the commandments of the Torah as a means of purifying themselves, of curbing wicked instincts, and resisting evil. Through such discipline Jews are more likely to achieve moral excellence and serve as an example to the whole of humankind. The practices enjoined in the Bible and the Talmud, wrote Mendelssohn, are necessary to maintain Jews as a people until the Messiah comes.

Mendelssohn proposed in *Jerusalem* that the organized Jewish community should be abolished, making an end of its power to discipline individual Jews. Mendelssohn was well aware that every state dominated by a church had persecuted Jews and that the organized Jewish community had played, and was still playing, a similar role; it continued to excommunicate heretics and to exercise physical punishment against transgressors. Mendelssohn found these practices intolerable, insisting that any compulsion is illegitimate: "The church's only rights are admonition, instruction, reassurance and consolation; and the citizens' duties towards the church are an attentive ear and a willing heart."

Mendelssohn bet the future of the Jews on their continuing, with their legendary stubbornness, to choose to be other in a free and open society. Judaism would be sustained by the faith and fortitude of individual Jews. In his circle in Berlin, even those Jews who no longer believed in the literal revelation of the Bible continued to live according to the laws and traditions of their ancestors. But when Mendelssohn died, the dam broke. The move toward conversion became a stampede among the younger generation of Berlin's Jews. In the new age one was no longer forced to be a Jew; so why follow the commandments that were so precious to Mendelssohn? The next generation of Berlin's bourgeois Jews—men in powdered wigs and glittering coats and women in hooped gowns—saw as their Messiah the new age of the Enlightenment. Little of their Jewishness had any meaning for them. Of Mendelssohn's own six children, only two, one son and one daughter, remained Jews. After his death, the others assimilated into Prussian society through conversion to Christianity. The motives were mixed. Two of his children accepted the pervasive premise of the Enlightenment, that all religions were equally true or equally false; at their best, they all taught the same universal morality, and therefore there was no longer any reason to suffer the slings and arrows of outrageous fortune by remaining a Jew. The other two became very pious Christians.

These breaks with the Jewish past were happening amid radical change in the world at the turn of the century. In America a handful of Jews had already been given equal citizenship, but, more important, they were reputed to be living comfortably among the gentiles. In Europe itself the old lines seemed to be breaking down. The old order fell dramatically in France, when the revolution deprived the nobility and the clergy of their special privileges, and by 1791 all the Jews in France were given equality by law. By 1812 the armies of the French had marched victoriously through Europe all the way to the outskirts of Moscow. Everywhere, these armies brought with them the doctrine of "liberty, equality, fraternity."

Even among the nations that had resisted France, the new, revolutionary spirit had substantial influence, at least among the upper crust of society. In Berlin especially, literary and political salons became the rage. Some of the more famous ones formed around brilliant Jewish women, such as Rahel (Levin) Varnhagen (1771–1833), who had converted to Protestantism. To these continuing soirées and conversations, people came without distinction of religion or class. In this environment, being Jewish—certainly being Jewish in any serious sense—was an encumbrance, a kind of an inherited disease. So intermarriage flourished, especially between Christian men and Jewish women, who were usually heiresses of great wealth. It was in these salons that the outcry was coined "Judaism was not a religion; it was a misfortune." But we know from surviving letters and diaries that some of these women were not at peace with the abandonment of their Jewishness. Rahel Varnhagen came to admire the religion she had earlier described with disgust as "one long bleeding." On her deathbed she confessed to her husband that "the thing which all my life seemed to me the greatest shame, which was the misery and misfortune of my life—having been born a Jewess—this I should on no account now wish to have missed."[2]

FRIEDLANDER'S FAMOUS PETITION

For a Jew to become a Christian in the name of universal morality was, at best, self-delusion. The Jews who converted were being asked, in fact, to assent to Christian beliefs and practices, which were no more defensible before the bar of "enlightened reason" than the religion they were abandoning. This fallacy led David Friedlander (1750–1834), a wealthy businessman and disciple of Moses Mendelssohn, to address an open letter, in 1799, to Pastor William Abraham Teller, provost and head of the Berlin consistory of the Lutheran Church. Friedlander asked Teller, who was himself a man of the Enlightenment (he was the leading modernist among the Christian clerics in Berlin), to be allowed to join the church without accepting the faith in the divinity of Jesus. Friedlander made it very clear, on his own behalf and "in the name of some Jewish householders" whom he represented, that the sole purpose of their wanting to join the church was to enter the majority society and culture. Why adopt Christian dogma, asked Friedlander, when "Enlightened Jews" and Protestants shared the monotheism of Moses? He was thus the first major figure to insist that Jews ought not surrender their specialness unless the Church did the same. What Friedlander really wanted was a new world in which there was neither Jew nor Christian, only enlightened men and women who shared a belief in biblical monotheism. Friedlander's solution was a muted replay of what had happened a few years earlier at the height of the French Revolution. All religion had been abolished and had been replaced with "the religion of reason." The great cathedral in Paris,

Notre Dame, had become the Temple of Reason, and the calendar had been changed so that the day of rest was every tenth day. This revolutionary attempt to reorder culture was suppressed by a counterrevolution after a few years, but the hope lived on that a new society that had broken with the past could be created by human effort.

Teller rejected Friedlander's petition, though he did not require that Friedlander and the others literally accept every dogma of Christianity. In his response, Teller did agree that Friedlander and his friends would not be constrained to believe in the doctrine of the incarnation. Nonetheless, Teller could not accept their petition because, even in Teller's liberal mind, there was one impassable barrier. To become a Christian, Teller insisted, the convert would have to accept the superiority of Christianity over Judaism, that is, that the New Testament represented a moral advance beyond the Hebrew Bible. Teller understood that this was the central issue that still divided enlightened Christians from Jews. He had read Friedlander correctly: Friedlander was saying that Judaism and Christianity represented the same biblical morality and, by clear implication, that Christianity was a gloss on what had already been present in biblical Judaism.

This interchange prefigured the continuing battle between religious liberals in both camps. The Jews have kept insisting that the New Testament is really a set of sermons added to the ethical doctrines laid down at Sinai (maybe by God or by Moses or by the collective conscience of the Jewish people), overlaid with the moving pathos and imagery of the crucifixion and the resurrection. Christians have been insisting, from Teller at the end of the eighteenth century to Arnold Toynbee, the controversial historian of the first half of the twentieth century, that the incarnation may not be true, literally, but that Christianity represents a quantum advance beyond Judaism: it took the fate of a single tribe and made of it a universal religion; it insisted that "thou shalt love thy neighbor as thyself," defined "neighbor" not only as your kin but any and all human beings. To this, the Jewish liberals have responded, with equal insistence, that the universalism of Christianity was already present in biblical Judaism.

In Germany at least sixty thousand Jews left the synagogue for the church in the course of the nineteenth century, but only a minority believed in their newly adopted faith. Most assimilating Jews, like Moses Mendelssohn's banker son, Abraham, who was the father of the great composer Felix Mendelssohn-Bartholdy, simply regarded conversion as the admission ticket to the larger society. This attitude is articulated in a letter to his daughter Fanny: "We have educated you and your brothers and sister in the Christian faith, because it is the creed of most civilized people, and contains nothing that can lead you away from what is good, and much that guides you to love, obedience, tolerance, and resignation, even if it offered nothing but the examples of its Founder, understood by so few, and followed by still fewer."[3]

How did this social contract work? Not very well. To be sure, some of the friendlier gentiles pretended not to know that most of these conversions were career motivated, and many Jews wanted to pretend that conversion conferred upon them unquestioned acceptance and equality, but most knew that it was not so. Still, those Jews who wanted to enter the larger society kept hoping that baptism would end their otherness. Within this environment, David Friedlander was a conservative. He was trying to defend the Jews in his circle from completely going over to the other side. Friedlander's stipulation—that those Jews who want to enter society not be forced to become real Christians— was an attempt to save as much Jewish dignity as he could. He was not an assimilationist; he was the general of a defeated army, the army of Mendelssohn, and he was trying to defend the very last barricade against the rush to conversion. Friedlander was saying, if you must abandon Judaism, at least don't become unconditional Christians.

KARL MARX: LUTHER IN RED

And so in the early decades of the nineteenth century the stage was set in central Europe for two clashing and contradictory formulations of how Jews could shed their otherness. One possibility was to convert to Christianity; the other was to do away with both Judaism and Christianity and make a new society. On the one side stood Heinrich Marx (formerly Hirschel ha-Levi), the son of a chief rabbi in Trier in the Rhineland, who became a Deist, a man of the Enlightenment. He found it easy, in his indifference to all religions, to convert to Protestantism in 1817. This act allowed him to resume his career as a lawyer after the fall of Napoleon, when the Prussians reconquered the town and reinstituted all the old laws excluding Jews from the professions. Heinrich Marx then had his eight children converted, including Karl, who would become the preeminent theorist of modern socialism.

As an adolescent, Karl Marx was very busy internalizing his Germanness. Being an authentic Prussian meant being a Lutheran. Even after he had abandoned religion and consciously became a socialist, Karl Marx still spoke about Jews in the language of Martin Luther. The rhetoric of his essay "On the Jewish Question" was denounced as anti-Semitic from the day it first appeared in 1843. It was an anti-Jewish diatribe of a specific kind; it talked about Jews in the manner of a "proper German" of that day. Karl Marx was now trying to prove the truth of his conversion not by his piety but by his supposedly gentilelike anger at Jews. How could anyone imagine that he was still a Jew if he spoke like an anti-Semite? What greater, and more shameful, proof could he offer of his Germanness than these terrible lines about Jews?

> The nationality of the Jew is the nationality of the merchant. . . . What is his [the Jew's] worldly God? Money. . . . Emancipation from huckstering and from money, and conse-

quently from the practical, real Judaism, would be the self-emancipation of our era.

But in the midst of such outbursts Marx explained that the noun *Jews* was really a metaphor for the members of the merchant class, the bourgeois who lived by trade rather than by primary production. To be sure, Jews were very prominent in this group, but they were not the only "Jews." The permanent solution to anti-Semitism, Marx insisted, was to overturn the existing society and build a new one in which everyone could begin over again as equals. In theory, Jews would no longer be outsiders, and all religions would become obsolete. In practice, Jews remained outsiders, and their only available escape was conversion. But even that did not always work.

SHYLOCK AND FAGIN

Anti-Semitism had taken a fateful turn for the worse at the dawn of the modern era. This change became evident when we contrast the two most villainous Jews in Western literature: Shylock in *The Merchant of Venice* and Fagin in *Oliver Twist*. Shakespeare's Shylock is the Jew as depicted by medieval anti-Semites. He is a greedy and vindictive moneylender who hates Christians. But Shylock is redeemable. At the end of the play, he has become a Christian and presumably is on the way to losing his hateful characteristics. There is no doubt that his former tormentors will now welcome him. This outcome is prefigured in Shylock's very human lament about his terrible treatment as a Jew at the hands of Christians, when he tells us that he is a human being who is no different than anyone else:

Hath not the Jew eyes? Hath not a Jew hands, organs, dimensions, sense, affections, passions? . . . If you prick us, do we not

bleed? If you tickle us, do we not laugh? If you poison us, do
we not die? and if you wrong us shall we not revenge? . . . If we
are like you in the rest, we will resemble you in that . . . the vil-
lainy you teach me, I will execute, and it shall go hard. But I
will better the instruction. (Act III, Scene 1)

Charles Dickens's Jew, Fagin, is much more vile than Shylock. He
has every negative characteristic attributed to Jews by medieval anti-
Semites, including a foul odor. But the most fundamental change is
that Fagin is villainous *by his very nature* and beyond rehabilitation.
Society can only wall him off, preferably in a prison and, more surely,
in death. When Dickens was castigated by a reader for fomenting "a
vile prejudice against the despised Jews," he answered that he was
merely describing the situation as it was, that the "class of criminal
almost invariably was a Jew." This was not so, but the problem with
Dickens is not getting his facts wrong about criminality in London. He
was propagating the teaching of the most anti-Semitic figures of the
Enlightenment (and of the racists of his own day), who attributed to
the Jews not special virtue but a unique capacity for vice. These modern anti-Semites had given new currency to the ancient Hellenistic
canards of Manetho and Apion, who had declared the Jews to be infec-
tious lepers. The new leper was now named Fagin.

How did this fateful change come about? The dominant doctrine
of the Church had been and remained that a Jew once converted was
fully equal to all other Christians, but the process of demonizing "the
synagogue of Satan" had been going on for centuries as a powerful
countertheme within Christian society. Had not the Jews acquired
something ineradicable of Satan's nature? This hostile idea had been
the basis for a decree issued in Toledo, Spain, in 1449 against the thousands of Jewish converts to Christianity, most of whom had been
forced into the Church by the riots and persecution that had begun in

1391. The decree had announced a new doctrine of "purity of blood" *(limpieza de sangre)*. Only those who could prove that all four of their grandparents had been born Christian were permitted to exercise any significant authority within the society. This doctrine had become so ingrained that even as late as the middle of the nineteenth century, nearly four hundred years after all professing Jews had been expelled from Spain, no man who had Jewish blood in his veins could become an officer in the army.

But Spain was a backward country in the mind of the European intelligentsia of the eighteenth century, the leaders of the Enlightenment. They mocked the Church in Spain and Portugal and its Inquisition for continuing to burn heretics at the stake. Nonetheless, the arch-critic of these Spanish persecutors, Voltaire, seems to have embraced the doctrine that it was "in the very nature of Jews to be born with raging fanaticism in their hearts, just as the Bretons and the Germans are born with blond hair. I would not be in the least bit surprised if these people would not some day become deadly to the human race."[4] Voltaire was not alone in this assessment, though, fortunately, the majority of the men and women of the Enlightenment believed, like Shakespeare, that the Jew was a human being like everyone else and could be "regenerated."

The demonization of the Jews continued into the nineteenth century. The main source of the new anti-Semitism was the theory of race, the notion that humanity was divided into well-defined biological groups and that these races could be graded on a scale of virtue, intelligence, and usefulness. The new theorists of race, as we shall see later, were mostly from right-wing political circles; they were people who disliked the French Revolution and wanted to reassert the inherent superiority of their "Aryan" race and of their social class. They agreed that the Jews were at the bottom of the scale. But Charles Dickens did not construct Fagin because he had been reading writings about the inequality of races. Dickens was a reformer who knew very well what contemporary socialist thinkers such as François-Marie-Charles Fourier and Pierre-Joseph Proudhon in France had been saying about Jews. These revolutionaries were following after Voltaire in maintaining that the brave new world that humanity could and should create would be possible only if the Jews, wicked by nature, were walled off. Fagin was a creation of an early socialist idea that the utopia is so important that it must be created exclusively for those who are worthy of it, even if this dream can be realized only through the most extreme cruelty to those who do not fit and would subvert the dream. Dickens thus could describe Fagin as a foul and hopeless monster. I wonder if Charles Dickens, who thought of himself as the defender of virtue and the lover of humanity, could have imagined that he was opening the door a little bit wider to the racist horrors that were to come in the next century.

CHAPTER 12

REINVENTING
JEWISHNESS

We now, in this account of the Jewish experience through the ages, have reached the crucial turning point—from the medieval era into modernity. The conventional view is that Jews entered the modern era when they were emancipated, that is, when the long-existing special discriminations against them were revoked after the French and American Revolutions.

This account is based on the assumption that the Jews waited passively for many centuries and that only when they were finally allowed some access to Europe did they revive from their wretchedness and talmudic narrowness. The trouble with this account is that it depicts Jews as seen by those who proposed to "regenerate" them. It presupposes that the Jewish community was totally inert and reactive. Such a presumption is false. Jews have never been hostage to external events alone. As in every previous era, they have reinvented themselves, in large part, by the force of their own will.

At the beginning of the nineteenth century, as western Europe and the United States were moving into the modern age, the signature of the new era became voluntarism; it was now possible for individuals freely to change their beliefs and values. Most people chose to remain within the identities and traditions into which they were born, but the critical word is *choice*. Those who affirmed themselves in the ways of their ancestors could no longer do so without some reflection. This new freedom to make choices required that even those who insisted that nothing had changed were forced to recognize that they were standing pat in a world in which other Jews had chosen to question, even rebel against, the certitudes of traditional Jewish belief.

Among Jews, the usual image of free choice in religion has had a negative connotation. It is the story of a "free-thinking" yeshiva student, such as the young Spinoza, who falls into "evil ways" because he has surreptitiously read alien books. After Spinoza, such incidents occurred with some frequency—everywhere, until this very day—but they did not add up to the revolution that would redefine the mode of Jewish communal life at the dawn of modernity.

The shift to voluntarism among Jews began much more dramatically, during the great convulsions caused by the appearance of Shabbetai Zvi and, a century later, by the rise of Hasidism. Shabbetai Zvi had led a rebellion against the tradition, and although it was suppressed, it left behind the dramatic memory of Jews who had dared to revolt against the ways of their ancestors. The Hasidim were even more important because they could not be thrown out of the Jewish community. They appeared in communities that were tightly controlled by Jewish leaders who permitted no deviation from the older ways. The battle with the Hasidim began over their audacity to make even minor changes, but what embittered the fight was the fact that the Hasidic groups were voluntary associations. Individual Jews chose to adhere to the Hasidic movement and to identify themselves as followers of a particular tzaddik (holy man). Individual Hasidim were free to leave their rebbes and to follow another or to walk away from Hasidism altogether toward some modern ideology.

The ideological heirs of the Gaon of Vilna insisted vehemently that the old ways had to be maintained or Judaism would be swept away. This doctrine of categorical resistance to modernity was announced and practiced not in some far-off village in the Ukraine, where the Jews were still living a separate existence as a matter of course, but in Bratislava, (then called Pressburg) in what is now western Slovakia, not far from Vienna, the capital of the Hapsburg Empire. Here, on the very edge of European and Jewish modernity, Rabbi Moses (Schreiber) Sofer (1762–1839) announced that no deviation from the old ways, not even the slightest, was permissible. He forbade any encroachment of the Western style in clothing or manners. Only Yiddish could be spoken for everyday purposes, and only Hebrew could be used in prayer. He condemned secular education as a heresy, and he coined the slogan "anything new is forbidden by Torah." He even distanced himself from the battle for emancipation because Jews would come to know the gentiles and be seduced by their culture. His followers cut themselves off not only from the gentiles but also from most Jews. Sofer was creating a new kind of Orthodoxy. Unlike the rabbis of past centuries, Sofer did not pretend to worry any longer about all Jews; he was creating a separatist sect of "true believers." His heirs today are the *haredim*, the ultra-Orthodox Jews who have declared that all other expression of Judaism is false and dangerous.

Moses Sofer cast Mendelssohn as the ultimate heretic who had come to seduce Jews away from their ancient faith. Sofer was wrong. Mendelssohn had spent his life, and especially his later years, trying to create a new Jew who could fit into the modern age without assimilating. Mendelssohn's true ideological heirs are the three great Jewish movements that would emerge in the early years of the nineteenth century: Reform, Conservative, and modern Orthodoxy. Each, in its own way, answered the central question Mendelssohn had posed: What should the modern, affirming Jew look like?

SAMSON RAPHAEL HIRSCH, THE INTEGRATED OTHER

Some among the Orthodox refused to follow Rabbi Sofer into isolation. They insisted on entering the modern world without surrendering even the slightest bit of the inherited religion. The founder of this school of thought, Rabbi Samson Raphael Hirsch (1808–1888), personified the paradox of one who is a totally integrated German bourgeois and totally other as a Jew. The argument between Hirsch and Sofer was not primarily theological. All Orthodox Jews adhered strictly to the halachah, the religious law, which they believed to be divinely revealed and therefore unchangeable. A liberal interpreter might soften some rules, but Orthodoxy, even in its most relaxed versions, could not, for example, justify the abolition of the dietary laws or permit disobedience of the rules of Sabbath observance. Samson Raphael Hirsch affirmed God's law to the letter, but most old-line believers distrusted him because he was the first Orthodox Jew to break the accepted mold of the rabbi. Hirsch conducted services wearing a robe in the style of Protestant ministers, and he introduced some changes in the divine service. A choir sang in his synagogue, and the congregation sang along in precise musical order; Hirsch preached twice a month not in Yiddish but in German, "the national cultural language." He was even more upsetting to the older Orthodox rabbis because he insisted that secular literature and the arts were "uplifting works" that contributed to godliness.

Hirsch clarified his views in a pamphlet called *Religion Allied with Progress* (1854) in which he rejected any changes that would alter the principles of the Jewish faith or compromise Jewish law. He insisted that Jews, not Judaism, were in need of reform. What they needed most was "uplift"—to rise to the eternal ideas of Judaism—and not "progress," a favorite term of the reformers, which he identified as a code word for assimilation. Hirsch was particularly critical of the Reform practice of worship in German, insisting that knowledge of Hebrew was indispensable in maintaining the unity of the Jewish people in the Diaspora.

Hirsch's new Jew would have to be, as Mendelssohn had been, a thoroughly contemporary person who observed the divinely ordained ritual laws of the Bible and Talmud; these commandments could not be compromised in the slightest. To be a contemporary person, Hirsch wrote, the Jew must live in this world and within its culture and should make no effort to recreate a Jewish commonwealth in the Holy Land, for that is forbidden by ancient talmudic law (an oft-quoted caution in the Talmud forbade the Jews from "going up in a wall of people" to reconquer the land). The redemption would come at God's chosen time. But Hirsch insisted that the prayers for the restoration of Zion be kept in the liturgy and that connections to the Holy Land be maintained, including the sacred obligation of sending alms to institutions in Jerusalem and in the other "holy cities" in which pious Jews lived, prayed, and studied. In the Holy Land, Jews must support their own pietists, just as Christians remained connected with their monasteries, ministries, and churches. More fundamentally, Christians had always dreamed of the Second Coming, and they kept praying for that glorious event to take place and to bring on the end of days. At that point

Christians would no longer be ruled by kaisers and czars but by the King of Kings. These religious hopes did not call the patriotism of Germans or Austrians or Hungarians into question. Why should the religious hopes of Jews for "the end of days" make them less fit to be part of the existing society?

To be both modern and Orthodox was not easy. An Orthodox male wore a beard, because the Bible had forbidden shaving with a blade, but how could one fit into the culture of modern business and continue to look like a Jew who came from the older culture of apartness? Such men took to using depilatory creams, which their rabbis decreed to be in compliance with religious law, rather than razors, which were forbidden by the Talmud. During the three-week mourning period for the destruction of both the First and the Second Temples, when Jews are forbidden to wear fresh clothes because a new shirt is a mark of well-being, some of Samson Raphael Hirsch's more affluent followers put on and took off twenty-one shirts in a row on the eve of this period, so that, technically, they would not be putting on a fresh shirt during the mourning period. It was possible, Samson Raphael Hirsch demonstrated, to obey the letter of the law, that is, to find room in one's life for the most rigorous demands of Orthodox religious law, and yet enjoy the amenities, style, and attire of a modern bourgeois.

Hirsch won this battle. In all the major centers of Jewish life to this day, from New York and London to Tel Aviv and Johannesburg, there are synagogues that call themselves "modern Orthodox." Samson Raphael Hirsch himself was a man of both worlds. He believed that secular culture was worthy and important. He read Schiller and Goethe and quoted from them in his sermons. But nowadays, secular culture is much less respected among Hirsch's successors, who have been influenced increasingly by the move of the Orthodox to the religious right. Hirsch's truest heirs are to be found in Yeshiva University in New York, which has as its motto "Torah and Science." The core of the institution is its Orthodox rabbinical school, but it is the home, as well, of a nonsectarian law school and medical school. Here, too, the tide of the ultra-Orthodox is rising, for they keep attacking the respect for—and involvement—in Western culture that Samson Raphael Hirsch had advocated and that the seminal figure of the Yeshiva University faculty, Joseph Dov Soloveichik, represented in this time. The union between "modern" and "Orthodox" seems less possible today than it was in Hirsch's day. Those who are most vehement in the defense of Orthodoxy are, nowadays, equally passionate in their denunciations of modernity as a snare and a trap.

ABRAHAM GEIGER, RADICAL REFORMER

Hirsch's solution did not satisfy those Jews for whom the question was not how to live within religious law but whether it should be obeyed at all. The basic issue was not one of convenience; it was a crisis of faith. Orthodoxy of any kind was no longer an option for those who did not regard the Bible as the literal word of God. If the Torah is a human document, crafted for a certain time and a certain place, then it becomes possible to introduce radical change into Jewish practice. What people once made, people can now unmake. So Abraham Geiger (1810–1874), the most brilliant of the early Reform rabbis, argued that the Orthodox ritual system was of great importance in past centuries because it had defined the Jews in an age of apartness, when they had lived defensively in exile. But Jews now had entered the modern age of universalism, a time when eating only kosher food and other forms of separation contravene the unity of humankind; they are anti-God. Jews, therefore, had to be freed from all observances, even circumcision, that set them apart from the rest of society.

On the surface Abraham Geiger appeared to be intent on moving into the mainstream of German culture and society. Despite his profound knowledge of rabbinic texts and his fluency in Hebrew, he insisted that contemporary Jewish religion should express itself in German, as did other religious persuasions in Prussia. But Geiger's basic commitment was to the Enlightenment. He saw Judaism as the ultimate expression of religious universalism in an age of progress. This vision would eventually lift all of humankind; in the meanwhile, it was the mission, and responsibility, of the Jews—Geiger's Reform Jews—to carry them forward.

At one point Geiger's son, Ludwig, asked his father, Why continue Judaism at all if the ideal world is one of universal morality? Geiger responded that the triumph of universal liberalism was still a couple of generations away, and therefore Judaism had to be kept in business as a catalyst to that end. But progress was slow in coming. Jews were failing to win their way into European society. Near the end of his life, Geiger moderated his views. He retained some Hebrew in the liturgy, reinstated the second day of the festivals, kept Shabbat worship on Saturday instead of Sunday, and reaffirmed the rite of circumcision. In the end, the radical reformer moved back to some of the very rituals that for centuries had underscored the otherness of the Jews.

Geiger changed course because by midcentury his views had become somewhat outmoded in Germany. The new mood had begun in the first decade of the 1800s. Romanticism and nationalism had arisen as rallying cries against Napoleon Bonaparte, the military genius who had made himself into the emperor of France and had imposed his laws of human rights upon the conquered nations of Europe. In reaction, German nationalists began to idealize their national past. Suddenly medieval literature was in fashion and the spirit of the *Volk* (the people through the ages) was hailed and essentially worshiped. Feelings took precedence over reason and history over philosophy.

The new ethos was no longer forward looking; on the contrary, it derived its inspiration from the past, from the standards that had been fashioned by a people in the course of its historic experience.

ZACHARIAS FRANKEL AND ANCESTOR WORSHIP

Some modernizing Jewish scholars and rabbis, chief among them Rabbi Zacharias Frankel (1801–1875), applied romantic nationalism to Jewish history and culture. He challenged Geiger's assertion that God had chosen the Jews to be the prime bearers of universal moral absolutes. The history of the Jews, Frankel insisted, had transformed them into a specific and unique people; they are not just one among many religious denominations. The collective experience of the Jews, not theology, defines the Jewish character. Frankel believed that Judaism could and should evolve; some tinkering at the edges of the rituals was permissible, but nothing could be allowed that conflicted with the essence of Judaism as it had been formulated and practiced in the course of its long history.

Frankel, who was considered a moderate reformer, did not hesitate to take part with other modernizing rabbis in the meetings in the 1840s in which Reform Judaism defined itself. He acquiesced to proposed changes in the ritual of conversion to Judaism, though he protested. What finally drove Frankel to break with Geiger and the reformers was the suggestion that Hebrew be retired as the language of prayer. Such a step, he insisted, was an offense against the authentic Jewish spirit and the continuity of Judaism. This was the line Frankel would not cross.

Frankel was attacked from the right by Samson Raphael Hirsch and from the left by Abraham Geiger. Hirsch kept badgering Frankel with the question: Do you or do you not believe that the Torah came from God? Frankel never answered this question, nor did his disciples, who would found the Conservative movement (they called it "positive-historical" Judaism) in Germany in the mid-1800s and soon after in the United States. They kept saying that there is something of the voice of God in Jewish law, but it has been revised continually, age after age, by the best wisdom of the Jews. Where the boundary might be between these two impulses is beyond the power of the human mind to determine. From the other side, Geiger criticized Frankel as being old-fashioned and so mired in the ancient talmudic texts that he failed to respond to the spirit of the new age. Frankel was moving against the tide; he was reasserting the immemorial insistence of the Jews that they are, and should remain, other. Geiger agreed that the Talmud had performed a great historic service in protecting the separate existence of the Jews but that it was now time to move on to the next stage, that is, to liberate Jewish life from the outmoded laws that had kept Jews from joining the wider society and leading humanity to embrace the universal ideals of the Hebrew prophets.

ISRAEL JACOBSON, THE FIRST REFORM JEW

The movement toward religious reform in central Europe seemed to be led by modernizing rabbinic intellectuals, but its main impetus had come a generation earlier from laypeople such as the leaders of the Bordeaux Jews who removed Talmud study from the curriculum and Israel Jacobson (1768–1828), the first Reform Jew. An avowed follower of Mendelssohn, Jacobson was a citizen of the Duchy of Brunswick, which had been annexed to the kingdom of Westphalia in 1808 after the French conquest. All of the exclusions that had existed for centuries in this German principality were suddenly nullified under Napoleon's code of law. Jacobson was the acknowledged leader of the Jews in the region, chiefly because he was the wealthiest and the best connected to government circles. The Orthodox believers murmured against him, but they could do little in opposition because government officials had chosen Jacobson as the designated leader of the Jewish community.

Jacobson placed great importance on decorum. Proper worship, he insisted, required that Jews abandon the boisterous praying of the ghetto and behave with dignity in the manner of the Protestants. Following the lead of Naphtali Herz Wessely a generation earlier, Jacobson established a modern Jewish school in 1809, emphasizing vocational training and subjects pertaining to the majority culture. It was in the school's synagogue that Jacobson initiated unprecedented change. Here, for the first time, sermons were delivered in German rather than Yiddish, and Jewish children underwent a confirmation ceremony, as was the custom in the neighboring churches. A year later he established a school in Seesen that included a "temple" with a steeple; at its inauguration the bell was rung and songs sung in German with organ accompaniment. Jacobson presided over the event wearing the black robes of a Protestant minister.

Everything Jacobson had built collapsed when the Prussians retook Westphalia, and he moved to Berlin and organized a congregation in the home of a friend. After several months, it was shut down by order of the government, which prohibited the holding of services in private residences. In 1817 Jacobson established an avowedly Reform synagogue, but strong Orthodox opposition compelled the city to shut it down six years later. When Jacobson began making changes in the synagogue, he thought of himself as an enlightened and not as a liturgical innovator. In fact, this lay leader radically altered the service by shortening the liturgy, introducing choral singing with organ accompaniment, and adding prayers in the vernacular.

In Hamburg, Germany, a group of Jews went even further than Jacobson in reforming Jewish religious practice. Jews, they argued, had to give up their otherness by abandoning everything in their own tradition that might compromise their claim to being good Germans of the Jewish faith. Thus when the Hamburg reformers opened their temple in 1818 they abandoned the long-established Jewish custom of men wearing head coverings at prayer. In 1841 their new prayer book deleted the traditional prayers of longing for the end of the exile and return to Zion. In doing so, they demolished a central pillar of Jewish identity, the sense of the Jew as a distinct people waiting for restoration to the Promised Land.

Israel Jacobson and the founders of the temple in Hamburg and, for that matter, the modernist rabbis who assembled in synods in the 1840s to define Reform Judaism as a new version of the ancient faith did not have an assimilationist intent; on the contrary, they wanted to preserve Judaism by dressing it in universal garb. Why be baptized and become a Christian if you could be a good German, worshiping God in the manner of other Germans, and yet retain a direct line to your ancestors?

It is significant that the reforming rabbis appeared a generation later than the lay leaders who had initiated religious change at the beginning of the century. Laymen who wanted change also had dominated the "Grand Sanhedrin," the meeting that was convoked by Napoleon in 1807 to negotiate the terms by which Jews would be accepted as equal citizens in his domain. The laypeople were dragging the rabbis along to make some concessions to the "spirit of time." This assembly conceded that civil marriage would take legal precedence over religious ceremonies in France and in the kingdom of Italy. The Grand Sanhedrin declared,

It is a religious obligation for every Israelite in France . . . to regard from now on civil marriage as a civil obligation, and therefore forbids every rabbi or any other person in the two lands to assist in a religious marriage without it having been established beforehand that marriage has been concluded according to the law before a civil officer. The Grand Sanhedrin declares further that marriages between Jews and Christians which have been contracted in accordance with the laws of the civil code are civilly legal, and that, although they may not be capable of receiving religious sanction, they should not be subject to religious prosecution.[1]

The Jews of the Grand Sanhedrin had no choice but to recognize Napoleon's code, which included state control over all marriages. But the rabbis did insist on their right not to extend religious recognition to those acts that they could not accept. Since that day, the situation has remained the same everywhere among Jews in the western Diaspora. The civil law of the state regulates marriages and divorces, and religious authorities are free to impose their own rules only upon those who accept their authority. This distinction became particularly important in the United States, where the Jewish community was divided into several denominations. The Orthodox could no longer control what the majority of Jews were doing in matters of personal status. So Reform Jews could easily abolish the *get* (religious divorce) and, like the Protestants, accept the jurisdiction of civil law in matters of marriage and divorce.

In America, where Jews had to organize their communities voluntarily and from the ground up, the Judaism that soon evolved reflected the life of the laity on the frontier of European civilization and not the inherited traditions of the old country. As early as 1825, a group of younger members of the Beth Elohim Synagogue in Charleston, South Carolina, organized themselves to push for major reforms in the ritual of the congregation. They wanted the service to be read largely in English because they no longer understood Hebrew, and they wanted the doctrines that were reflected in the liturgy to be Deism or Unitarianism rather than the traditional Jewish faith in the God of the Bible. This group maintained a separate identity but never succeeded in becoming a rooted community, and it disbanded after a few years. The first congregation founded as a Reform synagogue, Har Sinai Verein in Baltimore, established in 1842 by a group of laypeople with no rabbi in sight, adopted the prayerbook of the Temple in Hamburg. Everywhere in America in the middle of the nineteenth century, congregational reforms were being instituted by lay leaders who felt the need for a "proper" form of Jewish worship that would not embarrass them if their Christian neighbors visited the service.

At first the changes were external; the reformers wanted to assume proper bourgeois manners and aesthetics. But inevitably questions of doctrine arose. How could these immigrants, in their gratitude for the opportunities that they suddenly and almost miraculously acquired in America, continue to end the service on the Day of Atonement or the Passover Seder with the proclamation "Next year in Jerusalem"? Kansas City or Dubuque or San Francisco had become their Jerusalem because America enabled them to make a new life for themselves. Some of the immigrants achieved prominence in civic affairs, becoming mayors of cities or activists in national politics. One or two of them even found their way into President Abraham Lincoln's circle of friends. The tension between the long history of Jewish otherness and its seeming end in America (anti-Semitism would not appear in strength until the latter part of the nineteenth century) was so substantial that it demanded reforms in the Jewish religion. And these Jews did not need rabbinic leadership to do the reforming, though that would change when rabbis started to appear in America from central Europe.

ISAAC MAYER WISE,
ARCHITECT OF AMERICAN REFORM JUDAISM

The most important of these religious leaders, Isaac Mayer Wise (1819–1900), arrived in New York in 1846 after having served as all-purpose officiant and teacher in the village of Steingrub in Bohemia. Wise studied at several yeshivot (Orthodox seminaries), but he probably never received ordination. Nonetheless, he called himself "Rabbi." Wise also took to calling himself "Doctor," although his university career in Prague had lasted less than a year. In those early days the appearance of clergy with dubious credentials was not unusual on the American frontier. Christian preachers kept springing up, called by the "pure spirit" without claim to ordination or even formal religious studies.

The first ordained rabbi to settle in the United States was Abraham Rice. A disciple of Rabbi Moses Sofer and himself a staunch defender of Orthodoxy, Rice had a brief and unhappy career in Baltimore. He wrote in utter despair to a friend in Germany,

> I dwell in darkness without a teacher or companion. . . . The religious life in this land is on the lowest level; most people eat forbidden food and desecrate the Sabbath in public. . . . Under these circumstances my mind is perplexed, and I wonder whether it is even permissible for a Jew to live in this land.

He resigned his position as rabbi in 1849 and supported himself and his family for the next thirteen years as a storekeeper. When he died in 1862 his colleague, Bernard Illowy, preached the eulogy in the darkest accents: "We must acknowledge to our shame that since the downfall of the Jewish monarchy there has been no age and no country in which the Israelites were more degenerated and more indifferent toward their religion than in our own age and in our own country."[2] Such complaints had precedent in America. In 1783 Haym Salomon, the Jewish businessman who helped finance the America Revolution, wrote back home in Yiddish to his father in Posen advising him that Philadelphia would not be a fit home for any of his brother's children because they would find "little Jewishness."

The clerics on this frontier were expected to make peace with whatever changes their lay employers were ordaining. To be sure, some rabbis were, at times, even more eager to make changes than were their congregational boards, and on occasion their differences resulted in heated clashes. Such was the case in 1850, when Isaac Mayer Wise, serving as rabbi of the Beth El Synagogue in Albany, had his eye on the more prestigious and the now avowedly Reform pulpit, Beth Elohim, in Charleston, South Carolina. In his trial sermon Wise asserted that he believed in neither the coming of the Messiah nor the resurrection of the dead. Wise would decline the position in Charleston (he was afraid of the inner divisions in that congregation), but the "heresies" that he had professed in South Carolina scandalized the traditionalists of his home synagogue in Albany, which at that time was Orthodox. The membership split down the middle into two hostile factions, one side demanding that Wise be fired and other standing with their rabbi. The synagogue board fired Wise, but the legality of the decision was called into question. Wise notified the president of the congregation that "according to the law and at the request of the trustees, he shall remain in office and perform all the duties pertaining thereto." And so, on the eve of Rosh Hashanah, the Jewish New Year, Wise came to synagogue and ascended the pulpit. "A general melee commenced," reported *The Albany Evening Atlas* on September 7, 1850.

Argument, persuasion, and conciliation were dispensed with, and angry words, threatenings, and even blows were resorted to, and several severe assaults were committed. The peace of that portion of the city finally became so alarmingly disturbed, that it became necessary, for the safety of the public, and for the belligerents themselves, to call in the interposition of the police authorities. Sheriff Berdsley repaired promptly to the spot, accompanied by a strong force, and soon cleared the synagogue of both parties, locked the doors, and took the keys in his possession.[3]

The newspaper did not report, perhaps because it was too embarrassing, that the Reverend Mr. Wise and the president of the synagogue also had engaged in a fistfight. In the aftermath of this fiasco Wise established his own synagogue, but he soon left Albany for Cincinnati, "the Queen City of the West." There he would become rabbi of Congregation B'nai Jeshurun and eventually would organize a nationwide association of synagogues, the Union of American Hebrew Congregations, and the first Reform rabbinical seminary to be established in the United States, the Hebrew Union College. (Wise no doubt preferred to identify his institution with the proud, biblical "Hebrews" because "Jew" connoted the anti-Semitic image of the groveling ghetto "yid.")

After the Civil War Wise's congregation erected a new sanctuary on Plum Street at the very center of this bustling river port. As part of the economic power elite, the Jews of Cincinnati felt that their house of worship needed to be at the intersection where the major Christian denominations had built their sanctuaries. The dedication of Wise's temple in 1868 was a major civic affair. The governor of Ohio was present, along with many other dignitaries. In his dedicatory sermon Wise emphasized that this temple was not the synagogue of past sorrows; it was a house of worship that would glory in the freedom of America.

Wise's story is the story of his generation, the central European Jews who began to come to the United States in substantial numbers in the middle of the century. From 1825 to 1875, the number of Jewish immigrants (the large majority of them from German-speaking countries) grew from 5,000 to 150,000. They were typically the younger children of poor Jews who could not stay in the town of their birth because the number of Jewish families was severely restricted. In a generation or two, the most ambitious of these immigrants remade themselves in America as owners of department stores, bankers, and financiers. Anti-Semitic prejudice began to take hold in America, but the absence of economic restrictions in law and the principle of a career open to talent allowed Jews to achieve success more easily in America than anywhere else in the world. These new Jewish arrivals, therefore, confidently expected that in the new world they would be part of "Americans all."

The Jewish immigrants from German-speaking lands were not, in their majority, assimilationists. Some of them, of course, did want to be just like everybody else. They disassociated themselves from other Jews and disappeared. Within the organized community itself, a few wanted to think of themselves as universalists. Felix Adler, the son of Rabbi Samuel Adler of Temple Emanu-El, in New York City, founded a new movement in the 1860s called "Ethical Culture," in which like-minded people of both Jewish and Christian backgrounds could join in the pursuit of universal moral ideals. But the overwhelming majority of the German-speaking Jews felt most at home in the flourishing Reform movement. Those who created these congregations had a profound sense of belonging to the Jewish community worldwide, even as they deleted the prayer for the return to Zion from their liturgies. They took the lead in protesting the murderous pogroms against the Jews in Russia in 1881–1882, and they never wavered in regarding the czar and his oppressive government as their enemy.

The acknowledged leader of these America Jews was the financier Jacob Schiff (1847–1920). He was as imperious and temperamental as

Doña Gracia had been three centuries earlier. She had fought the pope, while he took on the czar, but in his time he was much more successful. He made it clear that he was acting as a Jew when he decided to punish the Russian government for its unrelenting and bloody attacks on Jews. In 1904 Schiff approved a two-hundred-million-dollar loan to the Japanese government, which was at war with Russia. After Japan's victory, he was awarded a medal and became the first foreigner to dine at the imperial palace.

Even the most successful Jews on the American scene in the nineteenth century—including the powerful Jacob Schiff—had no illusions; they knew that being a Jew meant that they were different. They had to organize their own society parallel to that of their gentile peers, who had very little to do with them except in business. But they would not let go of their deepest aspiration: they wanted America to think of them as part of its elite. It was no accident that Isaac Mayer Wise and his congregation chose the Moorish look for their sanctuary on Plum Street. They were evoking the Golden Age in Spain, when Jews had been ministers to Muslim caliphs and Christian royalty. These peddlers, who had risen to be merchant princes in America, could achieve such aristocracy only by claiming that they were the upper crust of a great people. They wanted to gain respect in the general society by portraying themselves as a people of noble inheritance.

BENJAMIN DISRAELI, THE PRINCE OF PARLIAMENT

The astonishing idea that the long-despised and persecuted Jew is, in fact, the ultimate aristocrat was best personified in the nineteenth century by a former Jew, the prime minister of England, Benjamin Disraeli (1804–1881). It could have been expected that he would try to hush his Jewish origins as had so many converts to Christianity or, like Karl Marx, dissociate himself from the Jewish people by becoming an intemperate anti-Semite. On the contrary, Disraeli flaunted his Jewish origin and made of it an armor with which to deflect the darts and arrows of his anti-Semitic detractors.

Instead of becoming a bar mitzvah at age thirteen, Benjamin was baptized in the Church of England. His father, Isaac D'Israeli, was by conviction a Deist who had been a member of the Spanish-Portuguese synagogue in London until he got into a bitter dispute with its leadership. The congregation offered him the choice of becoming the synagogue warden or paying a hefty fine of forty pounds. Isaac D'Israeli said no to both, emphatically, and the argument dragged on for several years. When his Orthodox father died, Isaac resigned from the synagogue and had his five children converted to Christianity. Isaac, himself, remained a nonpracticing Jew, and he wrote articles and books on Jewish subjects, including a tribute to Moses Mendelssohn.

Young Benjamin received a thorough education in the Christian faith, and he actually seemed to have taken his new religion quite seriously. Nonetheless, he kept reading Jewish books from his father's library. Benjamin soon turned to writing novels in which his protagonists revealed a passionate undercurrent of Jewish emotion. Even as he lived his life as a believing Christian, Benjamin remained to the very end of his days a Jew at heart, even a chauvinist.

How did Benjamin Disraeli deal with this paradox? He embraced the notion that the essence of a people is determined by its genetic inheritance, by its blood. The idea of race was becoming popular in Europe at the time. Some socialists were agreeing with the reactionaries who had condemned the Jews as the most obnoxious and destructive of all the races. Disraeli, who looked classically Semitic, with black hair, full lips, and curved nose, advanced his own theory—that the Jewish race is the most supremely talented in the world, a prime example being the illustrious Disraeli himself!

In Disraeli's first novel, *Alroy* (1831–1833), the Jewish hero leads a rebellion to reconquer the Holy Land from the Babylonians. Alroy's lust for power leads to the defeat of his army. But he achieves personal redemption by refusing to commit apostasy (this comes strangely from the pen of Disraeli, the convert). Through the character of Alroy, Disraeli casts himself as the leader of the Jews who would bring his people back, sword in hand, to Palestine. There is defiant boldness in Disraeli's publishing such a novel at a time when he was striving to launch a political career and win a seat in the British Parliament.

In Disraeli's novel *Tancred or the New Crusade* (1847) his hero protests, "Why do the Saxon and Celtic societies persecute an Arabian race [the Jews] from whom they have adopted laws of sublime benevolence, and in the pages of whose literature they have found perpetual delight, instruction, and consolation? That is a great question, which in an enlightened age, may be fairly asked." Disraeli regarded the Jews as the most aristocratic of peoples because, in his view, they constituted the most powerful and most creative element in every human endeavor. The Rothschilds, he observed, were the single most influential family in Europe, and all the great singers, writers, soldiers, and even churchmen were Jews, crypto-Jews, or of Jewish descent. "Power is neither the sword nor the shield," he wrote, "for these pass away, but ideas . . . are divine, and in the realm of ideas the Jews were outstanding. For God had revealed himself to one race only—the Jews." Disraeli even enlisted his adopted religion to prove the spiritual superiority of the Jews by pointing out that Christians were worshiping two Jews—Jesus and Mary.

What purpose did this doctrine of superiority serve? Disraeli thought of himself as the leader of the Jews, even at the beginning of his career, when "all London" regarded him as a flamboyant fop. (He was once described as wearing "a black velvet coat lined with satin, purple trousers with a gold band running down the outside seam, a

scarlet waistcoat, and long lace ruffles, white gloves with several brilliant rings outside them, and long black ringlets rippling down his
shoulders.") Disraeli was playing the Oriental prince, and the women
swooned. As he fought in British politics for the leadership of the Tory
party, the political expression of the landed aristocracy, he made much
of his Jewish ancestry to disarm those who tried to undercut him as a
proper Englishman. At the very height of his career, which included
two terms as prime minister, Disraeli became a close friend of Queen
Victoria. He flattered and charmed her, and part of that charm was
his continued insistence that he was heir to the most ancient and
exalted "Arabian" stock. Disraeli, who had become the first Earl of
Beaconfield, felt that he was entitled to his position among the upper
crust because he was a descendant of David and Solomon, and as such
he represented the lasting nobility of the Jews.

Disraeli did not shy away from the Jewish questions in domestic or
in international politics. At home he led the fight for the full inclusion
of Jews in British society. He came to the defense of his friend Baron
Lionel de Rothschild, who had won four elections but could not be
seated in Parliament because to take the oath of office upon the
Christian Bible would be to surrender his dignity as a Jew. There is
something of Disraeli that still endures in the box in front of the
Speaker's desk in the House of Commons, where a Hebrew Bible,
which is used by Jewish members in taking their oath of office, rests
beside the King James version of the Old and New Testaments.

At the Congress of Berlin in 1878 Disraeli met with the redoubtable
Count Otto von Bismarck, the chancellor of Germany. They created a
balance of power in Europe that lasted for a generation, until Kaiser
Wilhelm II led Germany into the First World War. At the meeting in
Berlin, Disraeli refused to recognize an independent Romania unless
that nation constitutionally guaranteed civil rights to the Jews. The
Romanians protested, but in the end they had to accept Disraeli's

terms, though they did not, in fact, honor their promise. At that great diplomatic meeting, Bismarck spoke admiringly of Disraeli: "The old Jew, that is the man." He accepted Benjamin Disraeli as the ultimate wise man of Europe.

Disraeli remained a practicing Christian until the end of his days, but he insisted, perversely and persistently, in defining himself as a Jew—as other. Disraeli couched this affiliation in exaggerated rhetoric about the superiority of the Jewish race. He expressed this view in romantic and sentimental language, but Disraeli knew what was unique about the Jews: Their religion had begun as an act of criticism against paganism, and it continued as a call to all of humanity for moral responsibility. Disraeli was among the first of the moderns to realize that the connection of the Jews to their ancestral home, to the Holy Land, was central to the uniqueness of the Jews. As early as the 1830s he seized upon the theme of modern Zionism, that a Jewish commonwealth should be reconstituted in the Holy Land. And he brought England into the sphere of Middle East politics by arranging with Baron Lionel de Rothschild to finance the Suez Canal project.

Disraeli seems never to have made the same kind of connection between his Jewishness and his social conscience. Nonetheless, he was the founder of the school of conservative thought that insisted that the upholders of the inherited structure of society must provide for the poor. In moving the British Tories, at least some of them, away from the narrowness of defending privilege and toward a sense of noblesse oblige, Disraeli was reflecting a basic Jewish religious doctrine. In Judaism, charity is prescribed as an obligation. The town that does not take care of its poor is defined in the Talmud as "a godforsaken city." Disraeli probably had never studied this text, but he confronted the Tories with the Jewish principle that had been formulated twenty centuries earlier by the sage Hillel: "What is hateful unto you, do not do to others."

It was not Disraeli's intent to construct a model of how Jewish otherness would express itself in succeeding generations, but he essentially defined the modern, secular Jew. The basic ingredients of this
identity would consist of pride in the Jewish past; a sense of specialness; defense of Jewish rights; protection of the poor; and the professed
longing for a return to Zion. It is intriguing, even ironic, that this formulation of Jewishness had been presaged by a convert to Christianity.
What Disraeli affirmed as Jewishness amounted to group pride, Jewish
nationalism, and social conscience. He omitted Jewish religion and
Jewish culture because they had no special meaning to him. The same
may be said for many Jews today. They are "proud to be Jews," suffering the woes of all Jews, but they have no time for Jewish study, and
they avoid that primal authority figure, the God of their ancestors.

CHAPTER 13
TWO RADICAL SOLUTIONS

During my college years I continued to live at home within the deepest Hasidic Orthodoxy. My heart was still there—in fact it still is—but my head was taking me on a different journey. It had begun even earlier when I was a ninth or tenth grader in high school. I had expressed my adolescent rebellion by joining a socialist-Zionist youth group called Gordonia, which had been named after A. D. Gordon, the preeminent and spiritual leader of the "back to the land" movement in Jewish Palestine. At college I was soon immersed in left-wing thought because, in the thirties, a proper intellectual embraced leftist politics.

Those were the days of the Civil War in Spain, when the boldest among this crowd volunteered to fight on the side of the Spanish Republic against the fascist insurgents led by General Francisco Franco.

Toward the end of my first year at Johns Hopkins, I confronted, very personally, the modern Jewish crisis, the clash between head and heart, between my deepest commitments and the values and purposes of a modern ideology. The leader of the Communists on campus wanted to recruit me. He was a "big man on campus" so I was honored that he would take any notice of me. But I had some questions for him. I wanted to know if he really believed that the revolution might succeed in America. He was confident that it would because American capitalism had been irretrievably discredited by the Great Depression. I asked him further: Will religion be essentially outlawed as it was in the Soviet Union? He answered, without hesitation, that this would be done by the revolutionary government when it took power in the United States. So what would happen to my mother and father? I asked the question to make the point that they would never surrender their faith. He told me that they would probably wind up in the American equivalent of Siberia, perhaps in some camp in Idaho. Or, he hinted darkly, worse things would happen to them if they were counterrevolutionaries. I replied that he really was inviting me to help those who would destroy the lives of my parents. That was too high a price to pay for all the supposed wonders and glories that the revolution would bring—and so I never became a Communist.

After that conversation, I even became less of a socialist Zionist than I had been just a few days earlier. I had come face-to-face the terrifying reality that radical solutions to the problems of society always come at terrible cost to somebody. Some Jews were willing, even eager, to turn Communist because they wanted to break totally with the world of their ancestors. This kind of rejectionism was even present within the Zionist movement. Some Zionists were proclaiming themselves to be "new Jews." They were saying to their followers: Let us leave the Diaspora and its sick culture behind. Let us bury the past and create a totally new society in Palestine, which will be Jewish in a way our ancestors could not even imagine. Theodor Herzl, the founder of political Zionism, had no personal antipathy to the Jewish past, but he had come to Zionism from a life so completely outside of the Jewish tradition and community that he imagined the future Jewish state to be a version of Western society with no particularly Jewish character.

The Zionists and the Jewish Communists were expressing a modern Jewish response to anti-Semitism: they were fighting back. Leon Trotsky and Rosa Luxemburg were going to make the world revolution for all of humankind and create a new society in which anti-Semitism would be eradicated along with religion. Herzl was going to move the Jews out of all the existing societies in which the anti-Semites might continue to attack them. Concentrated in a state of their own, Herzl said, Jews would have the power to fight back. His first order of business as he was turning Zionist was to encourage Jewish university students to organize dueling societies. Had Herzl and Trotsky ever met, they probably would not have liked each other, but they both believed that Jews could no longer sit by and wait while others decided their destiny.

Throughout the nineteenth century most Jews continued to live their lives in central and western Europe with the assumption that the drums of Jew-hatred eventually would be stilled, but instead they grew louder and more persistent. In the final decades of the century, anti-Semitic political parties were organized in Germany and Austria. In France both the right and left wings adopted anti-Semitic platforms. Some Jews began to think that a radical solution was needed to end anti-Semitism once and for all. If the great battle of the modern Jews to achieve equality could not be achieved through assimilation into the gentile society, then the Jews would have to create a national state of their own, which would be as Jewish as Germany was German. The emancipation would be achieved by the bold, startling act of walking out on those who had refused to accept Jews as equals. The supreme expression of this attitude came in the brief, meteoric, and incandescent career of Theodor Herzl (1860–1904). In the previous generation, Benjamin Disraeli had imagined himself a Semitic prince heroically leading the Jews back to Zion. Theodor Herzl, who was just as self-consciously a theatrical figure, cast himself in the same role. With his long, squared-off black beard, Herzl looked the part of a king of ancient Israel. The critical difference was that Disraeli (whose novels Herzl had read) acted out this fantasy only in his fiction; Herzl, who was not distracted by having an empire to run, actually took steps to realize his dream of creating a Jewish state.

Until he became a Zionist in 1895, Theodor Herzl's career was not remarkable. He had written plays that commanded little attention and charming essays and perceptive dispatches from Paris for the Vienna-based newspaper the *Neue Freie Presse*. As a playwright and journalist, Theodor Herzl would not have been remembered as one who had shaped twentieth-century history.

What set Herzl apart was his epic quest to find the antidote to anti-Semitism. He had encountered Jew-hatred all his life, from his school days in Budapest through his university studies in law and during his career as a writer in Vienna. Herzl was not amenable to conversion, though he did give the idea fleeting consideration. He wrote in the opening entry of his famous diary, in 1895:

At first the Jewish question vexed me bitterly. There was perhaps a time when I would have gladly slipped over into some corner of the Christian fold. But, in any case, this was only a faint vagary born of adolescent weakness. For I can say to myself with honesty ... that I never thought seriously of becoming baptized or changing my name.

Nonetheless, in 1892 Herzl's first reaction to the rise of Jew-hatred in Austria had been to propose the conversion of Jewish children en masse. He described the imagined spectacle in his diary:

> In broad daylight, on twelve o'clock of a Sunday, the exchange of faith would take place in St. Stephen's Cathedral, with solemn parade and the peal of bells. Not with shame, as sorry individuals have hitherto gone over, but with a proud gesture. And because the Jewish leaders would remain behind, conducting the people only to the threshold of the church and themselves staying outside, it would elevate the whole performance to a display of utter sincerity. We, the steadfast leaders, would have constituted the final generation. We would have remained within the faith of our fathers. But we would have made Christians of our children before they reached the age of independent decision—after which conversion looks like an act of cowardice or calculation.[1]

Herzl quickly realized that such a "solution" would not work. Many Jews would reject conversion, and even those who did join the Church still might not be left in peace.

Herzl's faith that anti-Semitism was a curable social disease was shaken in January 1895, when he reported on an especially nasty scene. While a foreign correspondent in Paris, Herzl watched as Captain Alfred Dreyfus was degraded on the parade ground of the École Militaire and sent off into exile in a prison on Devil's Island. Dreyfus, the only Jewish officer on the General Staff of the French army, had been falsely accused of selling secret documents to the German enemy. The sound of the mob shouting invectives at Dreyfus and "Down with the Jews!" caused Herzl to redouble his efforts to find a solution to the "Jewish question."

In the beginning of June 1895, Herzl met with Baron Maurice de Hirsch, the preeminent Jewish philanthropist of the time, and asked him to take the lead in acquiring Palestine for the Jews. The baron dismissed the journalist as an impractical dreamer. This setback did not diminish Herzl's resolve. He immediately began to compose a memorandum to the Rothschilds, but he could not convince anyone to act as an intermediary with the French branch of the famous banking family. In angry disappointment, Herzl turned away from the elite and appealed directly to the Jewish masses. He expanded the memorandum into a short book, *Der Judenstaat,* which was published in February 1895 and immediately translated into five other languages. Herzl proposed to the Jewish public that the only cure for anti-Semitism was to reestablish the Jews as a "normal nation" in a state of their own. So long as this ancient people continued to be a minority everywhere, it would, at one time or another, be persecuted as aliens. The Jewish people would be safe only if it became the majority, preferably in its ancestral homeland.

As Herzl envisioned it, the Jewish state would need no particular cultural content. It would be founded as a Western democracy, on advanced principles of social justice; citizens would be free from cultural constraints and from religious coercion. Attending to the imperatives of national politics and civic life (not religious faith or study of the sacred texts) would become the principal occupation of the Jewish people in their own state.

Herzl's book created an immediate sensation. He was denying what had been the basic premise of Jewish politics throughout the nineteenth century: that society was moving toward tolerance and democracy and that any lingering anti-Semitism was an aberration, a vestige of medievalism. Herzl denied that the source of anti-Semitism was the accusation of rejecting Christ. He insisted that Jewish hatred in its modern form was an expression of xenophobia, hatred of the other. The Jews were the prime target because they had been a minority longer and in more societies than any other group in history. Unknown to Herzl, this argument had been made already in 1882 by Leon Pinsker in a pamphlet called *Autoemancipation,* but Pinsker was from Odessa in the Ukraine, and he had written in reaction to the massive pogroms sweeping through czarist Russia. Herzl recognized that the anti-Semitism in Vienna and Paris, these jewels of enlightened Western society, was essentially no different from that of the Ukraine backwater and that anti-Semitism would remain a powerful and dangerous impulse. Herzl concluded that the Jews had only two choices: either to get out and create their own national home or to assimilate totally into the majority culture.

Herzl could not be ignored because his proposal excited tremendous interest in eastern Europe, where the majority of world Jewry still lived under the brutal fist of the czar. He also attracted passionate followers in Germany, France, England, Austria-Hungary, and even the United States. In 1897 Herzl's supporters joined in founding the World Zionist Organization, which staged its first congress in Basel, Switzerland. On the opening night, he ruled that only delegates in formal dress would be permitted into the hall. The poor Jews who could not afford fancy clothes were offered the price of a rental from Herzl's own pocket. He wanted the world press to regard this gathering as the first session of a national parliament on the way to creating a Jewish state, and therefore the dignity of the meeting was of paramount importance. In his diary, Herzl wrote that in Basel he had founded the Jewish state, adding that in fifty years all the world would recognize what he knew that night.

Nearly fifty-one years later, on May 14, 1948, the State of Israel was proclaimed in Tel Aviv.

In the final eight years of his life (he died at the age of forty-four in 1904), Herzl created the Zionist movement and all of its basic institutions. The drama of these achievements was enhanced because Herzl made himself larger than life. His followers were mesmerized by his personality, and even many Zionists who opposed his policies regarded him as a modern Moses. The sultan of Turkey and the pope in Rome received him as a dignitary, even though he represented no existing power but only the dream of a Jewish state. The grief at his death was unparalleled in the modern history of the Jews. Many tens of thousands rushed to Vienna for his funeral, and memorial meetings were held in every substantial Jewish community in the world.

Herzl knew the meaning that he had chosen for his life with almost unmatched clarity. He was going to rescue the Jews from their otherness. Did Herzl succeed? The conventional answer is yes. He did create a national movement from nothing, and he became the founding father of the third Jewish commonwealth. But in the deepest aspiration of his life, the meaning that he himself gave to it, Herzl failed. Zionism did not end the otherness of the Jews. The state gave the Jews a renewed sense of pride, and it relieved them of some of the complexes and anxieties that came from being a powerless people, that is, a people that nowhere possessed the keys to a port or airfield to which it could admit Jews fleeing persecution. But the Jewish state has not made an end of anti-Semitism. The quarrel with the Arabs, which Herzl had hoped to avoid, has spawned intense Jew-hatred in much of the Muslim world. Israel's Arab enemies see themselves as defending the Holy Land, not from the Zionists, but from a world Jewish conspiracy against the Arabs. Ironically, Herzl's Zionism, which he had conceived as the way to end the tension between Jews and Christians, may only have transferred the problem from the Occident to the Orient.

In some ways Israel is an ordinary state with a Jewish president, prime minister, generals, ambassadors, and everything else that comes with sovereignty. And yet Israel is not just another state among states. Herzl dreamed of Jewish "normalcy," but he failed to understand that the Jews will never agree to be like everyone else, not in the Diaspora and not in their own land. The otherness of the Jewish people transcends boundaries; it is a state of mind.

The lasting problem of Herzl's life was his awareness that he could never escape the powerlessness of being a Jew. He knew that there were ways to wiggle out of the disabilities, primarily through baptism, but Herzl was a man of honor. He regarded baptism for the sake of becoming a professor or the director of the state theater as the peddling of one's soul. Such an act would be far more disreputable than peddling old clothes in the Jewish ghetto.

Herzl imagined the creation of the Jewish state not in some far-off time but in fifty years, conceivably in his own lifetime. One suspects that when he wrote this estimate in his diary, he added fifty to thirty-six, his age then, and imagined that he might live to see the event. In fact, the first president of the state of Israel, Chaim Weizmann, who had been involved in Herzl's movement from its very beginning, was not much younger than eighty-six when he assumed office.

Rosa Luxemburg: Blaming the Victim

If Zionism was the first radical response to the persistence of anti-Semitism in Europe, the second was socialist revolution, the creation of a "classless society." Most of the Jews who joined the revolutionary cadres were not just trying to cure anti-Semitism; they were desperately eager to cure themselves of their own Jewishness. Many brilliant young Jews joined the revolution and sacrificed their lives in failed plots to assassinate the czar or in the insurrections in Russia and central Europe.

The Jewish true believers in Marxism had no doubt that the revolution required that they sever all allegiance to the Jewish community and abandon their own group identity. This was clear in the case of the charismatic but ultimately tragic revolutionary heroine, Rosa Luxemburg (1871–1919). She was born in Poland in the town of Zamosc, the birthplace some years earlier of one of the great Yiddish writers, I. L. Peretz. Rosa Luxemburg's father, a wealthy merchant, moved the family to Warsaw when Rosa was three in order to get away from the Orthodox, Yiddish-speaking Jews who dominated the Jewish community in Zamosc. When she was still a schoolgirl, Rosa joined the Polish revolutionary movement in Warsaw. By 1898 she had moved to Germany and had become a citizen by marrying a non-Jew who was a printer—a member of the working class—as was fitting for a revolutionary of bourgeois origins. Luxemburg soon become a leading figure in the revolutionary left wing of the German socialist movement and a colleague of Vladimir Lenin and Leon Trotsky.

All her life, Rosa Luxemburg was uncompromising in her refusing to identify as a Jew or to deal with any political question, even fleetingly, from a Jewish perspective. She remembered as a child, in 1881, hiding in a doorway in Warsaw, as a mob ran by shouting "Kill the Jews." But she would blame the Jews for clinging to their otherness. The best way to avoid pogroms, she insisted, was to cease being Jewish: "Let them learn, speak, and think Polish, celebrate Polish holidays, and cease insisting on their Sabbath rest. . . . The apparatus of capitalist production and trade is under no obligation to accommodate the faith, customs, and calendar of the Jews."[2] Luxemburg opposed the creation of any specifically Jewish section of the socialist movement and remained a total assimiliationist to the end. During the revolutionary turbulences in Berlin at the beginning of 1919, Rosa

Luxemburg and Karl Liebknecht, with whom she edited a Communist newspaper, were arrested by army officers and murdered.

Leon Trotsky: Forever Bronstein

Like Luxemburg, Leon Trotsky (1879–1940)—he was born as Lev Davidovich Bronstein and changed his name to the Russian Trotsky when he became a revolutionary—insisted that the problems of the Jews could be solved only through world revolution. But Trotsky and Luxemburg responded to the Jewish question differently. She had no patience, and certainly no compassion, for the tribulations of the Jews as a separate people. Trotsky knew that it would take time to eradicate anti-Semitism, so he organized and armed Jewish groups in 1905 to defend themselves in anticipation of a pogrom. Six years later, when the medieval accusation of blood libel was revived by the Russian government in the Mendel Beilis case, Trotsky accused the czarist government of using this outrageous charge to make a scapegoat of the Jews.

As a rule, however, Trotsky did not let ethnic sentiments get in the way of his orthodox Marxism, even when he knew that his behavior was immoral by Jewish standards. After the revolution Trotsky's impoverished father needed a pair of shoes. His son, the second most powerful man in the land, refused to requisition them for his father. He would let the old man walk barefoot in the snow. "With so many people around without shoes," he explained, "how could I request shoes for my father?" When his malnourished father died of typhus in 1922, Trotsky would not bury him in the Jewish cemetery and ordered, instead, that the body be interred in the yard of the family farm.

Like Marx, Trotsky believed that religion is the opiate of the masses because it diverts attention from the revolutionary struggle by raising false hopes about the world to come. The salvation of humanity would be achieved only when the workers of the world would unite and establish a new world order based on the principle of economic justice for all.

After the Bolshevik Revolution, Trotsky refused to help Jews who pleaded with him to stop the shutting down of their synagogues and schools. When the chief rabbi of Moscow, Jacob Mazeh, implored Trotsky to spare his congregation, the revolutionary leader reacted with cold indifference and informed the rabbi that he no longer considered himself to be a Jew. Mazeh reportedly replied, "The Trotskys make the revolution, but the Bronsteins pay the bills." In the room that day two Jewish outlooks confronted each other. On one side of the desk sat Trotsky, the powerful war minister of the Bolshevik regime. He could have ordered the guards to take the rabbi to the cellar and shoot him as an intractable counterrevolutionary, which he was. But the rabbi was not afraid to tell Trotsky to his face that the revolution would not make the "Jewish question" disappear, because those who were being shoved out of their positions by the "dictatorship of the proletariat" inevitably would blame the Jews. Trotsky knew that the rabbi was telling him the truth. The White Russians' armies, which were still fighting the civil war against the revolution, were making pogroms everywhere, and they specifically targeted the Jewish Communists.

Trotsky would remain forever Bronstein, even in the eyes of his comrades Vladimir Lenin and Josef Stalin. Vladimir Lenin once said to the writer Maxim Gorky, "Trotsky is not one of us—with us, but not of us." Stalin made no secret of his contempt for Trotsky as a "rootless cosmopolitan" and "a member of an alien race." Trotsky had spent great effort to eradicate his family name because he wanted desperately to lead the international revolution as a Russian. But he would remain all of his life an outsider. And as Rabbi Mazeh had predicted, Bronstein would pay dearly for his life as Trotsky.

In the 1930s the Soviet press announced that Trotsky's younger son, Sergei Sedov (he used his mother's maiden name), was arrested for plotting to poison a group of workers. The Soviet secret service made a point of publicizing that Sergei's real name was Bronstein. Trotsky, who was living in exile in Mexico, complained bitterly about this propaganda campaign "to emphasize my Jewish origin and the half-Jewish origin of my son." He accused Stalin of reviving the "medieval charges" against the Jews as poisoners of wells. Stalin was not content to kill the younger son; he eventually had all of Trotsky's children executed. One great-grandson is known to have survived, and he is believed to be living in Israel as an Orthodox Jew. The drums announcing Trotsky's Jewishness beat very loud during the show trials in Moscow from 1936 to 1938. A number of old Bolsheviks who had been central to the revolution were executed for allegedly advocating "Jewish internationalism," which was viewed as an affront to the Soviet fatherland. Trotsky was found guilty in absentia and was condemned to death.

Trotsky foresaw that Hilter would annihilate millions of Jews in Europe, but he could never make peace with Zionism, which he kept insisting was a "tragic mirage." In July 1940, a month before his death, he warned that the Zionists had created a trap for several hundred thousands Jews who would fall into Nazi hands as Germany's armies swept into Palestine.

On August 20, 1940, in Goyoacán, Mexico, a Stalinist agent carried out the execution by plunging an iron ice pick into Trotsky's head. Six months earlier Trotsky had written in his last testament:

I shall die a proletarian revolutionary, a Marxist, a dialectical materialist, and consequently, an irreconcilable atheist. . . . Whatever may be the circumstances of my death, I shall die with unshaken faith in the Communist future. This faith in

man and in his future gives me even now such power of resistance as cannot be given by any religion.

If Trotsky thought that these words would convince the world
that Lev Davidovich Bronstein was gone and forgotten, he was mis-
taken. Winston Churchill knew that the anti-Semites would never let
Trotsky cease being a Jew. "He was still a Jew," wrote Churchill.
"Nothing could get over that. Hard fortune when you have deserted
your family, repudiated your race, spat upon the religion of your
fathers, and trapped Jew and Gentile in a common malignity, to be
bilked of so great a prize for so narrow-minded a reason!"

The tragedy of Trotsky is a recurring Jewish theme in the modern
era. Ever since Spinoza, some of the most brilliant and daring Jewish
thinkers conceived of a new world in which there would be neither
Jew nor gentile. But this dream of universality was denounced everywhere by the old elites and by the mob as a Jewish plot against the
existing order of society. These Bronsteins who wanted to be Trotskys
were hated all the more because they were demanding of the gentiles
that they, too, surrender their past.

CHAPTER 14
HARD TO BE A JEW

My portrait gallery of modern Jews is not yet complete. We have looked so far at Jews who were willing to disappear into the majority society by total assimilation and those who insisted on living as if they were still in the sixteenth century. We have encountered a number of Jewish thinkers who tried to mediate between these two extremes and define some version of a modern Jew. And we have examined larger-than-life figures, such as Theodor Herzl and Leon Trotsky, who wanted to solve the "Jewish problem" in one bold stroke. What we have not yet encountered are those—and they are many—for whom being a Jew in the modern world is an insoluble problem, a hopeless personal pain, a misfortune, like being born with some incurable disease.

The German-Jewish writer and philosopher Theodor Lessing (1872–1933) defined this affliction in his book *The Self-Hatred of the Jew* (1930), a study of Jewish intellectuals who had descended into self-contempt. He asserted that Jews had been forced to live on the margins of European and Asian culture, which caused them to become "over-spiritualized and decadent." As a young man, Lessing converted to Lutheranism to leave his Jewishness behind, but with the rise of Zionism, he returned by identifying with the new Jews who were creating the farming communes in Palestine. Theodor Lessing never "ascended" to Zion. He was assassinated in 1933 by the Nazis. His contemporary, Otto Weininger (1880–1903), a Viennese psychologist and philosopher, could not make peace with his Jewishness. He converted to Christianity on the day he received his doctorate; published his major work, *Sex and Character* (1903), an anti-Semitic and woman-hating polemic; and then permanently solved his Jewish problem at the age of twenty-three: he killed himself.

Franz Kafka once observed,

> Most young Jews who began to write in German wanted to leave their Jewishness behind them. . . . But their hind legs were still mired in their father's Jewishness and their thrashing forelegs found no new ground. The ensuing despair became their inspiration.

In this metaphor, Kafka captured the essence of Jewish self-hatred. Such Jews curse the image they see in the mirror, the one from whom they cannot escape. And they blame their parents who brought them into the world as Jews—and gave them little Jewish pride and much pain.

Those unfortunate souls, who regard their Jewishness as a mark of Cain, want to erase the memory of their ancestors, but often they cannot. I have encountered this phenomenon up close a number of times in my wanderings. Those for whom being Jewish has been mostly a tormenting memory have saddened me, very deeply, and perhaps that is why I remember them.

One such encounter happened in the late 1940s, when I was rabbi in Nashville, Tennessee. The political liberals in town were not a very large band, and I got to know them quite quickly. One of them was the scion of a famous political family, but he had never succeeded in living up to the accomplishments of his forebears. When I met him, he was finding some consolation, between glasses of bourbon, in telling stories about his ancestors. One day he invited me to visit the family mansion in a nearby small town. After we settled down in the living room over the inevitable bourbon and branch water, he led me to a small storage room filled with paintings in the rear of the house. The most striking canvas was that of a man with a black beard and sad eyes. I instantly identified him as a Jew and asked about the painting's provenance. He told me it was a portrait of his grandfather, a Jewish peddler who had found his way to Tennessee in the 1850s and converted to Christianity when he got married. My host added that no one in the family had ever shown this portrait to an outsider. He knew that this patrimony was no asset; to display it would only give his enemies more ammunition. So why did he show it to me? He said that he wanted someone to look at his Jewish grandfather with sympathy for the lonely life that he must have lived in Tennessee, far away from the Jewish world he had left behind. To this day I wonder: Was my host feeling the pain of having been denied a part of his past, or was he ashamed of himself for still keeping his Jewish grandfather in the closet?

I could tell many similar stories, but it is best that we turn now to four major cultural figures who wrestled with this kind of Jewish ambivalence, which, at its worst, turned into self-hatred.

HEINRICH HEINE: "BAPTIZED BUT NOT CONVERTED"

Heinrich Heine (1797–1856), next to Goethe the greatest poet in the German language, had a serious Jewish problem, and his conversion to Protestantism only made it worse. Heine desperately wanted to find a home in German letters, but he was never fully accepted as a legitimate German literary figure; he remained "the Jew Heine." He thus became the archetype of the most tortured of the Jewish moderns: the marginal Jew who feels intense discomfort within Judaism but remains chained to Jewish destiny.

Heine was, from the beginning, ill equipped to be at home in Jewish life. Growing up in Düsseldorf, Germany, which was then part of the Napoleonic empire, he was sent by his parents (his mother was a Deist and father a believing Jew with bourgeois ambitions) to a school run by Franciscan priests. His teachers did not try to convert the boy because, as disciples of Voltaire and the new age of the Enlightenment, they tended toward universalism. Heine did receive some Jewish instruction, but it was fragmentary and disconnected from his daily life. As a young adult, Heine felt increasingly alienated from his Jewishness. Tired of being always an outsider, he joined an avowedly anti-Semitic, Christian fraternity during his first year as a student at the University of Bonn. He soon became disillusioned with the group's mean-spirited chauvinism and insistence on celibacy. His enemies spread a rumor that he had contracted a venereal disease, a tale that his fraternity brothers chose to believe, and so Heine was expelled for being unchaste.

Heine completed his studies in Berlin, where he met a group of intellectuals, led by Leopold Zunz, who wanted to bring about a Jewish renaissance. He became an officer of their society for "the scientific study of Judaism" and began to study and teach Jewish history. But he eventually lost interest in academic Judaism; he much preferred the old-fashioned shtetl Jews of Poland to the fat Jews of Germany.

"The Polish Jew," he wrote, "with his filthy fur, his infested beard, his garlic-laden breath, and his jargon [Yiddish], is still dearer to me than many a German Jew in all the majesty of his government bonds." In these remarks, Heine did not disguise his contempt for the half-assimilated bourgeois German Jews who were his parents and relatives. He found a sense of authenticity only among the Jews he had encountered on a trip to Poland. These Jews had not adopted the non-Jews as the arbiters of their self-worth; they still stood unashamed before the God of their ancestors.

Heine was expressing a sentiment that would be espoused also in the first two decades of the century by Kafka and Franz Rosenzweig, both of whom were profoundly affected after meeting Yiddish-speaking Jews who were perfectly at home in their own skins. But Heine could not make himself part of that world because he had "not the strength to wear a beard, to fast, to hate, and out of hate to be forgiving." Frustrated in his failure to find a place for himself in the Jewish world, the poet declared himself "the born enemy of every positive religion."

Despite his anger at both Judaism and Christianity, Heine was required to show a certificate of baptism in order to qualify for his doctorate in law, so he converted to Lutheranism. It was a step he had been loath to take because he considered it "beneath my dignity and a stain on my honor to allow myself to be baptized for an appointment in Prussia." He would later write, "No Jew can ever believe in the divinity of another Jew." The baptismal certificate, which Heine had called his passport into Western society, brought him no advantage, only grief. Doors remained closed to him. Jews disdained him as an apostate; Christians dismissed him as an opportunist. "I am very sorry I had myself baptized," he confided to a friend. "I do not see that things have gone any better with me since. On the contrary, I have had nothing but misfortune. Is it not absurd?" he asked. "As soon as I am baptized, I am decried as a Jew. . . . Now I am detested by Christian and

Jew alike." Heine declared, "You can't change your religion. You can only renounce the one from which you are estranged for another to which you will never belong—I am baptized, but I am not converted." On his deathbed, in Paris, the paralyzed poet referred to himself as a "poor deathly-sick Jew." He reread the Hebrew Bible and praised its humanitarian teachings. When asked why he did not return to Judaism, Heine insisted that he had never really left it. When asked if he had made peace with God, the dying poet answered, "God will forgive me—that's His business." He was buried, according to his instructions, in a non-Jewish cemetery, but without Christian rites.

FRANZ KAFKA: METAMORPHOSIS IN PRAGUE

In the nineteenth century in central Europe, the father normally ruled unchallenged in the family. Therefore a revolt against the patriarch often represented a revolt against established order, including religion. The attempts to leave one's Jewishness almost always coincided with a break with the father, as in the case of the Czech-German writer Franz Kafka (1883–1924), who was the quintessential marginal Jew.

Emotionally estranged from the hollow Judaism of his bourgeois father, he nevertheless remained mired in his Jewishness. Indeed, Kafka's life seethed with feelings of guilt and loneliness, self-loathing and melancholy, anger and resentment. In a famous letter to his father, written in 1911 but never posted, Franz reflected bitterly on their relationship. He lamented that Judaism, which might have been a source of harmony between them, became instead a cause of acrimony. "I could not understand," wrote Kafka, "how with that insignificant scrap of Judaism you yourself possessed, you could reproach me for not ... making an effort to cling to a similar insignificant scrap." Declaring that his father's nostalgic traces of Judaism meant absolutely nothing to him, Franz decided that the "most effective act of 'piety' one could perform" is to "get rid" of everything Jewish "as fast as possible." Kafka was rebelling against the assimilationist aspirations of the Jewish business class in Prague, which idolized the German language and culture. He also resented the arrogance and hypocrisy of those Jews who spoke of lofty values in the synagogue (which they rarely attended) and then acted without a scintilla of compassion in their everyday lives. In his letter Kafka decried his father's callousness in describing how he spoke about a tubercular employee: "[the] sooner he dies, the better, the mangy dog."

Kafka's first positive Jewish experience as an adult was his encounter with a troupe of itinerant Yiddish actors who appeared at the Cafe Savoy in Prague. He recorded in his diary that a performance of *Der Meshumed* (The Apostate) "made my cheeks tremble." Kafka felt the intense passion for "people who are Jews in an especially pure form because they . . . live in [the religion] without effort . . . without any longing for or curiosity about Christians. . . ." One of the actors, Isak Lowy, made a deep impression on Kafka because the authenticity and energy of his art derived so naturally and spontaneously from the very core of his Jewishness. Stirred by Lowy's stories about Warsaw and Hasidic life, Kafka began to read Jewish literature and history, attended cultural events, and even overcame his intense shyness to organize and host an evening of readings in Yiddish.

Realizing the power of language to shape attitudes, Kafka reflected in his diary on how German had affected his feeling toward his mother.

Yesterday it occurred to me that I did not always love my mother as she deserved and as I could, only because the German language prevented it. The Jewish mother is no "Mutter" . . . [a word that] unconsciously contains, together with the Christian splendor Christian coldness . . . the Jewish woman who is called "Mutter" therefore becomes not only comic but strange. "Mama" would be a better name. . . . I believe that it is only the memories of the ghetto that still preserve the Jewish family for the word "vater" too is far from meaning the Jewish father.

Herman Kafka did not share his son's enthusiasm for Yiddish or for shtetl Jews; on the contrary, the presence in Prague of these impoverished Yiddish actors from Poland was a source of embarrassment to him. The elder Kafka scoffed at his son's cherished friend, the actor Izak Lowy, and dismissed him with the proverb "He who lies down with dogs gets up with fleas." It has been suggested by some Kafka scholars that the idea in the story *Metamorphosis,* of a man waking up in the morning as an insect, is rooted in the author's reaction to his father's "abuse, defamation, and denigration" of his "innocent" friend.

After three months of infatuation with the melodramatic Yiddish players, Kafka wrote in his diary: "When I saw the first plays it was possible for me to think that I had come upon a Judaism on which the beginnings of my own rested, a Judaism that was developing in my direction and so would enlighten and carry me farther along in my own clumsy Judaism; instead, it moves farther away from me the more I hear of it. The people remain, of course, and I hold fast to them." Kafka wanted these Yiddish actors to lead him to a form of Judaism in which he could believe. As he got to know these men and women better, he found that they themselves had strayed from the faith of their parents, which was why they spent their time on stage and not in the synagogue studying sacred texts. Kafka still admired them as Jews because they were steeped in an authentic Jewish culture, but he had not yet found a way of being Jewish in which he could feel at home. That would come when, under the influence of his friends Max Brod and Hugo Bergmann, he joined a circle of Zionist intellectuals who had formed the Bar-Kochba club.

At first Kafka rejected the Zionists as being out of touch with the Jewish masses, but he gradually moved into their orbit and became a serious student of the Hebrew language. It was not until he was dying of tuberculosis in a sanatorium near Vienna that he made peace with his Judaism. He dreamed of living in the Holy Land but had to content himself with "running his fingers over the map of Palestine." Franz Kafka died at the age of forty-one and was buried in the Jewish cemetery in Prague-Strashnitz. Today busloads of tourists to Prague make a pilgrimage to the tomb of Kafka, whose name is synonymous with the surreal struggle of the outsider who can find neither justice nor acceptance.

In his novels Kafka never referred directly to Jews, but his heroes suffered from the same nightmarish alienation that he experienced as a German writer who was not German, a Czech citizen who was not Czech, and a Jew who rejected the Judaism in which he had been raised. The writer's confidant and biographer, Max Brod, pointed out that "Kafka writes alongside the general tragedy of mankind, in particular the sufferings of his own unhappy people, homeless, haunted Jewry. . . ." His heroes often stood accused of some vague and inexplicable infraction, as in *The Trial*, which begins: "Someone must have been telling lies about Joseph K., for without having done anything wrong, he was arrested one fine morning." On one level, Joseph K. is every person who cannot understand why, if God is just and merciful, the innocent are made to suffer. On another level, the novel is about the endless victimization of the Jew as the outsider.

Kafka's unfinished novel, *The Castle*, can be understood both in universal and in particularist, Jewish terms. It is the story of land surveyor K, who tries desperately to reach the castle, but his every effort is resisted by vague forces, and he never arrives at his destination.

Thomas Mann defined the book's theme as a satirical portrayal of "the grotesque unconnection between the human being and the transcendental," as symbolized by the castle.

Max Brod saw such general religious interpretations of *The Castle* as correct but insufficient. Thomas Mann had universalized Kafka but had ignored completely the deep Jewish element in the writer's troubled soul. In his biography of Kafka, Brod pointed out that *The Castle* says "more about the situation of Jewry as a whole today than can be read in a hundred learned treatises. . . . Already in the introductory scene [K's first meeting with peasant farmers] one sees the position of the 'gentiles' with their calm rejection, and that of the Jew with his obligatory friendliness, pushfulness, indeed importunity described with shatteringly objective melancholy." The villagers did not want K among them. They joined with the castle in opposing the intruder.

In *The Castle* we find perhaps the quintessential statement in twentieth-century literature of the Jew as the dissenting outsider:

> You are not from the village, you are nothing. But unfortunately you are something after all, a stranger, a person who is superfluous, and always in the way, a person for whose sake one has continual vexation, a person whose intentions are obscure. . . . You think you know everything better than the people who live here. I am not saying that it isn't possible once in a while to get something done even in the teeth of every rule and tradition, but then it certainly doesn't come about in the way you are going on, by saying no all the time, and sticking to your own opinions.[1]

Max Brod comments, "K comes to grief in the most pitifully ridiculous way, despite the fact that he went at everything so earnestly and conscientiously. He remains alone. . . ."

K reminds me of Abraham in the land of the Hittites. He went about everything "earnestly and conscientiously"—and yet he remained an alien, and the Hittites never deigned to tell him why.

SIGMUND FREUD AND HIS FATHER'S FUR CAP

In the realm of human self-understanding, perhaps the greatest figure of modern times was the father of psychoanalysis, Sigmund Freud (1856–1939). He was the eldest of seven children in a Jewish merchant family that had come to Vienna from Moravia when he was four. The essential thrust of Freud's theory of personality was the assertion that each human being must be understood in terms of three universal forces: unconscious desires (the id), the values and conscience through which the id is restrained (the superego), and the self that emerges from this ever-raging conflict (the ego). Freud was most insistent that specific cultures and religions, including his own, are delusions that hinder healthy personality development. An avowed atheist, he dismissed religion as an infantile wish to overcome helplessness by connecting with an omnipotent father figure in heaven. Throughout most of his life, Sigmund Freud allied himself with the enemies of religion and cultural particularism in the name of a higher, universal truth. He moved the discussion from the rationalism of Spinoza and the economic determinism of Marx to the inner workings of the human mind.

Like Spinoza and Marx, Freud was judged by his contemporaries to be subversive. The sin of Sigmund Freud was his thesis that all human emotions express sexual impulses. When he presented this idea publicly in an academic paper, a leading professor of psychiatry at the Vienna Medical School denounced it as pornography—a matter for the police, not science. Psychoanalysis was assailed by its enemies as a Jewish assault upon the social norms and values of society. Freud was overjoyed, therefore, when figures like Carl Jung joined his almost all Jewish coterie of followers, and he put up with this Protestant from Switzerland even after he suspected that Jung might be not only a heretic from psychoanalytic orthodoxy but an anti-Semite as well. Freud wanted psychoanalysis to be regarded as a universal truth and not as a Jewish sect or, worse, a Jewish conspiracy.

Sigmund Freud was, at best, ambivalent about his Jewishness. He had received a reasonably good Jewish education, earning uniformly high grades in the Jewish classes that he took in the Vienna school system. (Every child was required to receive instruction in his or her declared religion.) Freud's father, who was well versed in talmudic learning, presumed that his son knew enough Hebrew to understand an inscription that he wrote in the Bible and gave to Sigmund upon his graduation from medical school. Sigmund's mother, who lived until 1930, could speak only Yiddish fluently. He could not possibly have communicated with her unless he understood Yiddish. But all these ties to his Jewishness seemed to be overshadowed by one incident that remained with him indelibly:

I may have been ten or twelve years old, when my father began to take me with him on his walks and reveal to me in his talks his views upon things in the world we live in. Thus, it was, on one such occasion, that he told me a story to show me how much better things were now [in Vienna] than they had been in his days. "When I was a young man," he said, "I went for a walk one Saturday in the streets of your birthplace [Moravia]; I was well dressed, and had a new fur cap on my head. A Christian came up to me and with a single blow knocked off my cap into the mud and shouted, 'Jew! Get off the pavement!'" "And what did you do?" I asked. "I went into the roadway and picked up my cap," was his quiet reply.[2]

Freud never forgave his father for his "unheroic conduct." He fantasized having a warrior father like the Carthaginian general Hannibal, who made his boy swear to take vengeance on the Romans.

Freud remained to the end of his life "an unbeliever," and he opposed all nationalisms as dangerous. But, as he explained in a speech to the B'nai B'rith Society in Vienna, he was irresistibly attracted to his Jewishness by

> many obscure emotional forces, which were more powerful the less they could be expressed in words. . . . And beyond this there was a perception that it was to my Jewish nature alone that I owed two characteristics that had become indispensable to me in the difficult course of my life. Because I was a Jew I found myself free from many prejudices which restricted others in the use of their intellect; and as a Jew I was prepared to join the opposition and to do without agreement with the compact majority.[3]

Freud thus acknowledged what defined him as a Jew: he had inherited the temperament of an intellectual and an outsider, for whom being in the minority was a familiar role. But what prevented this archexplorer of the unconscious from delving deeper into the "many obscure emotional forces" of his Jewishness? Such an investigation would have led, inevitably, back to his father and his father's God. He could neither break with them completely nor affirm them.

Like his father, Freud, too, would come face-to-face with an anti-Semitic assailant—the new rulers of Austria, the Nazis. In 1938 Freud sought refuge in London, but in order to receive an exit visa he had to go to Gestapo headquarters in Vienna and sign a statement attesting that he had been treated well by the authorities. Freud complied, and then he resorted to humor—what he had called the revenge of the weak. After his signature, Freud added, "I can heartily recommend the Gestapo to anyone." Would his father, the man who had said nothing as he picked up his fur cap from the gutter, have acted differently? In the end, Sigmund Freud was as powerless in the face of anti-Semitism as his father had been some seventy years earlier.

In the first years of the twentieth century Jewish modernity hit a blank and seemingly immovable wall. That was the somber and tragic meaning of Kafka's writing and, indeed, of his life. He could not become a gentile, either as a German or a Czech, and for most of his life he could not find the energy within himself to live his life as a Jew. The contemporary solutions that were being offered to this problem varied. Some Jews chose radical change, through the socialist revolution or through Zionism, but most stayed where they were or moved to America; that is, they chose to keep living as minorities in the Diaspora.

Two million or more Jews emigrated to the United States between 1882 and 1914. In the teeming immigrant neighborhoods, the "east sides," they felt a profound sense of loss of the warmth and values of the towns and hamlets from which they had come. There was special sadness at the sight of children being raised on the street, more by one another than by their parents, who were laboring in the sweatshops. This rift separating children from the culture of their parents was the theme of the first full-length "talking picture," *The Jazz Singer*. In this film Al Jolson (1886–1950) portrays a talented singer who is torn between show business and being a cantor in the Orthodox synagogue led by his pious father. At the climax of the story the Jolson character returns to the synagogue to chant the prayers of the Day of Atonement, the holiest day of the year, in place of his father, who is dying. He then goes back to the secular American life that he has made for himself as an entertainer. In essence, the film was a biography of

Jolson himself; he had sung in the choir of his cantor father before running off to become a black-face vaudevillian. Jolson lived his personal
life outside the Jewish community. In his will he instructed that most
of his three-million-dollar estate be divided equally among Jewish,
Catholic, and Protestant institutions. Jolson's disaffection from the
Jewish way of life was the norm in Hollywood in those days, where
celebrities routinely changed their names to blot out their Jewish identities. But in the next generation, one filmmaker made his Jewish neurosis a recurring theme.

THE SORROW AND THE PITY OF WOODY ALLEN

Woody Allen (born Allen Stewart Koningsberg in 1935) rebelled early
against the Jewish world of his youth in Brooklyn, New York. It is evident from his films and published interviews that Woody Allen has
little use for the old world manners and habits of his Jewish parents.
"Their values are God and carpeting," he once quipped. In his early
films, *Take the Money and Run* and *Bananas,* Allen portrays himself as a
whining Jewish schlemiel, an embarrassment to his parents. His later
cinematic self-portraits are darker; the balance keeps shifting from par-
ody to pain. In his 1997 film, *Deconstructing Harry,* his "father," wearing
a skullcap, is in hell for mental cruelty; he blamed his son for the death
of his wife in childbirth. But it is just as tragic and unfair to blame one's
father for siring a Jew.

Allen's highest aspiration as a comic has been to become like his
heroes, Charlie Chaplin, Bob Hope, and Groucho Marx, all of whom
transcended their ethnicities and the religion of their ancestors to
become universal characters. His biographer Eric Lax would have us
believe that Allen's "travails and foibles are not ethnic, they're universal. They are the same as Charlie Chaplin's pretensions and [Bob]
Hope's thinking he is a ladies' man. The three are little men, common

men, who see themselves as big and special and within that is the conflict and the joke."⁴ His screen persona tells a different story.

In his Academy Award–winning film *Annie Hall* (1977), Allen presented the discomfort of his Jewishness with stark clarity. At issue in the film is the failure of Alvy (played by Allen) to find common ground with his live-in gentile girlfriend (played by Diane Keaton), who is as different from him as she could possibly be. Allen depicts this by counterposing on the split screen two dinner scenes—Alvy's frenetic and loud Jewish family in Brooklyn and Annie Hall's unnervingly controlled family in small-town Wisconsin. In the cold gaze of Annie's anti-Semitic grandma, Alvy is reduced in his own eyes to a cowering Hasid with long beard and black caftan. There is venom in both depictions. Allen is saying, "a plague on both your houses." I am not going to trade Jewish insanity for gentile inanity. And so Alvy sadly goes back to Manhattan to sit in a darkened movie theater and see, again, his favorite film, Marcel Ophul's six-hour meditation on the Holocaust, *The Sorrow and the Pity.*

It seems that Allen cannot free himself from the memory of the Holocaust. Though he professes no religious convictions, Allen is concerned with the theological question: Where was God? In his most theological film, *Crimes and Misdemeanors,* Allen sets up a situation in which a Jewish ophthalmologist has his mistress murdered by a hit man and lives happily ever after. The moral of the story is that only those who get caught are punished because there is no God in the world. Ben, the rabbi in the film, is a model of moral correctness, yet he goes blind at the end of the story. Why did Allen strike the rabbi blind?

> Ben is blind even before he [goes] blind, because he doesn't see what's real in the world. But he's lucky because he has his naiveté . . . unless you have a strong spiritual feeling. . . . It's tough to get through life. . . .⁵

Allen's skepticism is sealed in *Crimes and Misdemeanors* when he has the Holocaust survivor, a philosopher who preaches love and hope, throw himself out of a window and die for no apparent reason. In the last scene of the film, the Woody Allen character sits alone, perplexed, and depressed.

For Woody Allen, God has failed the world. Judaism and Christianity are irrelevant. Woody is a confessed worshiper of Groucho Marx, who made the famous quip "I wouldn't want to join any club that would have me as a member." Apparently for Woody Allen, that club is called "Jews." In *Deconstructing Harry,* Allen portrays self-affirming Jewish characters as superstitious zealots who insist on creating exclusionary clubs and "force the concept of the other so you know clearly who you should hate." When his too-Jewish half-sister calls the Woody Allen character a self-hating Jew, he replies, "I may hate myself, but not because I'm Jewish." Woody Allen may deny the cause-and-effect relationship of self-loathing, but he has made it clear in *Deconstructing Harry* with unforgiving vehemence that any positive expression of Jewish identity is, at best, naive. Fortunately for Woody Allen, and for us, in all his years on the therapist's couch he has not lost his sense of humor—the revenge of the weak.

I believe Woody Allen keeps returning to dark Jewish themes in his films because he is deeply troubled by anti-Semitism. He knows that had he lived in Europe in the forties, he is too much of a schlemiel to have escaped the Nazis. In *Deconstructing Harry,* when the Woody Allen character is accused by his brother-in-law of being a Jewish anti-Semite who would even deny the Holocaust, he answers, "Not only do I know about the six million, but the scary truth is that records are made to be broken. I know what's out there. . . ." Someday, perhaps, like Kafka, Woody Allen will learn to respect the people from which he comes. Until that time, he will live only with the sorrow and the pity of his Jewishness.

∞   ∞   ∞

We completed the last few pages of this chapter early in the morning, so it was time for me to recite morning prayers. I repeated the words that Jews have been saying every day for countless centuries: "Behold how good is my lot, how sweet is my destiny, how beautiful is my inheritance." I have said these words thousands of times before, and yet on this morning I did not recite them as liturgical formulas. I remembered that through the ages these words had been said by refugees fleeing before pogroms, by people on ships taking them into exile, and in our time by believers packed in cattle cars on their way to Auschwitz. Under difficult or disastrous circumstances, these Jews wanted to belong to this tradition and to this learning. Most of those who have said these words, and say them today, are sustained by their faith in God. Some say these words because they belong, in love and pride, to their Jewish ancestors who stretch back to Abraham and Sarah. The Jews who repeat these words every day—and many others who identify with them—take somber pride in the rabbinic principle "It is better to be among the persecuted, and not one of the persecutors." How sad it has been for us to encounter, and try to understand, Jews who persecute themselves for the "crime" of having been born into this tradition.

CHAPTER 15

JUDAISM WITHOUT GOD?

Moritz Steinschneider (1816–1907) was the doyen of Jewish scholarship in the nineteenth century. In the course of his long life he compiled still-unsurpassed bibliographies of Hebrew manuscripts in the leading libraries of Europe, and his own literary output numbered more than 1,400 items. Steinschneider spent most of his life in Berlin in the midst of a Jewish community that was fast assimilating, and he presumed that this trend would continue until the whole of Jewry disappeared. So what was his rationale for recording all the evidence he could find of Jewish creativity in past centuries? When asked this question, Steinschneider always gave the same answer: "I am preparing Judaism for a dignified, honorable burial." His bibliographical volumes, it seems, were intended to be a museum in print, as much a memorial to an extinct people as the Egyptian mummies in the Louvre. One day Steinschneider received a visitor from Russia—Yehuda Leib Gordon, who identified himself as a poet in modern Hebrew. Steinschneider replied, "When did you die?" The scholar refused to believe that this culture, for which he was writing a learned obituary, could possibly be stirring into new forms of life. Mummies don't dance.

But Jewish mummies do dance. As we have seen, Nachman Krochmal made the observation that all other peoples go through one cycle of rise and decline, but the Jews repeat this cycle over and over again because God is present in their long historic journey, and every cycle of rebirth recalls the ways in which their Jewish ancestors had coped in the previous cycles. Krochmal's contemporary, Zecharias Frankel, made the ancestors into an object of veneration; he defined God as the force that links together the chain of Jewish continuity. Frankel seemed to be providing a new defense for faith in the Jewish God, but that defense raised some new and ultimately devastating questions. Frankel's critics maintained, quite correctly, that the "historical approach" allowed Jews to remake the inherited religion in their own image.

By the end of the century the most prominent exponent of historical Judaism, Rabbi Solomon Schechter (1847–1915), was writing elegant and often passionate essays asserting that the ultimate authority in Judaism was "catholic Israel"—the community of all affirming Jews. In each generation, the Jewish people defined and redefined their religious practices, and their decisions were guided by the spirit of the Jewish God. Schechter, too, defended this view with many examples of religious changes throughout the ages, but here again, the defense was questionable. In the past, changes had been made by learned rabbis in an effort, so they insisted, to discover the true meaning of the texts in the Bible. Schechter was saying that "the voice of the people is the voice of God." Schechter's theology essentially reflected the feelings of people who still cared deeply for the inherited traditions they had learned as children and young adults, even though they had left Orthodox beliefs behind them. So they tried to prop up the faith in God by invoking history or peoplehood.

The first major dent in the Orthodox consensus had been made by Moses Mendelssohn. As we have seen, he lived an impeccably observant Jewish life, but in defending his religious practice, Mendelssohn drew a distinction between the source of morality and ritual. Morality, he insisted, was universal, the same for everyone; Jewish ritual was what God, for unknowable reasons, had imposed on Jews to make of them a separate people until the messianic end of days. If that were so, what would be the role of God in the world? Surely it had to be more than the scorekeeper of the ritual behavior of the Jews. Mendelssohn's dichotomy did not convince most of his own children to keep the faith.

Nonetheless, modern Jewish thinkers, such as Krochmal, Frankel, and Schechter, followed in the path of Mendelssohn. They all invented a role for God that might satisfy Jewish doubters who were not content with the traditional proof—God's word as recorded in the Hebrew Bible. Krochmal turned to the "perplexed of his time" and said the Jews are not simply a religious faith; they are a people, a national community with a history through which God is progressively revealed. The revelation at Sinai, therefore, became one of many events that occurred in the cycles of Jewish history, all of which the people wove together to fashion its religious legacy. A thousand years earlier, the Jewish theologian Saadya Gaon had asserted that "our people exists only because we are the bearers of God's Torah." Krochmal had opened the door to the reverse assertion: the Torah exists because our people has created it. This view seemed all the more attractive because in the middle of the nineteenth century faith in God was waning markedly among the educated classes in Europe. Karl Marx had denounced religion as the opiate of the masses, and Charles Darwin (even though he was himself a Christian believer) was widely known to be proving that nature operated by the force of natural selection and not by divine purpose.

The doctrine that history and culture, and not theology, defined group identity attracted some modernist Jews who wanted to remain Jewish. It gave them license to retain the parts of their past that they wanted to preserve, to add new elements, and to discard the rest. This environment was fertile ground for the growth of modern Yiddish and Hebrew literature, created by Jewish nationalists who wanted to foster contemporary literature, art, and folklore of a renascent Jewish culture. But bitter battles soon broke out between the Yiddishists and the Hebraists. The Yiddishists maintained that the future of the Jews would be made, and guaranteed, by cultivating the language spoken by the overwhelming majority of the Jewish masses. The Hebraists insisted that Hebrew, not Yiddish, was the universal Jewish language. It had been known by all past generations of Jews, and it was still the lingua franca of the scattered Jewish people; therefore, a Jewish contemporary and secular culture could be fashioned only in Hebrew. The Hebraists were also insisting that a revival of Hebrew required a cultural center in the land of the ancestors, in Palestine. Some of these Hebraists wanted the new Zionist settlement in Palestine to break totally with the God-intoxicated Jewish life of the Diaspora. Young Hebrew writers, such as the essayists Micha Josef Berdyczewski and Joseph Hayyim Brenner and the poet Saul Tchernichowsky, kept insisting that the inherited God of the Jews stood in the way of a healthy contemporary Jewish life. The future belonged to the resurgent Jewish people, which would make of its life whatever it wished.

AHAD HA'AM, "ONE OF THE PEOPLE"

These younger writers were locked in battle with the leading Hebraist intellectual of the turn of the century, Asher Ginsberg (1856–1927), who wrote under the pen name Ahad Ha'am ("One of the People"). He was no less an unbeliever than his adversaries, for he was very consciously a follower of Herbert Spencer, the English thinker who had expounded Darwin to mean that nature, not God, ruled the world. Nonetheless, Ahad Ha'am knew instinctively that the Jews, whether they spoke Hebrew or Yiddish, could not survive as simply one among the many secular cultures. He therefore insisted that Judaism was headed for extinction unless it clung to the belief in the chosenness of the Jews. In some mysterious way, he asserted, Jews had created themselves to be different and often critical of the dominant values governing the societies in which they lived. The new Zionist settlement being established in Palestine should not lead the Jews to become "a nation like all others." This "spiritual center" of the Jewish people had to embody a unique culture in Hebrew based on the demanding moral values that had defined the Jewish character since antiquity. He fought a bitter battle against Berdyczewski and Brenner, who argued that since Ahad Ha'am denied the existence of a personal God, there was no logic in his assertion of Jewish chosenness. Ahad Ha'am disagreed vehemently. He kept insisting that the Jews had created their own chosenness by evolving a higher form of human morality, but he never completed a systematic proof of this proposition. One can only regard Ahad Ha'am's passion for the doctrine of chosenness as some interplay between his heart, which no doubt reflected his own deeply Orthodox upbringing, and his head, which told him that Jewish secularism unadorned had no future.

Ahad Ha'am's arguments in defense of chosenness were particularly unconvincing in America. The hundreds of thousands of Jews who had come from eastern Europe wanted very much to become part of this new world, in which pogroms were not an everyday threat. These Jewish immigrants did face the inevitable question: What were they to make of their Jewishness in America? This was not only a Jewish problem. In the early days of this century, America was a place to which Italians, Irish, Poles, Greeks, Russians, and every other national group in Europe were immigrating in substantial numbers. Each seemed to be facing the question: How do you become part of America while retaining some of the culture, values, and traditions of the old country? This question was particularly troublesome in the case of the Jews, who are not only an ethnic community but are also the bearers of a religious tradition at the center of which is the doctrine of their chosenness. How can you remain other in America when you have come to these shores to become part of "Americans all"? Ahad Ha'am's emphasis on culture was useful to Jewish intellectuals who were grappling with this dilemma, but the doctrine of chosenness was a bone in their throats.

MORDECAI KAPLAN, JEWISH RECONSTRUCTIONIST

The dominant American philosophy in the early years of the twentieth century was pragmatism, the emphasis on what people did rather than on abstract thought, on activism rather than contemplation or study. Activities that sustained a sense of community were far more important in America than theological affirmations. In describing his program for the reconstruction of Judaism, Rabbi Mordecai M. Kaplan (1882–1984) wrote, "Our problem is not how to maintain beliefs or uphold laws, but how to enable the Jewish people to function as a highly developed social organism and to fulfill the spiritual powers that are latent in it."[1] For Kaplan, those spiritual powers were not "the old religious guilt" of supernatural religion. "Contemporary Jewish life has to be made so attractive," he insisted, "that Jews will find rich, positive meaning in their Jewishness."

Kaplan was convinced that the new model of Jewish life in American society was cultural pluralism: every citizen should live within the common American culture, but each group had the right, and even the duty, to maintain its own community and its own sub-culture. Kaplan called this formulation "living in two civilizations." He was particularly troubled by the Jewish doctrine of chosenness. How can we live in a democracy as equal citizens, he asked, and continue to assert on religious grounds that our community is God's chosen people? Resolutely and in the face of great opposition, Kaplan deleted any mention of chosenness from the liturgy of his synagogue. He was willing to sacrifice a very precious part of classic Judaism, hoping for a counter offer from the Christian majority, so that these historic communities, which Kaplan did not want to merge, would at least live side by side as equals.

Mordecai Kaplan and Ahad Ha'am were wrestling with the same thorny question: What is the content of Judaism for those who no longer believe in a personal God? Kaplan wrote, "We are faced with a problem no less than that of transforming the very mind and heart of the Jewish people. Unless its mythological ideas about God give way to the conception of divinity imminent in the workings of the human spirit . . . the Jewish people has nothing further to contribute to civilization." Thus in Kaplan's "reconstruction" of the Jewish religion, the term *God* refers to the ultimate moral values of the community. The tale that God had once appeared at Sinai was a useful myth that the Jews had devised to grant authority to their highest moral values. The way to remain Jewish in America was by continuing the togetherness of the clan and some memory of its culture—without making Jews "other."

By the end of the nineteenth century, a hundred years after Jewish thinkers and theorists had begun to wrestle with the question of how to be a Jew in the modern age, the consensus among the majority of university-educated Jews basically followed the philosophical construct that had been defined by Spinoza and the Deists. The greatest heir of this idea among philosophers had been Immanuel Kant, and his most important interpreter was a Jew, Hermann Cohen, who taught philosophy at the University in Marburg. Cohen spent many years trying to show that the God of the Bible was identical with the one whom Kant had defined as the source of absolute morality. The problem with this construction was pointed out once to Hermann Cohen in a famous incident in a Berlin synagogue. A Polish Jew approached the revered professor and said to him, "Dr. Cohen, I think I understand your description of God, so please tell me, to whom does one pray? Who is the God to whom I can speak from my broken heart and ask him to help me?" Cohen did not reply, but there were tears in his eyes. Indeed, to whom could one pray? Certainly not to the God of Spinoza or of Immanuel Kant. Nor could one invoke the Jewish national spirit for consolation in times of pain and loss.

So at the end of the century Jews had many theologies that tried to make their religion philosophically respectable and contemporary and many ideologies that suggested that the Jewish people was a forward-looking and even revolutionary force in the world. But a deep yearning remained for the personal God who had been exiled into oblivion by the philosophers. The invitation calling upon the Jewish God to return was not couched in the older Orthodox rhetoric; it was the assertion that a Jew is not fully a Jew when estranged from God, and only in the company of the Divine can the Jewish community continue. More than anyone else, the philosopher who made this turn back to Jewish faith was Franz Rosenzweig.

THE EPIPHANY OF FRANZ ROSENZWEIG

Franz Rosenzweig (1886–1929) was born into an acculturated family of German Jews in Kassel. Early in his adult life, he wrote a brilliant dissertation on Hegel's philosophy, and he was clearly headed toward a career as a scholar of substantial influence and importance. Many members of his family and friends converted to Christianity, including his cousins the Ehrenberg brothers, one of whom, Rudolf, was being hailed as an important new voice in German Protestantism. The young Rosenzweig was attracted to Christianity, not for professional or social advantage, but because Christianity seemed to hold out to him the nourishment of the soul that he found neither in philosophy, which he knew well, nor in Judaism, which seemed to him "an empty purse."

In 1913 Rosenzweig was on the very verge of baptism, but he wanted to become a Christian from a Jewish rather than a pagan tradition. So the young philosopher decided, as a prelude to conversion, to attend High Holiday services at a small Hasidic synagogue in Berlin. There he found people who showed all the fire and passion of a people standing immediately before God; it was what he had longed for all his life. For the first time, Rosenzweig felt at home as a Jew. The young scholar no longer needed to leave this past behind in order to find God, for he had discovered an authentic Jewish connection among the very people whom his family and their friends had snooted as backward and uncouth. Rosenzweig would write to his cousin Rudolf Ehrenberg, "Becoming a Christian no longer seems necessary to me . . . and no longer possible. . . ."

Rosenzweig's encounter with the Hasidim brought him to the realization that the Jewish calendar, the Sabbath, the festivals, and the entire rhythm of Jewish life are all a reflection of eternity. The Jew, therefore, lives in two dimensions—the now and the forever. Jews have lived within changing and often tragic circumstances, but their religion has lifted them up to another realm in which nothing changes. The holy days and the commandments that Jews observe are timeless. Historical events are fleeting. The Zionist settlement of Palestine is no more important to the continuity of Judaism than the revolt against Rome or the expulsion from Spain or the pogroms in Russia. Rosenzweig's exalted vision of Jews as a people living beyond history follows the conviction of the masters of the Talmud that chronology is irrelevant in the study of Torah; all of its divine teachings and interpretations are eternal values that transcend time. For Rosenzweig, therefore, the obsession with the "Jewish question"—with Jews rather than Judaism—was a misstatement of the very essence and character of this unique people.

Rosenzweig did not presume to affirm or practice what he could not yet comprehend, but he insisted that the texts not yet understood or the commandments whose meaning were still obscure needed to be held in abeyance. We must leave open the possibility that as we learn more of Judaism, we will embrace the values and the practices that the texts command. Therefore, the whole of the tradition has to be kept alive through study.

In 1920 Rosenzweig moved to Frankfurt at the invitation of Dr. Nehemiah Nobel, one of the leading rabbis of the city, to direct a non-denominational institute for adult Jewish education called the Freies Jüdisches Lehrhaus (the Free Jewish House of Learning). Its faculty, which included Martin Buber, Gershom Scholem, and Erich Fromm, would teach the meanings of classical Jewish texts in an environment in which teacher and student were bound together by reverence for Jewish learning and the desire to understand the texts to the best of their ability. All kinds of Jews, whatever their ideology or however rich or poor their Jewish education might have been, could unite in study. They could freely choose to adhere to as much formal religion as spoke to them at that particular moment in their Jewish journey. Typical of their generation, most of the students no longer knew Hebrew, so Rosenzweig decided that he must translate Jewish classics into German. He collaborated with his friend Martin Buber in creating a new German translation of the Bible, but the work was interrupted by the untimely death of Rosenzweig in 1929. It was finally completed by Buber in 1961, long after the German Jews for whom it was intended had been exiled or murdered in the Holocaust.

Rosenzweig's journey led him into "orthodoxizing," as he described it, but not into Orthodoxy. He accepted the theory of the modern biblical critics, who had long been insisting that the Five Books of Moses were not a unitary document. These scholars had undermined the Orthodox belief that God had dictated this text verbatim to Moses. Rosenzweig agreed that the Bible had been written at various times by various hands and that it had been combined into one text perhaps in the sixth century B.C.E. But Rosenzweig offered his own interpretation of this process. He noted that modern scholars of the Hebrew Bible denoted the editor with a capital letter *R* as shorthand for *Redactor*. Rosenzweig said, Why not think of this *R* as referring to *Rabbenu,* our teacher? The Redactor who had decided what to include as holy writ from the various scrolls in which traditional memories were recorded had heard the voice of God. This person had been guided from above while editing the various scrolls and fragments into the text that has been hallowed as the Five Books of Moses.

In 1922 Rosenzweig became aware that he suffered from progressive paralysis. The disease eventually left him with no movement except the blinking of an eyelid. His wife, who understood the signals he was giving, typed his essays and translated for those who came to learn from the great man. Rosenzweig was trapped in a devastated body, but he did not feel sorry for himself, knowing that he lived in two dimensions—the now and the forever.

MARTIN BUBER, ZIONIST IN SEARCH OF GOD

Rosenzweig had returned to Judaism from the near total assimilation of his parents and their entire circle. This was not true of his closest colleague, Martin Buber. Though born in Vienna, Buber had spent much of his childhood in Lemberg, one of the major cities of Galicia, the part of Poland which then belonged to the Austro-Hungarian Empire. The young Martin was schooled under the direction of his grandfather Salomon, who was both a very rich businessman and a redoubtable Hebrew scholar. At the age of nineteen, Martin Buber joined the immediate circle of Theodor Herzl and became first his assistant and then his successor as editor of *Die Welt*, the weekly that Herzl founded to propagate Zionist ideas. Buber was restless working with Herzl. Various explanations have been given for the tension between them, usually emphasizing the difference between Herzl the statesman and Buber the young man in search of God. Their temperaments were bound to clash, for Herzl was impatient and more than a little imperious, and Buber was something of a contrarian.

But the fundamental reason for the inevitable break between Herzl and Buber was that even though they were near contemporaries (Buber was less than twenty years younger than Herzl), they belonged to different eras. As a man of the Enlightenment, Herzl still believed that society could be perfected, that progress was the wave of the future, and that anti-Semitism could be solved by rational means: removing the Jews from all the Diasporas and creating a Jewish state. Buber, on the other hand, was fleeing from the emptiness of a world in which secular ideologies had failed to perfect society. Buber was turning to God.

While some Jewish seekers were looking for religious inspiration in the East, especially among the Buddhists and Confucians, Buber looked to the biblical prophets for inspiration. He learned from them that the essence of the religious experience was to hear God with total attention and complete surrender. At age twenty-six, Buber found in the Hasidic rebbes a usable past for himself and for others who yearned for a spiritual life within their own Jewish heritage. Buber's epiphany came when he read about the teachings of the Baal Shem Tov:

> It was then that . . . I experienced the hasidic soul, the primally Jewish opened to me. . . . Man's being created in the image of God I grasped as deed, as becoming, as task. . . . I recognized the idea of the perfected man. . . . I became aware of the summons to proclaim it to the world.[2]

Buber did not retreat from modern society into the world of the Hasidim. His ideal became the kibbutz movement in Palestine, with its emphasis on pure and equitable interpersonal relationships, which he saw as a manifestation of the divine spirit. No matter that the members of these agricultural collectives were, almost without exception, nonbelievers. Buber defined such encounters in his most famous book, *I and Thou*. On its surface, this book is free of any specific Jewish content. He was saying that I-Thou relationships are not found primarily in the obvious places—in churches, in synagogues, or in mosques—but in places where the divine spirit is manifest in living realities. "Real faith does not mean professing what we hold true in a ready-made formula," he wrote.

> On the contrary: it means holding ourselves open to the unconditional mystery which we encounter in every sphere of our life and which cannot be comprised in any formula. It means that, from the very roots of our being, we should always be prepared to live with this mystery as one being lives with another. Real faith means the ability to endure life in the face of this mystery.[3]

Buber was popular among the younger Jewish intelligentsia because he offered a version of Judaism that allowed them to feel the mystery of Judaism without any obligation to practice Jewish rituals or to live according to the rhythm of the Jewish religious calendar. They could read his *Tales of the Hasidim* and appropriate the rebbes as he imagined them to be—warm, loving, romantic, and forgiving masters. In reality, most rebbes had been authoritarian figures who taught absolute commitment to their interpretation of how God needed to be served.

For Buber, Israel was the ultimate Jewish destination. In their reencounter with the land, Jews could achieve a sense of spiritual wholeness; they would live by the highest ideals of the Hebrew prophets. Buber emigrated from Germany to Israel in 1938, after the Nazis forbade him to continue lecturing on Judaism. He taught at the Hebrew University, and he became the first president of the Israel Academy of Sciences and Humanities. Buber used his prestige to found Berit Shalom, "the covenant of peace," a group that sought a peaceful and morally acceptable peace with the Arabs. To be the authentic Jewish state, he insisted, Israel had to be constructed upon a foundation of justice and compassion for all. "Israel can endure only if it insists on its vocation of uniqueness, if it translates into reality the divine words spoken during the making of the Covenant."[4]

Buber's own religious position was elusive. He wrote, over and over again, that the experience of God is personal; it is to be found by each individual as he or she stands alone, to hear what God is saying. And yet Buber never quite let go of the Jewish idea that God is experienced in law and that the individual encounters God through obedience. But he quickly added that law is what each individual hears for himself or herself; it is not an objective standard that all must obey in the same way. Buber was a Zionist who believed that the individual

Jew could find God in the new Zionist communal settlements on the land. But here, too, the decision belonged solely to the individual, and most Jewish individuals felt no compulsion to join a kibbutz. Thus, both as a theologian and as a Zionist, Buber was so much the individualist that Gershom Scholem could call him a "religious anarchist."

And yet Buber turned a historic corner. He told some of the Jewish intelligentsia that they need not be lonely and insecure. They could commune with God, and the God whom they would encounter is no stranger but the One who had spoken to their ancestors.

RABBI ABRAHAM ISAAC KOOK: PREPARING FOR THE MESSIAH

Like Buber, Rabbi Abraham Isaac Kook, the first chief rabbi of Palestine (1921–1933), took the kibbutz founders to his heart, not because he saw them as the harbingers of a new Jewish spirituality, but because they were recovering the land of Israel for the Jewish people. The Holy Land could be cast temporarily in the role of a modern, secular society, but Kook did not believe that such a Jewish state could last. The inherent sacredness of the place would prevail eventually. Therefore, from Kook's perspective, the Zionists, who were reviving the language and cultivating the land as part of the renascence of Jewish life, were unwitting instruments in a divinely appointed drama. "It is pointless to wage a bitter and ill-conceived war against those who are loyal to one aspect of the Jewish character, " Kook wrote. "No matter what they may think, the particular element of the Jewish spirit that they may make their own, being rooted in the total life of our people, must inevitably contain every aspect of its ethos."[5]

Kook saw the Zionist enterprise in Palestine as proof that the coming of the Messiah was imminent and that human effort could bring that day closer. After the mass slaughter of the First World War—this "war of Gog and Magog"—Kook believed that the Messiah of the Jews

would surely appear to redeem all of humanity, which had erred trag-
ically in placing its faith in Western culture. The modern State of
Israel, Kook asserted, would lead the way to the healing of the world:

> The securing of the structure of the world, which is now tot-
> tering in the bloody tempests of war, demands the upbuilding
> of the Jewish nation. . . . All the civilizations of the world will
> be renewed by the renascence of our spirit. All quarrels will be
> resolved, and our revival will cause all life to become lumi-
> nous with the joy of fresh birth.[6]

Rabbi Abraham Isaac Kook never wavered, even for a moment, in
his faith in God. On the contrary, he was both a profound scholar of
the Talmud, totally obedient to all of its prescriptions in the mode of
the Gaon of Vilna, and a kabbalist who followed in the footsteps of
Isaac Luria to redeem the sparks of holiness that were scattered and
obscured in the world and to prepare for the redemption that was
coming very soon.

Martin Buber, on the other hand, had never been an observant
Jew, not in his childhood in the home of his assimilated parents and
not even after he declared God to be at the very center of human
life. Nonetheless, the subtext of their writings is the same: a pro-
found disappointment with European civilization and a call to action.
Modernity had promised peace and progress, and it had held out to the
Jews the hope of finally being freed from centuries of persecution.
Theodor Herzl attracted the young Buber to his side because the
Zionist visionary had the courage to say that anti-Semitism was incurable in the foreseeable future and, therefore, the best solution was for
Jews to leave Europe. Both Buber and Kook believed that the world
needed redemption, and it could be achieved only through an
encounter with God.

∞   ∞   ∞

Near the beginning of this book I insisted that the Jewish character had to be understood in the image of a river reaching back to Abraham: the situations and troubles of modern Jews are a delta, in which that river has divided into many streams, but the impulse still emanates from the source. I proposed this metaphor as a critique of the more contemporary idea that one begins with the present, with the contemporary Jewish scene, and then either ignores or reinvents the past to suit one's needs. Now, nearing the end of our journey downriver, it is time that I point out sharply what is the basic difference between these two perspectives.

The essence of the matter is that the great river of Jewish life was contained throughout all the ages by banks, which compelled Jews to remain within their Jewishness. In the believing ages, even the sectarians among the Jews had no doubt whatsoever that God had commanded them. In the nineteenth century, an age of growing disbelief, the banks of the river still held because God had been replaced by anti-Semitism. As the voice of God became fainter, the shouts of the anti-Semites were heard ever louder. And so a Yiddish folk song of the nineteenth century could announce that "we are whatever we might be; but we are Jews." That is, what individual Jews believe is irrelevant; we share a problem and a destiny to stand up together against our enemy. Thus, for more than a century, the battle of the Jews for total emancipation and a state of their own dominated Jewish life, and these struggles gave Jews the sense of a shared and inescapable destiny.

The existential crisis in Jewish identity began when Jews no longer believed in God and began to feel that anti-Semitism was no longer permanent. This optimism gave many Jews, both in Palestine and the Diaspora, license to refashion their Jewishness as they pleased. In the United States, during the mass migration from eastern Europe at the turn of the century, democracy seemed to promise the end of persecution and complete freedom and equality for the Jews. The "new Jews" no doubt would use major elements of the past, but the basic criterion would be to keep whatever added dimensions of joy to their lives.

Rabbi Mordecai Kaplan anticipated this possibility when he once said to me that Judaism could no longer be summarized in the phrase "I must," because in a democracy an individual who no longer believed in a personal God and who was ever more at peace with the rest of society was beyond compulsion. If Judaism was to survive in a free environment, Kaplan insisted, the only phrase that could be used is "I ought." But how, I asked him, does one persuade Jews to say "I ought"? There is always the danger that, in freedom, they might prefer alternative experiences to any form of Judaism. Kaplan's response was that the Jewish experience had to be made so rich and compelling that Jews would choose to live at least part of their lives within it and not go elsewhere. The attempt to define Judaism without compulsion was inevitable in the open society, but does it have the slightest chance of rebuilding banks that will keep the ancient river on course? I think not.

People change their minds about what makes them feel good and about their aesthetic tastes. If Jewish loyalty is based on nothing more than the hope that Jews will continue to choose Jewish music and art or Jewish religious rituals because they make them feel better as people, the hope is vain. My commitment to Judaism has nothing to do with any notion that Jewish rituals are more edifying or aesthetically more interesting as pageant than the rites of other communities. I do not go to synagogue on the eve of Yom Kippur because I want to hear Kol Nidre as deeply moving music. As a descendant of Hasidim, I am very moved by Hasidic dance, but not because I think that it is a more compelling ballet than the Bolshoi or the dances of the Sufis. For that matter, I do not eat chicken soup on Friday night because I think it tastes better than gazpacho. If Judaism is in competition with other religious forms to make the individual feel spiritually or culturally enriched, the Jewish experience will no doubt win some of the time, but today, when one can summon up instantly by computer the cultural and religious experiences of a hundred peoples, Judaism will not necessarily always compete well. Those Jews who feel now like having their spiritual needs met by a half hour of Kabbalah may wake up one morning in an ashram in northern India. By its very nature, new age religion, for which the wants, needs, yearnings, and heartaches of the individual are the ultimate standard, is a very porous form of Jewish commitment.

This awareness was at the very core of the thinking of Buber and Rosenzweig. Buber knew that the individual had no handhold left in a world in which the gods of modernity had failed, so he turned to the God of Israel. Buber did not allow himself an easy life, not in Germany and not in Israel. He worked to the very end on the tasks to which he felt commanded: to bring back a generation of Jewish intellectuals to their Jewishness, to translate the Bible into an entirely new mode, and to fight for peace between Jews and Arabs. Rosenzweig had been raised in an environment so assimilated that his leaving the Jewish community would have created no ripples in his family or in his circle. He was free to do anything he wanted. When Rosenzweig returned to his Jewishness, he wanted to find in the Jewish texts what was required of him.

Rabbi Abraham Isaac Kook seems to have come from an entirely different religious situation, because all his life he was a totally committed believer, but he, too, was deeply aware of the modern situation. He knew that the makers of the overtly secular modern Zionist settlement in the Holy Land had proclaimed themselves to be a people who were free to make their lives into whatever they wished. He insisted, however, that these men and women were part of a divine plan; they were reviving Hebrew and reclaiming the ancestral land because these purposes were the lasting impulses of the great historic river that is the experience of the Jews. They might think they were acting out of their own volition, but the deepest Jewish tide was carrying them along. Like Buber and Rosenzweig, Kook knew that the Jews could not exist without the profound sense that they were commanded.

After a century the question is still unanswered: What is the source of such compulsion? Is it within the nature of the Jews, as Ahad Ha'am had insisted? Or, perhaps, have the Jews been behaving like Jonah in the Bible, who, when commanded by God to go and prophesy in Nineveh, ran away and wound up in the belly of a big fish? There, finally, he cried out, "God, save me." Is the Jewish God inescapable? My answer is a resounding yes—but not for the reason that is usually given. I do not have to prove that the God of the Jews exists. Every Jew who behaves as if he or she were commanded to be a Jew is affirming God.

Debates about whether nonbelievers can be "good Jews" are irrelevant. There are only two kinds of Jewish disbelief. One is the version held by those who believe vehemently that there is no longer any special virtue or necessity in remaining a Jew; they have already provided the rationale for their assimilating out of the Jewish community. The second kind of disbelief is the rejection of the specific rituals enjoined by Judaism. But these unbelievers busy themselves with nearly superhuman efforts in defending the State of Israel, in creating Jewish schools and cultural institutions, and in volunteering for various Jewish political organizations. The people who perform such tasks sometimes have trouble producing a coherent rationale for clinging to their Jewishness, but they feel compelled and even possessed to do so. They could be doing something else for the public good or nothing at all, merely enjoying themselves, but they have chosen Jewish tasks. The people who engage in such labors are asserting their commitment to the continued existence of Jewish otherness, and they continue to destroy idols. I do not care what such Jews say they are doing. If they are raising their children to follow after them in these compulsions, the God of the Jews is alive and well among them.

Every Sabbath in the synagogue a prayer is said for the congregation of all the Jews. Its climactic phrase is the prayer for "all those who busy themselves with the concerns of the community." The liturgy asserts that *acting as a Jew* is a sign of loyalty. The Jews who keep insisting that secular nonbelieving Jews are at least as good as the believers are absolutely right, so long as these nonbelievers continue to assert their Jewishness in deeds. I would say, therefore, to those Jews who ask me to condone their agnosticism: What are you teaching your children and your grandchildren that they must continue to do as Jews? The ancient rabbis had the boldness to put this very idea in the mouth of God: "I would not mind if they forsake Me provided that they adhere to My commandments" (Eichah Rabbah Petichah 2).

CHAPTER 16

FORSAKEN

In their first years of power, even the Nazis did not seem far different from earlier persecutors. Jewish gains had been reversed in the past. At one time or another during the Middle Ages, Jews were expelled or had to flee from almost every place in Europe. That the Nazis would organize the mass murder of Jews was unthinkable, until almost the very day when the first Jewish communities were rounded up for deportation or the *Einsatzgruppen* in Poland, the Baltics, and the western parts of the Soviet Union began to murder Jews wherever they found them.

On the morrow of the Holocaust, there no longer could be any doubt that Jews were irretrievably other. The Nazis had forced all

Jews—the conductors and the opera directors, the professors and the bankers, the avant-garde artists and the universalist philosophers—into the same cattle cars with the Hasidim and misnagdim. They were all Jews. No doubt as they stood jammed into cattle cars on the way to Auschwitz, many wondered why they, the cultured and the Westernized, the model Frenchmen, German, Dutch, Italian, or Hungarians, should be on the way to their deaths as Jews.

The Orthodox believers had never doubted that Jews were other. They had been chosen for a special role by God, one that brought them not only blessings but suffering. The Orthodox did not think of the Holocaust as unprecedented, and they resisted any attempt to label it as unique. For them, the Holocaust was the most recent in a long line of tragedies, beginning with the destruction of the Temple, and those who would make of it something special were really dealing with their own deep disappointment in Western civilization. It is for this reason that most Orthodox Jews refused to participate when the secular Israeli government declared an official annual day of commemoration of the Holocaust, on the day that the revolt in the Warsaw ghetto finally was stamped out by German troops. Instead, the Orthodox would say some additional prayers during one the traditional days of contrition, such as the fast day of the Ninth of Av, the day commemorating the destruction of both Temples and other great Jewish tragedies. The Orthodox were simply saying that for them the Holocaust was not new; they had been to an Auschwitz before.

The forced journey back to their Jewishness was most difficult for those who had moved furthest away from the faith of their ancestors. In France one of the nation's most distinguished historians, Marc Bloch, was about to be executed by a Nazi firing squad. He was offered the services of the rabbi to accompany him in his last moments. Bloch refused, insisting that he was dying as a Frenchman. Even Jews who had converted to Christianity would not escape the Nazi inquisitors who served the god of racial purity. In the Warsaw ghetto, to which the Nazis had deported only those whom they regarded as Jews, two Roman Catholic churches existed to the very end. Their congregants were converts, and so were the priests. I wonder what those who kept going to services in these churches were thinking and feeling, knowing that on the other side of the wall their Nazi guards were participating in the same rituals.

The case of the German philosopher Edith Stein (1891–1942) is perhaps the most tragic of all. She had become a Carmelite nun in the 1930s after a deep religious crisis that led her from an Orthodox family into the Roman Catholic Church. In 1938, in an attempt to escape the Nazis, she fled to a monastery in Holland. In retaliation of the Dutch bishops' condemnation of Nazi anti-Semitism, the Gestapo arrested her and other nuns and priests of Jewish origin. Edith Stein was murdered in Auschwitz. Pope John Paul II has hailed her as a holy martyr to her Christian faith, and in 1998 she was declared a saint of the Roman Catholic Church. This estimate sits very badly among Jews, who know that Edith Stein was not sent to Auschwitz for her Christian convictions or piety; she was forced to her death because she had been born a Jew. As she inhaled the Zyklon-B in the gas chamber, did Edith Stein really think that she was dying as a sacrifice for the Church?

Since the Holocaust, innumerable questions disturb our conscience. Was the Holocaust a unique event? How deep are the roots of anti-Semitism? Why did the various governments that could have helped avoid their responsibilities? Did American Jews and those in Palestine extend themselves enough in pushing their governments to intervene? These questions are beyond the scope of this book, but I do want to address three questions: How did American Jewry respond in the aftermath of the Holocaust? Were the Christians on the wrong side? And where was God?

In the mid–1940s the United States was the great victorious power. American Jews wanted to be thought of as part of the Allied victory, and rightly so; Jewish GIs had fought with courage in the war. As Americans, they were among the great winners. As Jews, they were identified with the corpses, not with General Eisenhower standing and looking horrified at the pile of bodies at the liberated death camps. The rent in the heart of American Jews was between their desire to identify with the Allied victory and the knowledge that, as Jews, they had lost the war. American Jews also felt a need to suppress their own guilt for not having saved more of their relatives. Therefore, in the 1940s they exerted themselves prodigiously in the battle for the creation of Israel. But they could not yet deal with the inescapable message of the *Shoah*—that Jews are other. So they forbade teaching of the Holocaust in their religious schools; it was a subject better to forget.

This taboo began to lift in the 1960s. By then, Jews had achieved essential equality in American society. The social barriers had only half fallen, but it made little difference that certain country clubs still would not admit Jews. The professional and political barriers had come down sufficiently to give Jews an unprecedented sense of self-confidence. In the 1960s, especially after Israel's military triumph in the Six-Day War, it became possible for American Jews to redefine their relationship to the *Shoah*. The Holocaust survivors began to tell their stories and write memoirs. After two decades in America, many of them had achieved material success, and they felt secure enough to organize themselves into a national organization. The bulk of the survivors were entering middle age; thoughts of their mortality and of what messages they were passing on to their children began to trouble them. The survivors had to tell their tale, at the very least in order to hand on the memory of their unique tragedy, and perhaps even to make some sense of it.

A new generation of American Jews was growing to maturity by the end of the 1960s and into the 1970s. For these baby boomers, the Holocaust and Hitler were not a living experience or a living memory. Their elders feared that this generation would become indifferent to Jewish concerns and marry outside the faith. The American Jewish response was to make them painfully aware that the Jews are beset by mortal enemies. The characteristic American Jewish organizations formed at the turn of the century—the American Jewish Committee, the Anti-Defamation League, and the American Jewish Congress—had long been in the business of fighting anti-Semitism, but what could they say to the postwar generation, which was entering college without the slightest concern about the anti-Jewish quotas that had kept many of their parents out of Harvard, Yale, and the other Ivy League schools? These young people might have to face some social anti-Semitism, but they were on the way to professional or business careers on the strength of their skills and talent. Yet the American Jewish community kept telling its young: Don't imagine that the world is a safe place for Jews. What better proof than the Holocaust?

Suddenly the *Shoah* became a usable past for the American Jewish community. By the mid–1970s the Holocaust was becoming a staple of Jewish education. The widespread pressure for Jewish studies programs usually began with a grant to a college or university from the local federation of Jewish philanthropies to teach courses on the Holocaust. A younger generation, which had little or no personal experience of anti-Semitism, was being told about it vicariously but searingly through the study of the Holocaust. Resisting anti-Semitism was invoked again and again as the principal force uniting Jews; it was even offered as the reason to remain Jewish.

But fear of anti-Semitism and pride in Israel did not make an end of assimilation. On the contrary, more and more young Jews were marrying out of the faith. By 1990 a population study done on a large scale by the Council of Jewish Federations and Welfare Funds established beyond a doubt that a significant minority of the Jewish community was in various stages of ceasing to care about its Jewish identity. The reaction to this upsetting knowledge shifted the emphasis from fighting anti-Semitism to a new obsession: promoting Jewish "continuity." So, in the last decade of the twentieth century, the focus on how six million had died shifted to interest in how they had lived. Before 1939 the center of Jewish culture, in all its versions, was not in Tel Aviv or in New York; it was in central and eastern Europe, especially in Poland. The Jewish people lost not only one-third of its entire population, but also the essential center of its spirit and culture. Many American Jews now have recognized that to remember the Holocaust requires that they link their lives to the traditions, the beliefs, and the texts that the Nazis had tried to destroy.

The most painful memories of the Holocaust were experienced and continue to be felt in Europe, in the very places where these terrible events happened. At the end of the Second World War, few Jewish survivors remained in the lands of their birth. In the decades after the *Shoah* it was not easy to answer the question: How can you, a Jew, live among the murderers of your people? The citizens of almost every country in Europe faced equally difficult questions after the war, but often the deepest moral issues were avoided. The Germans have gone furthest in coping with the Nazi past because they could not pretend that the Nazis were not their own. And so the German government, with majority support, has been dealing with its national guilt by making large restitution payments to the surviving victims of the Holocaust. The French, Italians, Austrians, Dutch, Norwegians, Swiss, Ukrainians, and other Europeans know that there were Fascists among them who collaborated with the Nazis, just as there were some who rescued Jews. But throughout Europe the story is essentially the same: almost every society wants to maintain that its majority was on the side of the angels and that those who helped the Nazis were an unrepresentative minority, an aberration. Almost everywhere there has been a reluctance to make peace with the past. But one after another, European governments have been forced by embarrassing revelations to confront the failure of their leaders to give a full and honest account of their nation's complicity in the plunder and murder of the Jews during the Holocaust. None of these societies will be at peace with itself until this dark chapter of its history is brought to light in a spirit of contrition and deep moral reflection.

Volumes have been written about what the Catholic and Protestant Churches did or did not do to help the Jews during the *Shoah*. Much less has been said about the Holocaust as a crisis for Christian religion and culture. Almost all the perpetrators had been baptized. How can a religion that teaches love and peace produce so many mass murderers? There is, of course, a ready defense: Christians sometimes fall away from grace and are unworthy of the teaching that they have learned. But for some Christian theologians this response does not absolve their religion of responsibility. For them, a terrible doubt has been sown by the Holocaust. Did the crucifixion happen again from 1939 to 1945 with the Christians on the wrong side?

The scene of the Jews forced to march to the railroad sidings through silent or jeering crowds was eerily reminiscent of Jesus carrying his cross along the Via Dolorosa on the way to Golgotha. Even the scene at the foot of the cross, when lots were cast for the disposal of Jesus' cloak, had its parallel in the eagerness with which Jewish property was divided moments after the Jews were torn from their homes. The thought has not escaped serious Christians that perhaps the Jews were reenacting the continuing Jewish role of suffering and dying alone, outside society. Had those Christians who allowed it to happen, including many priests and ministers, failed their own humanity?

Thoughtful Christians cannot avoid asking themselves: Did the drama of Jesus occur only once nineteen centuries ago, or have the Jews been reliving it, century after century, through all the persecutions they have suffered? These are the questions that keep burrowing under the very self-respect of the majority society. So in recent years the major branches of Christianity have been asking forgiveness for the anti-Semitism they once taught and for their inaction during the years when the mass murders were being carried out in the very sight of the churches. The Lutheran Church has now disavowed Martin Luther's anti-Semitism, and the Vatican has announced its repentance of all the negative aspects of its relations with Jews through the ages. After the Holocaust, Judaism and Christianity have been moving toward each other. This is a happy development—but was the price too high?

The terrible aloneness of the Jews during the Nazi genocide has forced Jews to face an equally devastating question: Where was God? I have never found a way to absolve God. I find no consolation in the theological formulation that God is a limited power who encourages humanity to do good but is not responsible for the pain and evil in the world. Long before the Nazis appeared, Mordecai Kaplan was talking of a "limited God" as an answer to the problem of evil. But such a God is created essentially in the image of a preacher who has the power to exhort but not to command and therefore bears no responsibility for what is happening in the world.

The most elegant version of this idea was fashioned by Martin Buber in his book *Eclipse of God* (1952). Buber invoked the kabbalistic image that God sometimes "hides His face" from the world, and at such times darkness reigns. Buber modified this notion to suggest not that God had chosen to go away, but that some dark power had eclipsed him for a time. But what right, I once asked Buber, did God have to go away or to permit himself to be eclipsed, while my grandfather and all of my mother's brothers and sisters and their children were being murdered in concentration camps?

I have always been even angrier with those who find reasons with which to justify the way God had acted in the 1930s and 1940s. In the Bible, as we have shown, the usual explanation for the suffering of the Jews is that they had disobeyed God and thus deserved to be punished. What sin was deserving of six million deaths? The ultra-Orthodox Jewish theologian Rabbi Joel Teitelbaum, the rebbe of Satmar, insisted in his book, *On Salvation and Redemption* (1967), that the Jews were punished by God for the sin of Zionism, for refusing, as they had been commanded, to wait passively for the Messiah; the Zionists had rebelled against God by creating the State of Israel by their own hand. Many Zionists, including David Ben-Gurion, argued the opposite, that the Holocaust was punishment for failing to learn the lessons of history, for remaining in Europe after the rise of Hitler in 1933 instead of joining the builders of the Jewish national homeland. I find both of these answers—blaming the victims for being either too Zionist or not Zionist enough—to be not only arrogant but also obscene.

Another answer is to deny God. A number of my friends who were firmly Orthodox before 1933 became fierce atheists. I have not joined them because I keep rereading the book of Job in the Bible. Every conceivable woe happens to this righteous man. What could he have done to deserve such suffering? He rejects all the explanations that his solicitous friends try to offer him. Job appeals to God for an answer. Replying out of the whirlwind, God assures Job that there is meaning to the world, and even to Job's dreadful suffering, but any explanation is beyond human understanding. Job knew that he could not continue to scream. He began a new family, acquired his flocks and herds, and opened his tent to all who came into his sight. Job remembered what he had lost, but he lived on. And yet, even as I read these verses over and over again, I keep asking the question: What about Job's children? Job survived the tragedy of their deaths, but could he ever forgive God?

The conversation about the Holocaust that lives with me—and haunts me—is one that never took place. Rabbi Aaron Rokeach, the rebbe of Belz in southeastern Poland, lost his entire family—his wife and all his children and their children—in the *Shoah*. He never again mentioned them or even said prayers in any visible ritual in their memory. I was in his presence in Tel Aviv in the summer of 1949. I tried to get the rebbe to talk to me about my grandfather and my uncles, who had been his disciples and friends, but he simply did not respond, not even with a gesture. The dead were too holy, so his closest associates explained, to need words. The rebbe of Belz had accepted the tragedy—his and everyone else's—in silence, even as he was rebuilding his Hasidic court in the Holy Land. Silence and rebuilding: that was how he spoke for his faith in God.

Even though I was once overwhelmed by the silence of the rebbe of Belz, I cannot join him. I must light candles in memory of those in my family who died in the *Shoah,* and I continue to grieve over the horror of their deaths. The Jew within me cannot forget the gas chambers, but what I most want to remember are the children who published a newspaper in Theresienstadt; the inmates of Auschwitz who held forbidden prayer services; and the heroes of the Warsaw ghetto, who conducted schools in defiance of Nazi edicts.

Faith after the Holocaust cannot be found in some theological formula. It is manifest in the courage of those who lived as Jews to the last moment and the courage of the survivors, who found the will to begin again.

CHAPTER 17

THE FUTURE

At the end of the nineteenth century Jews were frightened and uncertain. In czarist Russia Jews knew that the government was on the side of the makers of pogroms. In central and western Europe anti-Semitism was on the rise again in the very lands in which it was supposed to be evaporating. Everywhere long-accepted religious truths were in question. In response, the Jews were splintering into conflicting political and religious factions. Each seemed to offer hope and faith, but could any one of the new ideologies really raise the Jews beyond fear and despair? The mood of the 1890s was captured in a famous Hebrew novel, Mordecai Feuerberg's *Le'an? (Whither?)*, about a young man who is tormented by the counterpulls of all the competing ideologies faced by the Diaspora Jew in the modern world. So he asks himself: Where next? In what direction am I to go?

It is now a century later. The Jews are no longer powerless. They have a state of their own, and in the Diaspora Jews are more at home, everywhere, than they ever were before. But Feuerberg's question lingers, and it still demands an answer. The greatest threat today is not from the anti-Semites, for they are less powerful now than they were at any point in this century. It is not even from assimilation, because such losses have occurred before in Jewish history, and the continuity of this people has been guaranteed by the Jews who have chosen, and keep choosing, to affirm themselves as Jews. The explosive problem today is the age-old disease of factionalism. The latest outbreak is as sharp as it has ever been in Jewish history, and it threatens the very future of the Jewish people.

ISRAEL AT FIFTY

In 1948 the Jews of the world were more at peace with one another than they had been for centuries. The new State of Israel became the central focus and concern of world Jewry because its doors were open to any Jew who needed a haven and a home. Immediately after the state was declared in 1948, hundreds of thousands of Jews poured into the Jewish homeland from refugee camps in Europe, from Arab countries throughout the Middle East and North Africa, and in smaller numbers from the Western democracies. In recent years, hundreds of thousands of Russian and Ethiopian Jews have surged into Israel, bringing the Jewish population to nearly five million. Culturally, too, Israel's achievements have been impressive; its universities and research institutes are part of the international grid of technological development. Its writers and musicians have achieved world acclaim. And the revival of traditional Jewish learning in Israel's religious academies, the yeshivot, and in non-Orthodox institutes of Jewish studies have surpassed all expectations.

The vast majority of Israelis are confident of their nation's economy and its strength to stand up to its enemies, and the Jews of the Diaspora remain devoted to the only state in which Jews are the majority and in which Saturday is the day of rest. These are indices of a confident future, and yet, on the happy occasion of Israel's jubilee year, Jews everywhere were asking themselves and each other the old question: "If it is so good, why is it so bad?"

It is so good because Jews in this century have reasserted their legendary power to rebuild after the *Shoah,* to reaffirm themselves as Jews. Yes, there have been disaffiliations; some, like the parents of the United States Secretary of State Madeleine Albright, have walked away from their Jewishness. However, most Jews, especially the survivors of the Holocaust, rebuilt whatever they could of the Jewish life that had been destroyed. The State of Israel is the major monument to this power of regeneration, but this has been evident everywhere in the Jewish world. The rise of the Jews in the United States to an important role in most aspects of American life has been extraordinary. That the Jews in the former Soviet Union found the will to assert themselves as Jews is a near miracle. It is just as startling that, in the countries in Europe in which Jewish communities were totally destroyed by the Holocaust, a remarkable rebirth is beginning to take place. The Jewish populations are small, but the fact that they care to reestablish their Jewishness is another manifestation of the age-old capacity of Jews to rise from the ashes.

So the question needs to be asked again: With all that has happened in the last fifty years that is so good, why is it so bad? Because the Jews have reasserted their unceasing capacity to be at war with themselves. And most tragic of all, these factional battles keep being waged not by wicked people who set out consciously to harm other Jews, but by well-intentioned people who believe they are acting in God's name. The rebbe of Kotzk once said that when Satan wants to destroy, he does not ask you to commit an evil deed, he sends you to do a good deed at the wrong time and in the wrong place.

Nothing was more virtuous two thousand years ago than to rebel against pagan Rome in the name of pure Jewish monotheism, and nothing could have been more destructive. Nothing could seem more virtuous today than to cry out, "I want the Messiah now," but to act out this messianic wish in the occupied West Bank is to court death and destruction. If the Messiah is coming soon, why make any accommodation with the Arabs? Why give up an inch of the Holy Land? God will save the faithful from the consequences of their actions. The armed prophets on the West Bank and their ultranationalist supporters are staking the Jewish future on the same bet that the Zealots made when they rose up against Rome—that God could not possibly let Jerusalem be destroyed. Such thinking is nothing short of madness; it is the wild streak taking hold of a Jewish sect of true believers that claims to know God's intentions.

I have been warning the Jewish world for many years that the God who could sit silent while the Jews of Europe were destroyed gives no guarantee that the Jewish settlements on the West Bank and, for that matter, the cities of Israel would be saved in the wars of Gog and Magog. The point must be made openly and unmistakably. The greatest threat to the Jewish people today comes not from the outside; it comes from the element of the Jewish people that regards itself as beyond criticism and sees itself as the judge and jury of all the rest. I am speaking of some of the ultra-Orthodox and of the ultranationalists who are convinced of the manifest destiny of Israel.

The famous historian of the Kabbalah and of Jewish messianism, Gershom Scholem, warned many times against calling the State of Israel "the first root of our redemption." The Jewish nation, he insisted, is a human solution to contemporary political problems. To make of it an instrument of the messianic drama is the greatest of heresies. The Jews must create a just and decent society for all its inhabitants; only then will it be a reflection of the Jewish spirit.

It is no exaggeration to say that the contemporary Jewish messianists who wrap themselves in the cloak of legitimacy and claim to be safeguarding Jewish continuity are really the lineal heirs of Shabbetai Zvi, the false messiah of the seventeenth century. Then, as now, many eminent rabbis were seduced by those who proclaimed that the Messiah was at hand. The time has come for the Jews in this generation to realize that anyone who would condone the assassination of Israel's prime minister and would fan Arab angers in the nuclear age is living with the presumption that the Messiah will arrive before the bill for their actions comes due in the form of devastating terrorism and war against the people of Israel. Those who say that their political doctrine is what God intends always fail, and they always bring tragedy. May the leaders of Orthodox Jewry, and all other Jews, have the wisdom and the courage to raise their voices against the new Shabbateans before it is too late.

If Israel is to prosper in its second fifty years and beyond, it also must free itself of certain long-held assumptions inherited from its secular Zionist founders. Theodor Herzl created the Zionist movement at the end of the last century on the assumption that nation-states, each representing the traditions and culture of the overwhelming majority, are the ideal form of social organization. Today, almost every developed nation, including Israel, is becoming more multiethnic. But more important, more than 700,000 Palestinian Arabs (20 percent of the population) are citizens of Israel. If Israel is to be a "Jewish and democratic state," it must heed the ancient outcry of the prophet Amos—"Behold, you are to me just like the Ethiopians"—and treat Arabs and everyone else as equals. It is immoral to proclaim the

Palestinians to be interlopers in the land that God gave to the Jews. Those who act on this assertion have forgotten that God gave the Holy Land to the Jews on condition that the stranger be protected, "for you were once strangers in the land of Egypt."

The world is one, and not only morally. It is also true, very tangibly, in the economic realm. In the next century, as the world increasingly becomes a global village, the rules of economic survival will be radically different than they were in the centuries of mercantilism, when the objective was to strengthen one's own national economy at the expense of another in a zero-sum game; the global market is now too interlocked to play by the rules of previous centuries. Therefore, the Jewish state is already moving away from the separatist, self-sufficient economy that the Zionist pioneers had envisioned. An enormous effort and huge amounts of money had gone into making the desert bloom, but producing corn or wheat in Israel through irrigation simply does not pay. Israel now imports much of its food. Like most postindustrial nations, Israel will depend less and less on primary production and more on technological advances and on trade with the nations of the world and, when peace comes, with its neighbors.

Yitzhak Rabin was shot because he knew that Israel could not survive alone and defiant. Those who agree with Rabin and those who do not are now in violent confrontation, and the strife is worsening. The moderate majority of the Jewish world must not give in to the "armed prophets." Their messianic delusions threaten to plunge Israel into civil and regional war.

THE END OF JEWISH UNITY

The new messianists, and the ultra-Orthodox who are often their kindred spirits, are not only misleading Israel, they are also threatening the Jewish world as a whole. Perhaps the greatest achievement of the

Jews in the modern era is that they redefined the principle on which to base Jewish unity. For many centuries the unifying principle had been strict conformity to religious faith and practice; anyone who dissented, such as Uriel Da Costa and Baruch Spinoza, was excommunicated. In the nineteenth and twentieth centuries, this form of coercion fell out of favor, and Jewish communities became voluntary associations. Increasingly, semibelievers and nonbelievers took active roles in Jewish communal affairs without being subjected to any religious tests. When Theodor Herzl founded political Zionism, he insisted that his movement was wide open to all who affirmed Jewish nationalism. The tent of the Jewish national revival would be large enough so that all factions could dwell in it, and indeed the Zionist movement has remained to this very day a place where representatives of most Jewish ideologies and religious positions coexist. The vast majority of Jews today agree that they are bound together by many practical concerns, chief among them support for the State of Israel and the rescue of imperiled Jews wherever they may be. But this coalition also harbors a deep sense that the Jews have a long and indissoluble connection with the ancient sacred texts. Even those who do not read them as a code of religious conduct remember this learning and these traditions as the inheritance of all Jews.

To be sure, this coalition was always untidy. It was boycotted with special vehemence by religious minorities who barricaded themselves against everything new. Nonetheless, a turn was made in the modern era: the Jews refashioned themselves to include every individual who thought of himself or herself as a Jew for whatever reason. This was proved in the 1950s, when the first prime minister of Israel, David Ben-Gurion, sent a questionnaire to the leading scholars and thinkers of that day, asking them how they would define Jewish identity. Most agreed that anyone who asserts that he or she cares as a Jew is part of the Jewish people.

The great turning came in the aftermath of the Six-Day War in June 1967, when the messianists began to settle the West Bank. Since that time, the pluralist consensus has been under vehement attack both in Israel and in the Diaspora. The new Shabbateans have denounced their opponents—that is, most Jews—as the enemies of God. Some of the ultra-Orthodox (chiefly the followers of the Lubavitcher rebbe) have joined the messianists in insisting that the West Bank must be held by Jews, for that is God's will. The bulk of the ultra-Orthodox have become more separatist and more insistent that they are the only true Jews. These zealots nearly dominate the Orthodox community as a whole. As a result, the more liberal, "modern Orthodox" element, which has been part of the broad Jewish coalition, has been moving ever more into this separatist camp.

The surest barometer of the breakdown of Jewish unity since 1967 is in the radical change of the religious Zionists. At its very beginnings nearly one hundred years ago, this group, which was then called Mizrahi, broke with most of the rabbis of that day by joining the World Zionist Organization, led by the notoriously secular Jew, Theodor Herzl. In the politics of Israel from 1948 to 1967, the National Religious Party (which represented Mizrahi in Israel) was in every coalition government led by the Labor Zionists. The essential policy of Mizrahi was to defend the inner life of Jews in the larger pluralist society; its leaders made no claim on the foreign policy of the government of Israel in the name of a higher truth or the imminence of the messianic redemption. Today the religious parties hold enough seats in the Jewish parliament to bring down any government that strays too far from their vision of the Jewish state.

Whatever courtesy had once existed among the various Jewish religious movements is now essentially gone. I will cite just a few examples. In Germany, when the Nazis came to power in 1933, the chief rabbi of Berlin was Leo Baeck, a Reform rabbi whose authority on communal matters was almost universally accepted among the Jews. Today in Germany, the Orthodox leaders of the organized Jewish communities are distinctly unfriendly to the emerging Reform congregations. In Great Britain, the Jewish service celebrating the twenty-fifth anniversary of King George V was presided over by the chief rabbi of the major Orthodox community, Dr. Joseph Herman Hertz, who invited the leading rabbis of both the liberal and the Reform Jewish communities to take part. In 1997 when Hugo Gryn, the rabbi of the West London Synagogue (Reform), died, the present chief rabbi, Dr. Jonathan Sacks, assured the ultra-Orthodox rabbis in London that in eulogizing the deceased at a memorial meeting he would praise Gryn as a Holocaust survivor, but he would not grant him any legitimacy as a rabbi. Even as Sacks bowed to sectarian pressure, he was trying to maintain some civility within the coalition, but the task had become infinitely harder. In the United States, the Synagogue Council of America had existed for many decades as a kind of holding company to which the rabbinic and congregational associations of the three major denominations—Orthodox, Conservative, and Reform—all belonged. Orthodox representatives had long sat on this body, but the council was disbanded when the ultra-Orthodox insisted that working together with Reform and Conservative rabbis on religious issues might be regarded as legitimizing "the destroyers of Judaism."

THE ASCENDANCY OF WOMEN

And yet, surprisingly, despite the increasing and embittered divisions among the Jewish religious groups, there is a deeper tide moving the various elements in the religious spectrum in the same direction— toward an intensification of Jewish learning and practice and toward more inclusion of women in Jewish life. In the next century most synagogues, of all persuasions, will no longer be dominated by men. This change will refashion Judaism.

Orthodox men who have entered the secular world know that their daughters, almost all of whom will receive higher education, cannot be treated as if they were still living in the mythical Anatevka of the last century. Some Orthodox moderates have opted, therefore, to celebrate bat mitzvah in a private ceremony at home or in some manner in the synagogue, even though they know (or have suppressed the knowledge) that the rite, invented by Rabbi Mordecai Kaplan in 1922, had been denounced by Orthodox rabbis as a heretical act. What has kept the modern Orthodox from allowing girls the same honor accorded to boys is the truth expressed by the sociologist Emile Durkheim, who observed that religion is the slowest element in society to change. Nonetheless, the change toward gender equality is inevitable because the religious laws, which essentially treat women as not much wiser or more mature than children, are untenable. Those strict constructionists who defend the status quo by asserting that the oral law is divinely ordained and immutable, whatever anguish it may cause, misunderstand the intent of the very texts they so venerate.

The ancient rabbis who created the oral law were not Orthodox hard-liners; they were religious revolutionaries who opposed the orthodox leaders of their day—the entrenched priests of the Temple, who regarded the early rabbis as interlopers and as traducers of the inherited religion. On a number of critical issues, the rabbis followed their moral sense by interpreting away the plain meaning of Scripture. For example, the biblical law of the "rebellious son" was nullified by the rabbis of the Talmud, who declared that the right of the father to have a disobedient child put to death was not to be taken literally, for such an act is morally repugnant. The "rebellious son," they agreed, is really a parable to frighten those who would disobey their parents. In the second century C.E. Rabbi Akiva effectively abolished all the executions by making the law of evidence in capital cases so strict that no court could ever find a defendant guilty. He declared that any court that sentences a defendant to death even once in a generation is to be regarded as an evil court. Obviously, Rabbi Akiva had examined the death penalties prescribed in the Torah and, in the name of the repeated calls in the Bible for mercy and love of all God's children, found them to be morally unacceptable.

The rabbis whose arguments are recorded in the Talmud were equally revolutionary in protecting the rights of women. In the Hebrew Bible there is no limit on the power of the husband to divorce his wife and to leave her without any means. The rabbis therefore created the *ketubah* (marriage contract). Every groom had to agree that he would not capriciously divorce his wife and that he or his estate would be responsible for her well-being. The rabbis even insisted that no marriage could be permitted without such a contract. Here, too, the rabbis of the Talmud were expressing a moral commitment that went beyond what they could find in the biblical text.

In modern times, the movement for the inclusion of women was initiated by some of the great Orthodox figures of this century. In the first decades of the twentieth century the then-rebbe of Belz (with whom the rebbe of Gur, in Poland, and the Hafetz Haim, in Lithuania, publicly agreed) encouraged the creation of schools for girls in which they would study Torah. The reason given was that times had changed and therefore the old assertion in the rabbinic sources that teaching a girl Torah was no better than teaching her foolishness could no longer be followed. In more recent decades the Lubavitcher rebbe insisted that young women should be taught the "inner meaning of the Torah." The rebbe recognized that women were now becoming highly educated, and they needed to have an equally deep Jewish education because they continued to have primary responsibility for raising children. Women, therefore, should be taught Talmud, even though such practice had been barred for many centuries. These great men did not shrink from saying that a changing society required committed Jews to discard well-established prohibitions.

The sorrow of our time is that the halachists of today, who claim to be their successors, lack the moral courage to rise above a strict constructionist view of rabbinic precedent. At this moment, the great issue for Jews who want to live within the tradition is equality and dignity for women. This can be achieved only if every aspect of Jewish law and practice that demeans women is nullified. This effort will succeed because Jewish women have been at the forefront of this struggle for the past three decades, and their gains thus far have been impressive. Since 1972 women have been ordained as rabbis in all but the Orthodox movements, and today two Orthodox synagogues in New York City have commissioned learned Jewish women to perform some restricted rabbinical functions, even though these women have not been ordained. Change is coming in all parts of the Jewish world. The rationalizations may differ, but everywhere law is following life.

ORTHODOX TRIUMPHALISM

Hard-liners among the Orthodox would have us believe that only their brand of Judaism is authentic and viable. They divide the Jewish people into two camps: the Torah-true faithful and the Godless heretics who will vanish from the Jewish fold. This thesis ignores the fact that the Jewish people has never been a monolith. Before the destruction of the Second Temple, the Jews were composed of many rival sects. The Temple itself was in the hands of the Sadducees, a priestly party consisting of strict constructionists who did not accept many of the interpretations of the Pharisees, the party of rabbis. In addition, there were the Essenes, the name given to monastic groups that lived under rules of stricter purity than those the rabbis imposed upon themselves.

The Pharisees proved viable because they redefined Judaism around the synagogue, a kind of portable Temple, the perfect format for an exiled people. Having taken command of Jewish communal life, the rabbis kept a watchful eye on all Jewish dissident factions. They banned all contenders for legitimacy, including the Karaites, a sect that refused to follow rabbinic interpretations of biblical texts; the kabbalists, who searched for the profound secrets in the texts of the Bible; and the various messianic movements, which held that redemption was near. To all of these dissenters the Orthodox power structure said: You are heretics, you represent the revolt against God's word. You must be cut off—excommunicated.

Rabbinic triumphalism has declared essentially that everything pluralistic in Jewish experience is inauthentic or heretical and therefore must be disavowed. The function of this Orthodox account of Jewish history is essentially to delegitimize all of the modern Jewish movements from the time of Moses Mendelssohn to our own day. All who stray from the true path of Orthodoxy will fall away; their descendants will be lost to Judaism. In the Diaspora this argument is buttressed with statistics showing that the intermarriage rate is far higher among non-Orthodox Jews. The incontrovertible fact is that all of the modern Jewish movements, the very ones from which Orthodoxy proclaims it will save us, arose because in the course of the nineteenth and twentieth centuries Orthodoxy could not keep most of its children within its ranks. Therefore, can the Orthodox establishment really claim that its version of Judaism is the only effective antidote to assimilation?

The story that is very seldom told in the Jewish community is the movement *away* from Orthodoxy. Every recent study of the Orthodox in the Diaspora, and especially in the United States, has concluded that this group as a whole is not growing in relationship to all the other major Jewish denominations. Even as the ultra-Orthodox have been growing in strength, numbers, and vibrancy, the modern Orthodox seem to be declining. In his analysis of the 1990 National Population Survey of American Jewry, the sociologist Egon Mayer found that of the respondents who were raised "Orthodox," only 22 percent still identified with that branch of Judaism. Of those who said they were raised Conservative, 57 percent still identified themselves as such. And in the case of the Reform, the percentage jumped to 78 percent. As the birthrate among the Orthodox is at least twice as high as among adherents of other movements in Judaism, the proportion of the Orthodox should be rising from year to year, but it has not. In 1970 the National Jewish Population Survey found that 11 percent of the respondents identified themselves as Orthodox; twenty years later the figure had dropped to 6 percent. The only possible explanation is that there is a substantial and continuing exodus from the Orthodox fold.

If Orthodoxy is not the answer to Jewish continuity, what is? For the past two centuries, the organizing principle of modern Jewry has been pluralism; people who do not believe in one another's Jewish legitimacy in theory are nevertheless partners in practice. They share the same affirmations that held together the Jewish factions two thousand years ago. Both the Zealots who initiated the revolt against Rome and those who opposed military action agreed that the Jewish religion and culture were different from all the others in the world of their day. They disagreed only as to whether that difference was best preserved by war or by political accommodation. The Zionists, the Orthodox, and the religious liberals today have different assessments of what Jews should do, but their purpose is the same—to preserve the Jewish people as a unique and distinct entity in the world.

The second core value that Jews have always shared is the belief in chosenness. It does not really matter who chose the Jews. What does matter is that they have this angel or demon, conscience or neurosis, always riding on their back. The idea of chosenness has held the Jews together and has kept them going. From ancient times to this very day, the Jews—other and chosen—have continued to argue with one another and to live in tension with the world around them. Jews cannot leave one another alone because they are the heirs of many generations of ancestors who have yet to reach full agreement as to what the exact duty of the Jew should be. They cannot leave the non-Jewish world alone because they are heirs to an idea that pursues them relentlessly and is held aloft in pride: the Jews have an indispensable role in perfecting the whole. Jews of all persuasions continue to hold fast to the dream of their ancestors that at the end of days hatred, poverty, and injustice will be no more. Jews have often despaired of reaching that day, but they have always known that they must work to perfect and redeem the world.

In the decades following the Holocaust, some Jewish theologians were talking of the death of God or of a limited God. Or the ineffable was reduced to some pious rhetoric about our highest ideals for the remaking of society. We thought that therapy would bring us to psychological balance without having to bother with questions of conscience or faith. But God has returned from exile. According to the 1997 Annual Survey of American Jewish Opinion, conducted by the American Jewish Committee, 63 percent of the respondents agreed with the statement that there definitely is a God, and another 22 percent said probably; only 3 percent said definitely no. These results were unexpected. Most American Jews do not attend synagogue often, and they show few external signs of piety. And yet the majority affirms God. Why? Because there must be more to life than two careers, two BMWs, and two psychiatrists.

This turning back to God and tradition is occurring among all the major Jewish factions. Orthodox yeshivas and day schools are proliferating all over the world. Jews everywhere are returning to adult study. The individuals, mostly Orthodox, who are faithful to the *Daf Yomi* (daily study of Talmud) now number many thousands. A new literacy initiative that Reform Jewish leaders have launched to bring Jews home to Torah is attracting a growing following. Reform and Conservative Jews are forming Torah study groups in their homes, at their places of work, and on the Internet. Even Mapam, the ultrasecular, left-wing party in Israel, now holds a *tikkun* (an all-night study session of classic Jewish texts) in Tel Aviv on Shavuot, the festival celebrating the giving of the Torah. Everywhere there is a marked revival of interest in traditional religious texts by people who want to understand themselves as Jews. The sacred literature and traditions of Judaism are not the domain of any single branch of the Jewish people; they belong to all Jews.

But why at the end of the twentieth century are these ancient texts so precious? Because they are the key to understanding what the God of our ancestors demands of us. To be a Jew is to be commanded; to take actions because they are right, not because they bring personal comfort or material gain. Had Abraham wanted tranquillity and prosperity, he would have carried on his father's idol business. To be a Jew is to open one's tent on all four sides so that any stranger in need of food and shelter can enter from every direction. To be a Jew is to believe in *tikkun olam*, that the world can be redeemed. To be a Jew is to be carried by the current of the ancient Jewish river that keeps on flowing. The journey will continue.

CHRONOLOGY OF JEWISH HISTORY

BCE

Ca. 2000	Time of Abraham and Sarah
1004–928	Reigns of David and Solomon
722	Destruction of Nothern Kingdom
586	Destruction of Jerusalem; Exile to Babylonia
520–15	Temple Rebuilt
332	Alexander the Great Conquers the Land of Israel
167	Hasmonean (Maccabee) Rebellion Begins
164	Judah Maccabee Captures Jerusalem and Rededicates the Temple

CE

37	Caligula Declares Himself Deity; Herod Captures Jerusalem
38	Anti-Jewish Riots in Alexandria
50	Death of Philo
66	Revolt Against Rome Begins
67	Zealots Take Control of Jerusalem
70	Destruction of Second Temple
73	Fall of Masada
132–135	Bar Kokhba Revolt
390	Jerusalem Talmud Completed
499	Babylonian Talmud Completed
638	Jerusalem Conquered by Arabs
1096	Crusaders Massacre the Jews of the Rhineland
1105	Death of Rashi
1141	Death of Judah Halevi
1147–1149	Second Crusade
1189–1192	Third Crusade
1204	Death of Moses Mainmonides
1242	Burning of Talmud in Paris
1263	Disputation in Barcelona
1348	The Black Death
1391	Massacres and Forced Conversions in Spain
1492	Expulsion from Spain
1497	Expulsion from Portugal
1508	Death of Isaac Abrabanel
1544	Martin Luther Denounces the Jews
1556	Burning of Marranos in Ancona
1569	Expulsion of Jews from Papal States; Death of Doña Gracia Nasi
1572	Death of Isaac Luria

1581 The Netherlands Proclaims Independence from Spain

1590 Marranos Settle in Amsterdam

1609 Death of Judah Loew (Maharal of Prague)

1640 Suicide of Uriel Da Costa

1654 Jews Arrive in New Amsterdam (New York)

1656 Readmission of Jews to England; Baruch Spinoza
      Excommunicated

1665 Shabbetai Zvi Proclaims Himself the Messiah

1677 Death of Baruch Spinoza

1680 Death of Nathan Gaza

1760 Death of the Baal Shem Tov

1769 Mendelssohn-Lavater Controversy

1772 First Excommunication of the Hasidim

1776 American Declaration of Independence

1783 Mendelssohn Publishes *Jerusalem*

1786 Death of Moses Mendelssohn

1789 French Revolution

1791 French National Assembly Grants Jews Full Civil Rights

1797 Death of Elijah Gaon of Vilna

1799 David Friedlander's Letter to Teller

1807 French Sanhedrin

1812 Death of Shneur Zalman of Lyady

1818 Hamburg Reform Temple

1839 Death of Moshe (Schreiber) Sofer

1846 Isaac Mayer Wise Arrives in the United States

1856 Death of Heinrich Heine

1871 Pogrom in Odessa

1881 Death of Benjamin Disraeli

1881–1882 Pogroms Sweep Southern Russia

1894 Dreyfus Affair

1896 Herzl Publishes *Der Judenstaat*

1897   First World Zionist Congress

1903   Kishinev Pogrom

1904   Death of Theodor Herzl

1914   World War I Begins

1917   Russian Revolution

1919   Death of Rosa Luxemburg

1924   Death of Franz Kafka

1929   Death of Franz Rosenzweig

1929   Wall Street Crash

1933   Hitler Becomes German Chancellor

1935   Death of Isaac Abraham Kook

1936   Arab Riots

1939   Beginning of World War II; Death of Sigmund Freud

1940   Assassination of Leon Trotsky

1943   Warsaw Ghetto Uprising

1945   Germany Surrenders

1948   Establishment of the State of Israel

1955   Death of Albert Einstein

1965   Death of Martin Buber

1967   Six-Day War; Jerusalem Reunited; West Bank Occupied

1972   Hebrew Union College Ordains First Woman Rabbi

1973   Yom Kippur War; Death of David Ben-Gurion

1983   Death of Mordecai Kaplan

1998   Fiftieth Anniversary of Israel

NOTES

INTRODUCTION

    1. Ronald W. Clark, *Einstein: The Life and Times* (New York: World Publishing, 1971).

CHAPTER 1

    1. Introduction, *The Zionist Idea* (Philadelphia: Jewish Publication Society, 1997), 94.
    2. Ahad Ha'am, *The Zionist Idea*, 71–72.

CHAPTER 3

    1. Quoted from *De Superstitione* by Augustine in his *City of God*, 6.11.
    2. *Pro Flacco*, 28.69.

CHAPTER 4

1. Philo, *De Legatione ad Gaium*.

2. Josephus, *The Jewish War*, bk. 7, p. 494.

3. Reuben Ainsztein, *The Warsaw Ghetto Revolt* (New York: Holocaust Library, 1979), 36–37.

4. As quoted in Menahem Stern, *Greek and Latin Authors on Jews and Judaism* (Jerusalem: Israel Academy of Sciences and Humanities, 1974–), 2:103.

5. Salo Wittmayer Baron, *A Social and Religious History of the Jews* (New York: Columbia Univ. Press, 1952), 1:170.

CHAPTER 5

1. Jacob R. Marcus, *The Jew in the Medieval World* (Cincinnati: Sinai Press, 1938), 43–47.

2. Franz Kobler, ed., *A Treasury of Jewish Letters* (New York: Farrar, Straus and Young, 1952), 1:98.

3. Isadore Twersky, *A Maimonides Reader* (New York: Behrman House, 1972), 3, 4.

4. Salo Wittmayer Baron, *A Social and Religious History of the Jews* (New York: Columbia Univ. Press, 1952), 9:85.

CHAPTER 6

1. As quoted by David M. Gitlitz, *Secrecy and Deceit* (Philadelphia: Jewish Publication Society, 1996), 9.

2. Franz Kobler, ed., *A Treasury of Jewish Letters* (New York: Farrar, Straus and Young, 1952), 1:326–27.

3. Kobler, ed., *Jewish Letters*, 1:211–12.

CHAPTER 7

1. Cecil Roth, *Doña Gracia of the House of Nasi* (Philadelphia: Jewish Publication Society, 1948), 84.

2. Roth, *Doña Gracia*, 77.

CHAPTER 8

1. H. H. Ben-Sasson, ed., *A History of the Jewish People* (Cambridge: Harvard Univ. Press, 1976), 709.

2. From Franz Kobler, ed., *A Treasury of Jewish Letters* (New York: Farrar, Straus and Young, 1952), 2:526.

3. Thomas Yoseloff, *Gluckel of Hameln, Written by Herself* (New York: Thomas Yoseloff, 1965), 45–46.

CHAPTER 9

1. Quoted in Jacob R. Marcus, *The Jew in the Medieval World* (Cincinnati: Sinai Press, 1938), 166.

2. Marcus, *Medieval World,* 167.

3. Quoted from *Freiburger Rundbrief,* no. 3 (1997): 175.

4. Jacob Katz, *Exclusiveness and Tolerance: Studies in Jewish-Gentile Relations in Medieval and Modern Times* (London: Oxford Univ. Press, 1961), 167.

5. Katz, *Exclusiveness,* 168.

6. Abraham J. Heschel, *The Circle of the Baal Shem Tov: Studies in Hasidism* (Chicago: Univ. of Chicago Press, 1985), 40.

7. Spinoza, *A Theologico-Political Tractate,* trans. R. H. M. Elwes (New York: Dover Publications Inc., 1951), 54–56

CHAPTER 10

1. Quoted from Israel Cohen, *Vilna* (Philadelphia: Jewish Publication Society, 1943), 235–37.

2. Rabbi Yosef Wineberg, *Lessons in Tanya* (Brooklyn: Kehot Publication Society, 1988), 2: 483, 404.

CHAPTER 11

1. Arthur Hertzberg, *The French Enlightenment and the Jews* (New York: Columbia Univ. Press, 1968), 284–85.

2. Quoted by Hannah Arendt, *The Jew as Pariah* (New York: Grove Press, 1978), 48.

3. Quoted by Paul R. Mendes-Flohr and Jehuda Reinharz, eds., *The Jew in the Modern World* (New York: Oxford Univ. Press, 1980), 222–23.

4. Hertzberg, *French Enlightenment,* 300.

CHAPTER 12

1. Arthur Hertzberg, *Judaism* (New York: G. Braziller, 1961), 46.

2. Arthur Hertzberg, *The Jews in America: Four Centuries of an Uneasy Encounter: A History* (New York: Simon & Schuster, 1989), 115.

3. Sefton D. Temkin, *Isaac Mayer Wise: Shaping American Judaism* (New York: Oxford Univ. Press, 1992), 73.

CHAPTER 13

1. Marvin Lowenthal, *The Dream of Theodor Herzl* (New York: Grosset & Dunlap, 1962), 7 .

2. Joseph Nedava, *Trotsky and the Jews* (Philadelphia: Jewish Publication Society of America, 1971), 68.

CHAPTER 14

1. From *The Castle,* quoted by Max Brod, *Franz Kafka: A Biography* (New York: Schocken Books, 1960), 190.

2. Freud, *The Interpretation of Dreams* (New York: Avon Books, 1965), 229–30.

3. Speech to the Society of B'nai B'rith, Vienna, 1926, quoted in Jeffrey Wigoder, *Jewish Biographies* (New York: Simon & Schuster, 1991), 155.

4. Eric Lax, *Woody Allen: A Biography* (New York: Knopf, 1991), 165.

5. *Woody Allen on Woody Allen: In Conversation with Stig Bjorkman* (New York: Grove Press, 1995), 223.

CHAPTER 15

1. *The Menorah Journal* 6 (Aug. 4, 1920): 181–93.

2. Quoted in Donald J. Moore, *Martin Buber: Prophet of Religious Secularism* (Philadelphia: Jewish Publication Society of America, 1974), 25.

3. Moore, *Martin Buber,* 134.

4. Moore, *Martin Buber,* 78.

5. Quoted in Arthur Hertzberg, *The Zionist Idea* (Garden City, NY: Doubleday, 1959), 426.

6. Quoted in Hertzberg, *Zionist Idea,* 422–23.

INDEX